THE NEWSROOM

The Complete Scripts

by Ken Finkleman

Canadian Cataloguing in Publication Data

Finkleman, Ken
The newsroom

ISBN 0-7710-3224-2

I. Title. II. Title: The newsroom (Television program).

PN1992.77.N48F46 1997 791.45'72 C97-932029-1

Set in Minion by M&S, Toronto

The publishers acknowledge the support of the Canada Council and the Ontario Arts Council for their publishing program.

Front cover photo courtesy CBC-TV

Printed and bound in Canada.

McClelland & Stewart Inc.
The Canadian Publishers
481 University Ave.
Toronto, Ontario
M5G 2E9

1 2 3 4 5 01 00 99 98 97

THE NEWSROOM

CONTENTS

CAST OF CHARACTERS

Episodes 1-6

George Findlay, *News Director*	Ken Finkleman
Jeremy, *News Producer*	Jeremy Hotz
Mark, *News Producer*	Mark Farrell
Jim Walcott, *News Anchor*	Peter Keleghan
Audrey, *The Intern*	Tanya Allen
Rani, *On-Air Reporter*	Pamela Sinha
Dernhoff, *George's Boss*	Julie Khaner
Kris, *George's Assistant*	Lisa Ryder
Sandra, *George's Assistant*	Kay Valley

Episodes 7-12

(There are some cast changes after the first six episodes.)

George Findlay, *News Director*	Ken Finkleman
Mark, *News Producer*	Mark Farrell
Karen, *News Producer*	Karen Hines
Jim Walcott, *News Anchor*	Peter Keleghan
Audrey, *The Intern*	Tanya Allen
Dodie Graham, *George's Boss*	Nancy Beatty
Gillian Soros, *Head of Regional Programming*	Elisa Moolecherry
Bruce, *The Weatherman*	David Huband

Episode 13

George Findlay, *Jim's Campaign Manager*	Ken Finkleman
Jeremy, *Campaign Staff*	Jeremy Hotz
Mark, *Campaign Staff*	Mark Farrell
Jim Walcott, *Political Candidate*	Peter Keleghan
Audrey, *Campaign Staff*	Tanya Allen

(appearing as themselves: Daniel Richler, Cynthia Dale, Linda McQuaig, Pamela Wallin, Eddie Shack, David Cronenberg, Jeffrey Simpson, Alex Gonzalez, Angelo Mosca, Bob Rae, Stephen Lewis, Hugh Segal, and John Haslett Cuff)

EPISODE 1

"The Walking Shoe Incident"

First Aired: October 21, 1996

Jeremy and George enter the newsroom, walking towards the reception desk.

JEREMY We just got the CNN feed out of Kinshasa on the train that plunged into the Congo River.

GEORGE Dead?

JEREMY Two hundred.

GEORGE On the nose?

JEREMY A guesstimate. It's Africa and CNN Give or take twenty bodies either way.

The receptionist hands George phone messages. They continue to walk.

GEORGE Are there piranha in the Congo?

JEREMY I wouldn't swim there.

GEORGE Make it "piranha-ridden" Congo.

JEREMY How about "piranha-infested Congo"?

GEORGE Better.

Jeremy walks away. Rani, at her workstation, swings in her chair towards George. She has her phone in her hand.

RANI George, your mother on four.

GEORGE Oh, tell her I'm in a meeting. No, no, no, no. Uh, tell her I'm, uh, bus– tell her I'm away, for a week. Two weeks. Tell her I'm away for two weeks.

Mark is sitting at his workstation while George leans on the desk.

MARK So do we go with the fight in city counsel about rezoning the waterfront, which is a big local deal, or do we go with a train wreck halfway across the world?

GEORGE We go with the train in the Congo.

MARK Uh, we're supposed to be doing the local news here.

GEORGE Yes, we're looking for a local hook. He's on the phone with this guy. *(points to Jeremy, who's on the phone at his workstation)*

JEREMY *(to George and Mark)* Okay, my guy says there may have been a Canadian on board.

GEORGE There. Okay? Is that local enough? Did he go into the river? Is he dead?

JEREMY I don't know. I'm on hold. We'll find out.

MARK *(reading copy)* Okay, hold on. Uh, "piranha-infested Congo" – who said there's piranha in the Congo River?

GEORGE Jeremy. *(Jeremy starts to protest but George over-rides him)*

JEREMY No, I never said that. I never said there were piranha in there. I said similar to –

GEORGE I'm saying let's use the word "piranha." It's higher concept, people identify with it, and we'll use something like "piranha-like." How's that – "piranha-like fish."

MARK We still haven't even confirmed that there's a Canadian.

JEREMY Well, we're hoping that there's a Canadian dead. I mean that that's –

GEORGE	We're hoping he's dead? *(Mark shakes his head)* Okay, how about that "Perhaps one Canadian was eaten by piranha-like fish."
MARK	I have a problem with that. I mean, uh, how do we know he was eaten?
GEORGE	"Perhaps one Canadian may have been eaten by piranha-like . . ."

Mark's phone rings. He takes it.

JEREMY	Or "Perhaps one Canadian may have been eaten by flesh-eating fish."
MARK	*(answering phone)* Hello?
GEORGE	I can live with "flesh-eating."
JEREMY	Yes.
MARK	*(holding the phone out)* Your mother's on four.
GEORGE	Okay, okay. Um, tell her I'm busy. Tell her I'm busy. Tell her I'm in a meeting. Actually, tell her I'm out of town for two weeks, okay? Three weeks. *(Mark rolls his eyes)*

George and Jeremy are in George's office, Jeremy is sitting on the sofa, George in his office chair. Jeremy is holding a shoe.

GEORGE	I just got those shoes. Uh, they're British. They're very hip.
JEREMY	If you like walking shoes.
GEORGE	Those aren't walking shoes.
JEREMY	Yeah, they're walking shoes. They got the spongy insole. And these little air holes.
GEORGE	Those aren't air holes.
JEREMY	Yeah, they're air holes. For odour.
GEORGE	They're a feature of the goddamn design.

Bill pokes his head in.

BILL Your mother is on my phone.

GEORGE I'm very busy, okay? I'm busy.

JEREMY Why don't you just talk to her?

GEORGE Talk to her?

JEREMY Uh-huh.

GEORGE You're missing the point, okay? The point is, that this place is too cheap to get me an assistant, okay? If I had an assistant she could talk to my mother. But because this place is so goddamn cheap, my mother has no one to talk to.

Audrey rolls in the door on her chair.

AUDREY Your BMW dealer on six.

GEORGE *(grabbing a phone – a big upbeat smile)* Henry! Yeah, no, I'm good. Yeah, no, a little problem. The window. When it goes up to the top, it pops out of the frame. Yeah, no, I know it's nothing. Well, I can't get it over to you. No, no. I don't have an assistant.

Audrey is on the phone at her workstation.

AUDREY Oh, you're his mother. Um, hang on a sec, I'll see if he's available. *(she puts her on hold)*

George is still on the phone with the BMW dealer. His head is bent in his hand, his back to his office door.

GEORGE Henry, this is a forty-thousand-dollar German car. And you're telling me you can't send someone over to pick it up? I don't have an assistant to do it. No.

AUDREY *(standing in the doorway)* Excuse me.

GEORGE *(paying no attention)* Hey, well listen, you had no trouble sending people to Poland.

Hearing George's comment, Audrey looks around to see if anyone heard.

GEORGE Um, yeah, I'm sorry. I didn't mean that. Can you hold on one sec? *(he turns to Audrey)* Do you drive?

AUDREY Uh-huh.

GEORGE Can you take my car over to BMW?

AUDREY That's not my job.

GEORGE It's not your job?

Jim knocks on the door and enters past Audrey. He sits on the sofa, paper in hand.

JIM Did you read *Variety* this week on the new Eisner/Ovitz plan for Disney, ABC? How much Eisner stands to make on this deal?

GEORGE Can you wait one second? We're, we're just a little . . . you know, okay?

(to Audrey) Listen, you're an intern, okay? And what your job is, is to do anything that's required to get the show out. I don't think that's unreasonable.

AUDREY You're mother's on eight.

GEORGE Shit, can you talk to her?

AUDREY It's not my job.

JIM *(seeing the shoes, picks one up)* Do you have new shoes?

GEORGE Yes.

JIM Yeah, that's what you call a walking shoe, right?

GEORGE No. We're busy.

Mark and George are at Mark's workstation. George has the shoe in his hand.

MARK — Yeah, that's, uh, I saw a guy yesterday wearing that same shoe. He had, he had a Tilley hat, you know? You know the Tilley hat. The big white with the thing around –

GEORGE — Yeah, I know the hat. I know the hat.

MARK — Have you ever noticed those guys who wear Tilley hats have really big asses?

GEORGE — What's your point here?

MARK — *(pointing to the shoes)* He had walking shoes just like that.

George is on the phone with the shoe store.

GEORGE — I didn't want a walking shoe. Well, I'm sure they're great walking . . . well, nobody said they were walking shoes when I went into the store. I haven't been able to get them back because I'm a news director on a television . . . yes, television news, and I've had a horrible week. It's been just an incredibly insane news week. Well, I don't think I have to justify my, my, my week to a shoe salesman. A train with two hundred people plunged into the Congo River, okay? It's full of piranha.

Audrey is at her workstation, phone in hand.

AUDREY — George, your mother on four.

GEORGE — Can you get my shoes back to the store?

AUDREY — I already told you I don't run errands.

GEORGE — Listen, I've got a news show to get out five days a week. This place won't get me an assistant, my mother is *harassing* me to death. I want the number into this show changed. She got the number, I don't know how she got the number.

AUDREY Well, I doubt you can change the number of a Crown corporation just so your mother can't reach you.

GEORGE Not the corporation. The number to the show. Our show number. I want it changed, I want it changed today!

AUDREY *(retreats, rolling her eyes)* Okay!

GEORGE Thank you.

(on phone) Mom? Yeah? No, it's good to hear from you.

George, Jeremy, and Mark are in the boardroom. Mark has a copy of the hiring guidelines. George and Jeremy are eating popcorn.

GEORGE Okay, I happen to think it's ridiculous that I can't have a secretary?

MARK Well, not at your executive level, okay. Not with the cutbacks.

GEORGE Well listen, the intern does nothing here. I have *no* idea why she's here, okay?

MARK You cannot have her perform staff tasks like secretarial or messenger. It just can't be done.

JEREMY I heard you sent her out for All-Bran.

GEORGE For muffins, okay! Muffins.

JEREMY My dad's addicted to that shit. Is it five grams of fibre, is it ten grams. President's Choice makes a fifteen-gram fibre cereal.

GEORGE Fifteen, really.

MARK *(reading)* "An entry-level research assistant." This is the person you need.

GEORGE I need a secretary.

MARK	You can *define* research, okay. There's no job description; it just says "research assistant."
JEREMY	There you go. You've got your loophole. Plunge in.
MARK	All you do is hire the type of person you work well with – you know, an attractive woman, who's subservient and not that bright.
JEREMY	Now maybe you'll get those shitty-looking shoes back.

Audrey is on the phone at her workstation.

AUDREY	What do you mean, you can't change a phone number. This is coming from the news director. He has his reasons. I can't say what they are but he has his reasons *(stumbling)*. Look, it's our direct line in. I'm not asking you to change the main switchboard. Know what, forget it. Just . . . give me your supervisor's name. *(she grabs a pen)*

In his office, George interviews his first candidate for an assistant – a woman of fifty. He has a yogurt in one hand and her CV *in the other.*

GEORGE	You know, this is a demanding job, research. There's a lot of running around. It's a big building and, um, basically it's a young person's job. I mean, I couldn't do it.
WOMAN	I rock climb.
GEORGE	Well, we have elevators in here.
WOMAN	*(no reaction)* I couldn't help noticing those shoes. They're the best walking shoe on the market. I have a pair for women, exactly the same style. Exceptional arch support and I like the fact they breath. Your feet don't sweat.

GEORGE Well, that's a design –

WOMAN Do you have foot problems too?

GEORGE *(pointing at the shoes)* No. No. These were a mistake. I, I ordered these over the phone.

WOMAN Shoes over the phone?

GEORGE Yeah.

WOMAN I think that's a mistake.

George interviews his second candidate – a male, twenty-six, blonde, wearing a leather jacket. Comes across sounding "Hollywood."

MALE Well, I worked for Goldie Hawn when she was up here doing a movie. That was about, uh, three years ago. There was a certain amount of research involved in that because she needed a good school for her and Kurt's kids when she was up here. Mind you, all our schools are fabulous, you know. And she was amazed at the level of Toronto's public school system. Not that she'd send her kids to a public school. *(he laughs)* Um, and I helped her get a cottage up in Muskoka. She wanted the same lake as Marty.

GEORGE Marty?

MALE Marty Short. Um, you know, she looks fabulous. Goldie Hawn is fifty-one if she's a day and she still looks thirty-nine, forty-five tops. And Kurt Russell – that computer's been wearing tennis shoes for years. *(He laughs. George tries to laugh back and gives a small frown.)* You know, I worked out with them both. I was kind of like a personal trainer for them. And they both have amazing, amazing bodies. Yeah.

GEORGE Have you done any research that's, uh, you know, news related?

MALE — Well, not like Bosnia. *(he chuckles)* But I assisted the booker on The Shirley Show. Um, it's often news related, yeah. Shirley looks fabulous.

George interviews his third candidate, Sandra, a twenty-four-year-old black female. George reads her CV.

GEORGE — Okay, you have a masters degree in African History, winner of a *Globe and Mail* short story contest in '93, uh, research assistant to the head of the department of economics at the University of Toronto, '94, executive assistant to the President of the Black Lesbian Coalition, '95. Um.
(looks up, a beat, then –) Do you ski?

SANDRA — No.

GEORGE — Oh, so I guess you've never skied Whistler then.

SANDRA — That would be a pretty good guess.

GEORGE — Whistler's, Whistler's, oh, great. *(he chucks her* CV *on his desk, getting into his story)* It's, it's really the best mountain in North America. If you go for six days you can expect three days of rain. That's really the only problem, you know. Which is really a hassle. It's got great restaurants on the hills. Amazing number of runs. There's Whistler and Blackcomb you know, side by side. You know, you see quite a few black people on the slopes. You know, I, that to just . . . the black thing. *(he's stumbling, trying to cover up his comment)* Anyway, you have a great CV, and the Black Lesbian Coalition, does this mean you're a . . . *(waits for her to finish it)*

SANDRA — A lesbian.

GEORGE — Right.

SANDRA — Is that a problem for you – black non-skier lesbians?

GEORGE	Absolutely not. No, no, no. I want to hire the best-qualified person for this job. I'm not looking for a woman to ski with.

George interviews his fourth candidate, Kris, a blonde, tall, attractive woman. Could work boat shows.

KRIS	Oh, Whistler's a killer.
GEORGE	Oh, Whistler's fantastic.
KRIS	Oh, yeah.
GEORGE	But there is a problem.
KRIS	What? The weather?
GEORGE	Yes! The weather.
KRIS	It's crazy.
GEORGE	I was gonna . . . you know. Like, you can even go in January for six days, right . . .
KRIS	. . . expect three days of rain. For sure.
GEORGE	Exactly.
KRIS	Yes!
GEORGE	I've had that same experience.
KRIS	Really?
GEORGE	Yes. I have, I have. It's odd.
KRIS	Who knows, eh?

Both acknowledge they're simpatico with a laugh.

GEORGE	So it says here you like horses.
KRIS	I love horses.
GEORGE	Oh, really.
KRIS	Yes.
GEORGE	You know, so do I. Horses are great. You know, there's a, there's a –
KRIS	Certain smell.

GEORGE	Yes, the smell of horses! That's the thing!
KRIS	I don't know. There's something earthy or –
GEORGE	Yeah, is there something –
GEORGE/KRIS	Sexual.
GEORGE	Yes. Talking in sort of a tangent from what . . .
KRIS	Sorry. Sorry.
GEORGE	. . . the job interview. But it is odd that we have that same kind of reaction to the smell of horses.
KRIS	Yeah.
GEORGE	You know, there's one thing, though. It doesn't mention anywhere on your CV that, uh, it doesn't mention that you've done any research.
KRIS	No, no I haven't. Is that a problem?
GEORGE	No.
KRIS	Oh, good.
GEORGE	No, no, no. *(smiling)* No it's not.

Dernhoff, the vice-president of TV *news, is sitting behind her big executive desk while George sits in front. She has an easy self-confidence.*

DERNHOFF	She's suing the network, you personally and me as the division head for hiring discrimination.
GEORGE	Well, she was wrong for the job.
DERNHOFF	She's black, female, with a post-graduate degree in history and a brilliant CV and you hired a blonde ski bunny.
GEORGE	You know this, this ski bunny thing. You know, I've heard this going around, it's –
DERNHOFF	George, George. You hired someone you think you can screw, admit.
GEORGE	That's not true. That's not true.
DERNHOFF	What happened with your last assistant?
GEORGE	You know that was an unusual –

DERNHOFF The legal department wants your side of this. They'll be down to talk to you after lunch.

George sits across from two lawyers, one male, in his late forties, the other female, around thirty. She takes notes, making George very nervous.

GEORGE First off, I want to say that I want to cooperate with the legal department on this. This woman is definitely not a ski bunny. She's a good skier, which I don't think should disqualify her from a job. *(female lawyer makes a note)*

. . . When I asked her if she had skied Whistler, uh, she said "yes" and I thought that was good. She answered correctly. She had skied Whistler and I thought that was appropriate.

. . . She volunteered that she liked horses. I didn't ask her "do you like horses." I think there's a big difference between my saying "do you like horses" and her volunteering that she liked horses because I think if I said "do you like horses" that would clearly be wrong in an interview for a researcher.

I think I eventually said, "Yes, I would sleep with you." I didn't say, "Could I sleep with you?" If I said, "Could I sleep with you?" I think that would be inappropriate in an interview situation. *(Male lawyer looks straight at George, tapping his finger on his pen)* I didn't say that. I never would.

. . . I found her attractive. Um, I find you attractive. *(to female lawyer, who writes again)* I'm not interested in sleeping with you. I don't think you have to write down, that I wouldn't sleep with you.

... She's obviously a black woman who's very insecure with her own homosexuality.

... Can we strike, can we just delete "black" and "homosexual" from that?

... I'm not caving in here. I, I, I've decided to hire the black lesbian woman. She's highly qualified and I think that, uh, she's what the corporation needs at this time. We're very white and actually very heterosexual, and I think more homosexuals might help the quality of our programming. On the entertainment side, obviously, that's not relevant to the news *(he looks about to see if they are buying his story)*

Audrey is on the phone at her workstation.

AUDREY It was a question. I said "Is this bureaucratic bullshit?" I, I didn't say "*This is* bureaucratic bullshit."

... I'm an intern. Yeah, hi, is this the supervisor? Yup. The problem is we need our show number changed. I understand that but under the circumstances. I mean, uh, a man, a man is getting death threats here. I mean, can't we make an exception? Yeah, death threats. Uh, the anchor actually. Yeah. I know, the world is full of kooks. It's very scary.

In the boardroom, Jim has just heard the news. He is pacing. George is standing, Jeremy and Mark are sitting at the boardroom table.

GEORGE Okay, now, I don't think this is a serious death threat. I think this guy's a crank. The guys who threaten are not the guys who pull the trigger. Am I right?

Mark points to George in agreement.

JEREMY Yes, of course.

JIM You know, I guess I've been blessed in my broadcast career. I've never ever had a death threat, not even an angry letter. I have never consciously offended or been controversial for the sake of, of, of any controversy.

GEORGE You're absolutely right about that. You know, I mean, you are, you know, a bland guy. *(to Mark and Jeremy)* Am I right?

JEREMY/MARK Yeah, yeah, yeah, yeah.

JIM Now, some psycho has my name on a slug. That's not from being bland.

GEORGE Well, I didn't mean bland. I didn't mean bland. I'm looking for a word here to describe you. I can't find the word at this moment. But the point is, the guys out there with an AK-47 are not looking at the television sets and getting pissed off because they see some guy who's basically very bland. You know?

JEREMY Right. Right.

JIM You said "bland" again.

GEORGE I did say "bland." I didn't mean "bland." I know I said "bland."

MARK Is this guy serious? He'll just stick a gun to your head and pull the trigger and boom, your whole head will be gone so –

JEREMY Yeah, you won't even feel it. I happen to know the human brain has no nerve endings. It's not like –

GEORGE Wait a second you guys. Thanks, Mr. Science, for that little bit of information. It's the guy's life, okay. I'm sorry. I apologize.

MARK Sorry.

GEORGE	People know that you're on some wacko's hit list. What are they gonna do? They're going to watch us. Our numbers go up.
JEREMY	Right. *(Mark nods)*
GEORGE	I think we play this.
JIM	You're a sick man, you know that, sir? You're a sick man *(he buries his face in his hands).*
GEORGE	Listen, you know what you are? You're a victim. *(he looks to Mark and Jeremy for help)*
JEREMY	Victim.
GEORGE	You're a victim. This is the victim decade.
JIM	People are going to be watching. The numbers are going to go up because they are waiting to see the bullet hit. Those kind of numbers I personally don't need.
GEORGE	Wait. You know something? I'm sorry. I'm not using the correct word here. And I realize I made a mistake there. I didn't mean victim, I meant martyr.
JEREMY	Martyr. Martyr's great.
GEORGE	That's the word. That's the right word I've been searching for here. You're a martyr of the free press.
JIM	*(nodding, like he likes it)* Martyr.
JEREMY/MARK	Martyr.
JIM	I still think I should wear a bulletproof vest.
MARK	A bulletproof vest is not going to protect you from a head shot.
GEORGE	I'm not going to nickel-and-dime my anchor, you know, over, over, over his life. But the fact is that vests are expensive and I don't know if I can justify it.
MARK	It's not just a vest, either, we're talking about. I mean, if we get Jim a vest, we're looking at more shirts –
JEREMY	Yeah.

GEORGE Why?

MARK Well, 'cause the shirts have to go over the vests.

GEORGE The shirt, that's right.

MARK I mean, bigger shirts.

JIM *(speaking calmly)* I have given my life to this corporation. My life. And all I've asked for in return, sum total, was a German car and a cottage and the right to enjoy them without thinking about anything. I know this.

Mark shrugs.

George and Dernhoff walk through the atrium hallway toward the elevators, then stop.

DERNHOFF This ski bunny is suing for wrongful dismissal.

GEORGE Oh, that's ridiculous. I fired her before she started.

DERNHOFF She's claimed you discriminated against her good looks.

GEORGE Okay, she wasn't that great. I mean, she was very nice.

DERNHOFF This is another lawsuit. How did you get the idea you could hire someone to pick up your laundry in the first place?

GEORGE *(oblivious)* You know those lawyers I had to meet . . . The woman . . . is she dating anyone now, is she connected or married?

Dernhoff shakes her head and turns away to press the elevator button.

George, Jeremy, Mark, and Jim are in George's office. Jim is standing holding a bulletproof vest. Jeremy and Mark are seated on the couch, and George is at his desk.

JIM	This thing is state-of-the-art. It'll stop most assault weapons.
MARK	It's not going to protect you from a head shot.
GEORGE	Is that going to go under your regular shirts?

Kris (the blonde skier) enters with the shoebox.

KRIS	Sorry.
GEORGE	Yeah, yeah. No, no, no. Come on in.
KRIS	*(standing at the doorway)* Do you have the receipt for this? Because I'll need it when I return them.
GEORGE	Oh, it's in the box.
KRIS	Oh *(claps hand to her head)*. I'm sorry.
GEORGE	No, no. That was a completely reasonable mistake. That's no problem.
KRIS	You know, I don't know why you're returning them. I think they're kind of sexy.
GEORGE	Sexy? Really? You do?
KRIS	Yeah.
GEORGE	Really? *(he chuckles)*
KRIS	Yeah, yeah. But then I'm into shoes. I kind of have a foot fetish thing. Or a –
GEORGE	A fetish? Really?
KRIS	Uh. *(she chuckles, feeling silly)*
GEORGE	No, no, no, no. It's not a problem. *(Jeremy and Mark are watching George)* It's a very, uh, natural, uh –
KRIS	Anyway. Is there anything else that you wanted me to do?
GEORGE	Uh. *(he looks at Jeremy, who shrugs at him)* Oh, you're learning the computer. How's that going?
KRIS	Not well.
MARK	She gave up.
GEORGE	Oh well, forget that. You know, the whole thing with computers and the Internet, you know. Who cares? I

don't care. *(Kris looks pleased)* Really. No, I think you're doing great. Thanks.

GEORGE *(after Kris leaves)* She's good.

JEREMY/MARK She's great. Yeah. She's really good at what she does.

They are interrupted by Sandra.

SANDRA Excuse me. I have your President's Choice Fibre First – fifteen grams of fibre.

GEORGE *(to Mark and Jeremy)* It's for muffins, okay?

SANDRA Is there anything else you want?

GEORGE Um . . . *(thinks hard)* No, no. You're fine. You're great.

SANDRA Okay.

GEORGE Thank you. You're great.

MARK *(after she's gone again)* So, you hired both of them?

GEORGE Is that a big deal?

MARK No, no, no.

GEORGE Is that a problem?

MARK/JEREMY No, no, no. Good solution. Good move.

JIM *(to Mark and Jeremy)* I just want to say something here. This whole bit with the head shot. It's a joke, right? You think I don't fuckin' know that's a joke? You guys are assholes. This is my fuckin' life. *(he storms out, kicking the door and throwing the vest to the ground)*

GEORGE *(after a long, awkward pause)* You guys wanna eat?

MARK/JEREMY Yeah. Yeah.

MARK Some sandwich this time?

JEREMY No.

GEORGE Chinese?

JEREMY No, I don't want Chinese?

GEORGE Sushi? How about sushi?

JEREMY/MARK Yeah. Yeah.

GEORGE Okay, let's go.

People drift out saying goodnights. Jeremy and George are walking through the newsroom.

GEORGE It was a good show tonight.

JEREMY Yeah, fifty-four dead. That cave-in didn't hurt us.

GEORGE It worked. I take it all back. Even though it was in Ghana, it was still very relatable. Okay? Goodnight.

JEREMY *(stopping at his workstation to pick up his coat)* Have a good weekend.

George is heading towards his office, but notices Kris putting her coat on at her workstation. He walks up to her.

GEORGE Uh, hi.

KRIS Hi.

GEORGE So, everything work out with the new desk?

KRIS I love my new desk.

GEORGE Oh, great. That's great. *(he makes to go into his office but stops and looks back at Kris)*
Are you skiing this weekend?

KRIS No.

GEORGE You're not?

KRIS No.

GEORGE Oh, so you'll be in town?

KRIS Yeah. Yeah. I'm getting a brand-new queen-size bed from IKEA.

GEORGE Oh, you are.

KRIS Yeah, I love a big bed.

GEORGE You do?

KRIS Yeah.

GEORGE You know, IKEA stuff is, uh, it can be very tricky.

I've assembled a lot of . . . you know. And they have that system, um, the um –

KRIS Oh, the Allen key.

GEORGE *(making hand gestures)* No, they have the Allen key, but they have this other weird system where you put this little screw into a hole and then there's another hole underneath and then you have to make sure that they actually connect.

KRIS Really?

GEORGE You don't need some help with assembling?

KRIS No, actually, you know what? Um, Sandra will be helping me.

GEORGE Sandra?

KRIS The other assistant?

GEORGE Oh, Sandra! Oh, yeah. She's good.

KRIS *(coming around her desk to stand in front of George)* You know, um, is there . . . Can I talk to you?

GEORGE Yes, absolutely.

KRIS About something personal?

GEORGE Sure.

KRIS *(trying to handle this delicately)* Um, George. I really appreciate this job. And, um, I feel very badly about the lawsuit. And, um, I just hope it doesn't affect our relationship?

GEORGE Oh, no, absolutely not. No, that's all part of the business, and I completely understand. And I keep business and personal separate.

KRIS Whew. Okay, good.

GEORGE You know. Actually, I'm just going to grab my coat and go out for a bite. Do you want to join me?

KRIS Right, I, um, okay. My personal life has really changed with this job, you know, both self-esteem-wise and sexually.

GEORGE *(pointing to his office)* Do you want to talk?

KRIS No, it's fine. I just wanted to say, um, Sandra and I have developed a relationship as partners and I just can't describe how that has changed my life.

Sandra walks up behind Kris.

SANDRA Ready?

KRIS Yeah.

SANDRA Goodnight.

KRIS Goodnight.

GEORGE *(watching them leave)* Goodnight, goodnight.

Audrey and George are in the boardroom. Audrey paces.

AUDREY *(uncharacteristically contrite)* There are no death threats. I made that up.

GEORGE You what?

AUDREY I thought you were going to fire me if I couldn't get the number changed. So I called the supervisor. You know, she had this sort of mood and I was nervous and she said I better have a damn good reason for changing the number. You know, I didn't think you'd like it if I told her that you didn't want to talk to your mother, because that would seem silly to someone who didn't understand the situation. So I said the first thing that popped into my head, which happened to be that Jim was getting death threats.

GEORGE So you made this up?

AUDREY I really didn't think it would go this far.

Mark enters.

MARK You know what they did? They changed our number because of this death threat.

George looks at Audrey.

MARK — This is a bigger hassle than if they just shot the guy.

Mark leaves, and Audrey looks at George with a grin.

GEORGE — My mother doesn't get this number, understand?

Audrey nods, pleased with herself.

Kris, standing, is on the phone at a workstation. Audrey is working on the computer at the workstation beside her.

KRIS — Can you hold for a second?
(to Audrey) Um, Audrey. Audrey, I have a call for George through the switchboard. How do I transfer it over to our new show number?

AUDREY — You can't. Just give 'em the new number.

KRIS — Okay.
(on the phone) Hi, our new show number is 205-8600. Okay.

AUDREY — Who'd you give that number to?

KRIS — Um, George's mother.

THE END

EPISODE 2

"Dinner at Eight"

First Aired: October 28, 1996

George and Jeremy are in the newsroom watching Jim's newscast on the monitor. Jeremy is drinking coffee. George is holding a bottle of water.

JIM *(on the monitor)* International aid agencies have found it almost impossible to distribute much-needed food and medical supplies, thereby leaving relief workers unable to cope with close to one million starving refugees.

(a pause, changes to upbeat) Now with sports – Jack McManus has just returned from the America's Cup sailboat race, and I know one thing, I'd rather be sailing than starving.

GEORGE How can he say he'd rather be sailing than starving?

JEREMY *(shakes his head)* He's an anchor. He's an idiot.

George and Dernhoff sit with agents, Carole and Leonard Ross. Both are in Armani clothes. Both are in their thirties, confident, direct, charming. They have brought with them a number of cassettes with prospective co-anchors for Jim. Carole is walking around the room.

LEONARD We think your decision to give Jim Walcott a female co-anchor is great. We *(he indicates Carole)* handle a number of women who can give that spot some real life.

GEORGE Uh, don't get us wrong. We think Jim's a great anchor.

CAROLE We'd love to represent him.

LEONARD Absolutely.

GEORGE Yeah, he's no genius, but viewers do like him.

CAROLE Well, intelligence intimidates, and Jim doesn't intimidate.

GEORGE The last thing you want is to come home after a hard day's work and sit down in front of your television set and be intimidated by, you know . . .

DERNHOFF By intelligence.

LEONARD *(together with Carole)* By intelligence.

GEORGE . . . by intelligence.

LEONARD Intelligence can be a bitch . . .

CAROLE . . . when you're tired.

GEORGE You know, intelligence is a bitch when you're tired. *(he points to Leonard and Carole in agreement)*

They watch an anchor's audition tape. She is black.

MONIQUE *(on monitor)* The annual East Coast –

CAROLE Monique is also very wonderful. She doesn't have an in-your-face ethnicity.

LEONARD No, exactly. Seventy-four per cent of her audience in Saskatoon actually thought she was white. It's a very subtle ethnicity.

CAROLE An almost subliminal ethnicity.

GEORGE Didn't Coke or Pepsi do some advertising like that? Subliminal.

CAROLE Does anyone want a Diet Coke?

Everyone drinks generic diet cola.

LEONARD Colour's great, but you don't want to hit the viewer over the head with it.

DERNHOFF I'm not sure if this look is going to work for us right now. *(looks at George)*

GEORGE	I think what Sidney is saying is that a black anchor right now . . . if I can just say the word "black"?
CAROLE	Okay.
GEORGE	Can I say the word "black"?
CAROLE	No, absolutely, that's fine.
GEORGE	. . . that a black anchor right now reads "equality," and equality reads "social spending," and a social-spending message in this deficit-reduction climate looks like we're taking sides, and we have to be objective. A white anchor, on the other hand, reads "deficit reduction." Which doesn't mean that equality isn't a high priority for us. *(Carole nods)* A black may be too aggressive a move right now.
CAROLE	*(smiling)* Well, if it doesn't work, it doesn't work.

Another female anchor is on the monitor. She's white, with blonde hair.

CAROLE	There she is.
LEONARD	All right, now, Lindsay's out of Edmonton. This lady is very, very special.
CAROLE	Yes, but she doesn't read "public broadcasting." She reads "Alberta," she reads "free market."
LEONARD	Exactly. She has what we call a "go for it" approach to news. She just "does it."
CAROLE	Absolutely.
LEONARD	Right now we can put her into any mid-size U.S. market – Baltimore, Cleveland, Kansas City . . .
DERNHOFF	*(looking at George, sounding interested)* U.S.?
GEORGE	The U.S.
CAROLE	Tell them about the crying.
LEONARD	Oh, she has this wonderful quirky thing where she . . . on a sad story, she cries. But it works.

GEORGE	What, like in that movie *Broadcast News*?
CAROLE	Exactly like in *Broadcast News.*
LEONARD	It works.
GEORGE	Well, if it works –
CAROLE	It works. And blonde doesn't intimidate.
DERNHOFF	Which is good for Jim.
GEORGE	Sit him down with an intelligent black woman and you've got a problem.
DERNHOFF	A non-threatening blonde I think is the answer.
GEORGE	It's not about black and white.
LEONARD	She's a great compromise.
CAROLE	And I *love* her name.

George sits at his desk. Jim is on the couch.

JIM	*(incredulous)* I find out reading a newspaper – I find out reading Sid Adilman's column – that I'm out on my ass. That I'm, that I'm losing my spot. To, to a chick?
GEORGE	You're not losing your spot. That's ridiculous. And when I saw that thing in Sid's column, I was absolutely shocked. I have no idea how it got there.
JIM	Audrey sent him *your* press release.
GEORGE	*(after a long pause)* Do you know the expression, No pain, no gain?
JIM	Yeah.
GEORGE	You know that expression?
JIM	*(shifting in his seat)* Yeah.
GEORGE	No pain, no gain. I think it was Vince Lombardi that said that. This co-host situation is very American, you know. This is going to be great. You'll be with this woman, you'll bounce stuff off this woman, you'll get a dynamic going, there'll be sexual, there'll be intellectual. You're going to be brilliant at this,

okay? Now I want to tell you something. If you don't like this woman, she's gone. You have my word.

JIM Your word?

GEORGE My word.

George gets up from his chair. Jim rises, and George puts a hand on his shoulder. They start towards the door.

GEORGE Now, you know how the corporation works. I don't have final say in this stuff, so my word is effectively irrelevant. But I want to make sure you're happy. Are you happy with this? *(they stop in the doorway)*

JIM Yeah, yeah.

GEORGE Okay?

JIM Yeah.

GEORGE We both could come out of this with new German cars. *(he pats Jim's back)* All right? *(he starts backing away into his office)*

JIM A Z3 would be nice, wouldn't it. *(George points back into his office, like he's got work to do)*

Have you see this thing? The new Bond car?

GEORGE I've got to make some calls.

JIM Blue convertible in the movie. Gorgeous thing. And they use it so little. Bond drives up in this car with his girlfriend, gets into a plane, CIA guy drives off. They never crack it up. It's interesting. They never crack it up. *(George starts to slowly close his door)* It's probably the only one they have because it's way back, it's a prototype.

GEORGE Uh-huh. Okay. *(he continues to close the door, but Jim is oblivious)*

JIM Gorgeous, gorgeous.

Mark and Audrey are at the coffee area in the newsroom. Mark is pouring himself a cup.

AUDREY If you had a testosterone problem, would that mean that you could . . . *(she makes an up-and-down motion with her finger)*

MARK *(smiling)* Uh, do you have a testosterone problem?

AUDREY *(smiles back)* Sure. No, uh, does this mean that I'm impotent or infertile.

MARK Uh, impotence. Does someone here have a testosterone problem? Is it someone I know?

AUDREY No, no. I just wanted to know. *(she turns around to leave)*

MARK Well, don't go. Does someone in the newsroom have a testosterone problem?

Audrey, not immune to the gossip impulse, finally gives in. She laughs.

MARK Well, I mean, I can help. You should tell me. You should confide in me.

AUDREY I just checked Jim's voice mail and there was a little –

MARK Jim?

AUDREY Oops. *(she puts her hand to her mouth and doubles over giggling. Mark laughs too)*

AUDREY Did I say that?

MARK Is it Jim?

AUDREY *(slightly hesitant)* Yeah.

MARK And what did it say on his voice mail?

AUDREY That he had it tested.

MARK Ohhh. Well, just a test. It's not a big deal. Doesn't mean –

AUDREY Do you get it tested regularly?

MARK — No. God, no. I don't get tested. *(his eyes bulge and he takes a sip of coffee)*

AUDREY — Really.

MARK — Uh-uh. No.

AUDREY — Wow. Maybe we should keep this between us.

MARK — Um. Yeah.

Mark and Jeremy are walking through the atrium hallway away from the elevators. They are carrying Styrofoam containers.

JEREMY — *(smiling)* So, so, so he's like a, he's like a donkey.

MARK — First of all, it's mule, all right? And he's not like a mule. He's impotent. Mules are sterile.

JEREMY — Yeah, but he, but he can't get it up. I mean –

MARK — Well, we're not sure. The doctor, the doctor left a message saying for him to call back. Now, if everything was fine, the doctor would have said, "Hey, everything's fine."

JEREMY — Oh, yeah, for sure he would have said.

MARK — We should maybe keep this between us.

JEREMY — *(slightly serious)* Yeah, yeah. I won't, I won't say anything. No.

George walks down the hall with the new co-anchor, Lindsay Ward. A documentary camera follows in front of her.

LINDSAY — News is presenting the story in such a way that a housewife in her kitchen peeling potatoes for dinner will suddenly stop and listen and think, *(she looks directly into the camera)* "My God, three hundred people were burned alive in that Bangkok fire! Thank God I wasn't in that building."

They enter the newsroom. Jim is looking over news copy.

LINDSAY My job is to capture the moment and somehow convey that moment to the viewer. *(she spots Jim)* Jim Walcott. *(she shakes Jim's hand)*

JIM *(looking up)* Yeah.

LINDSAY Always been a huge, huge fan.

JIM Oh, nice to meet you.

Lindsay continues walking.

JIM *(to George)* What's, what's with the camera here?

GEORGE Oh, they're doing a documentary on the history of news, and she's in it. Just ignore it.

JIM Oh, do they want something from me on this? *(he smiles)*

GEORGE No, no. They don't want anything from you. Just stay out of it, stay out of it, okay?

(in a slight whisper) Oh, by the way, I heard about your testosterone thing, and, uh, my door's open if you want to talk about that, okay? *(he starts walking away. Jim stops him)*

JIM Wait a minute. Wait a minute. Who told you about my testosterone test?

GEORGE *(in a slight whisper again)* Oh, it's going around.

JIM What?

GEORGE It's going around. Listen, listen. I know it's, I know it's hard but – *(he snaps his fingers realizing the word he just used)* It's difficult, it's difficult. I gotta do this.

George leaves Jim standing there, eyes wide open. Mark walks up with paperwork.

MARK Hey, Jim, sorry about your testosterone. That's a drag.

JIM Who told you about my testosterone test?

MARK *(stumbling)* Audrey. Did I, I wasn't –

JIM What does, what does Audrey know about my testosterone test?

MARK *(pointing to his paperwork, then to his workstation)* I have to put this over here. I, I –

JIM Who else knows about this.

MARK No one knows.

Lindsay is seated on the boardroom table. She picks up a bottle of wine and has a plastic glass in her hand ready to be filled. The documentary crew is shooting. George is watching from the corner of the room.

LINDSAY You know, Toronto is a world-class city. Driving in from the airport on the 401? *(looking back at George)* . . . the 401, we passed an overturned tanker truck that had crushed a car. Now, evidently three people were killed and I was just passing as a civilian.

(she pours some wine) I mean, not in a news capacity at all. There were three dead. That's a major market.

GEORGE Toronto's a great city, and I think that Lindsay's going to be a fantastic addition to it.

LINDSAY Well, thank you. I'd like to propose a toast. To a great new city and a great new team. Cheers. *(she takes a drink and George watches, smiling)*

Jim and Lindsay are sitting in front of the anchor desk, talking to a documentary camera. An oddly improbable staging, as if they are sitting for an "in-the-work-place" moment.

JIM	I wanna, I wanna say that I, uh, I have a confession to make about my first reaction to news that I was going to be splitting my duties with this lady at the newsdesk.
LINDSAY	*(she touches Jim's arm)* No, no, no. I am a huge fan and I absolutely, I *love* this man. I do. *(Jim chuckles)* And I just think we're going to have so much fun.
JIM	We are, we are. I just, I do want to say that I initially felt threatened. And I know it was partially a professional territoriality and partially a challenge to certain, I don't know, masculine impulses. *(he smiles)*
LINDSAY	*(laughing)* Now listen, I have seen you on camera and there's no doubt about your masculinity. None. *(to camera)* His testosterone is possibly right off the charts.
JIM	*(glaring at her)* This is bullshit. This is bullshit. *(he stands up and walks away)* Bullshit.

Jeremy is standing off to the side, leaning on a monitor, watching it all.

JIM	*(to cameraman)* I'm sorry. Could you cut that? You know, I'm dealing with a family tragedy and, uh, Jesus. Very busy, very busy. Excuse me, excuse me. *(he turns, pats Jeremy's shoulder, and walks away)*
LINDSAY	What did I say? Jim? *(to Jeremy)* Is he gay?

George and Jim are in the hallway in back of the studio. They are standing close.

GEORGE It was a complete coincidence. She had no idea you had tests done.

JIM It's not *tests*. It's not *tests*. It was a test. One goddamn test. I wish I never had it.

GEORGE Fine.

JIM Right in front of a documentary camera and I lose it.

I lost it . . . I lost it . . . I lost it . . . I lost it.

GEORGE Look, you didn't lose it. You had a very weak moment. That was good.

JIM I've never lost it on camera before in my life. Never. It's that testosterone. It's got to be. You know, am I, am I half a man? I'm half an anchor, that's for sure. *(he starts to walk away, then stops)*

GEORGE You're not half an anchor, you're a co-anchor. There's a big difference, okay? Now, we're on in ten minutes. I want you to calm down.

JIM I can't calm down. I can't calm down.

GEORGE *(taking a pill bottle from his pocket)* Okay, here. I want you to take this. Here. Come here, come here, come here, okay? That's a Demerol, and that's a Valium. These are heavy, okay? Here's another Demerol. I want you to take all that. Now I hesitate to give that to you 'cause I don't have many left. Okay. Don't drive. You can do the news but don't drive. All right, okay?

JIM I don't –

GEORGE No, no, just *(makes a "shooing" motion)* go.

Lindsay and Rani are in the make-up room. Lindsay is having her face touched up.

LINDSAY I have to admit, I was a little nervous about coming to Toronto at first, coming from Edmonton. A girl from the boondocks, you know? But everyone here's been so nice to me. It's great.

RANI Yeah, but this place can be very Machiavellian. And I'd be real careful who I said what to, if you know what I mean?

LINDSAY No.

Lindsay and Rani are now walking into the news-room.

RANI Oh, and one more thing. You should really not let George choose your wardrobe. His taste is shit. Good luck.

LINDSAY *(laughs)* Thanks.

Rani walks off to her workstation. Lindsay walks towards the anchor desk. Lynn, the floor director, is there.

LYNN Hey.

LINDSAY Hey.

(taking her seat) Is that my prompter here?

LYNN That's the one. *(she helps Lindsay with her mike pack)*

LINDSAY *(reading TelePrompTer)* Four homeless men froze to death last night in Toronto's east end when temperatures plummeted to –

(to floor director) Do I have too much lip gloss on?

LYNN No, you're perfect.

LINDSAY Okay, great.

(reading again) Four homeless men froze to death last night in Toronto's east end when –

LYNN — Can we get a level check?

LINDSAY — Sure.

(reading again) Four homeless men froze to death last night in Toronto's east end –

Lynn gives Lindsay the okay sign. Lindsay gives a thumbs-up back. George approaches the desk.

GEORGE — How do you feel?

LINDSAY — Great.

GEORGE — How's that chair?

LINDSAY — Excellent.

GEORGE — Good, good. Are you going to wear that?

LINDSAY — Yes.

GEORGE — Okay.

George crosses to Jim, who enters glazed, his eyes intensely focused on nothing in particular.

GEORGE — How do you feel? How do you feel?

JIM — There he is.

GEORGE — Did you take that stuff?

JIM — Oooh, yeah.

GEORGE — It's gonna work, it's gonna work.

JIM — Hey, there's the new anchor-bitch. *(he slides into his seat beside Lindsay)*

LYNN — Okay, you ready?

LINDSAY — Yeah.

LYNN — You've got ten. Here we go. *(she backs away from the desk)*

LINDSAY — I didn't know you were gay. I'm sorry if I said anything. *(Jim stares at her)*

LYNN — . . . in three . . .

Jim and Lindsay are seen on the monitor, being watched by George, Mark, and Jeremy at a workstation.

JIM — Good evening. Tonight it gives me, oh, great pleasure to introduce a new member of the City Hour team, Lindsay Ward.

LINDSAY — Thank you, Jim. It's a treat to be in Toronto. It's a competitive, world-class city with amazing opportunities for everyone.

(to camera) Good evening. Four homeless men froze to death last night in Toronto's east end when temperatures plummeted to minus thirty-six degrees with the wind chill . . .

George, Jeremy, and Mark watching monitor off set.

GEORGE — She's great. They're perfect. He's going to love her.

Jim and Lindsay have just stood up from their anchor chairs. Jim walks away, while Lindsay and Lynn chat in the background. Dernhoff walks by Jim.

JIM — *(to Dernhoff)* Hi.

DERNHOFF — Jim. Fabulous, fabulous program. You're looking terrific, you know?

JIM — Thanks. Did you think . . .

Dernhoff walks away from Jim in mid-sentence. She walks directly over to Lindsay. Jim turns and stops George, who's also on his way to see Lindsay.

JIM — Can I talk to you a second, please? *(he's distraught)*

GEORGE — Calm down, calm down, calm down.

JIM You know, that little piece of white Edmonton trash doesn't know how lucky she is to be sitting next to me. She really doesn't.

GEORGE That is a healthy attitude, I like that.

Distracted, George peeks over Jim's shoulder at Lindsay, who is being congratulated by Mark, Jeremy, Rani, and Dernhoff. Lindsay is praising Rani.

JIM You know, she takes a basically cerebral discipline like journalism and turns it into whose-tits-are-bigger-than-whose, which is exactly what she did there.

GEORGE Okay, our audience respects your intellect. Okay? You give her the tits, you take the mind, okay? Mind, body, I think that works for us. Excuse me. *(he notices Dernhoff and Lindsay are walking by)*

GEORGE *(to Lindsay)* Hey, that was a good show tonight.

DERNHOFF Gotta run, George. *(she and Lindsay continue on their way)*

JIM Do you have, do you have any more of those, uh, pills that you gave me before? You know, just to chill out. Not as a crutch or anything. I just, I just can't calm down.

GEORGE Okay, you're an adult. You can control it. I don't think we should be uptight about this.

JIM No, that's what I said. I just want to chill out, you know.

GEORGE Okay. I got a couple of Demerol and a Valium, okay? I'm very reluctant to give you this stuff, 'cause I'm running out of Demerol. But the Valium I can get more of. All right? Not as a crutch.

JIM No!

GEORGE — Okay, later. *(he walks off. Jim puts the pills in his pocket and leaves in the opposite direction)*

Jeremy, Mark, Audrey, George, Rani, and Lindsay are in a production meeting in the boardroom.

MARK — *(reading rundown)* So we're replacing the item on Mother Teresa with a lap-dancing story?

GEORGE — Yeah, book it.

Jim enters. The rooms falls silent. He sits on a table behind George.

GEORGE — Uh, what are you doing here, Jim?

JIM — I thought I'd sit in.

GEORGE — You never sit in, Jim.

JIM — Well, Lindsay's here.

RANI — She's observing.

LINDSAY — I'm just observing.

JIM — I won't talk. Yeah, I won't talk.

GEORGE — Let's move on.

JIM — *(leans in and whispers to George)* The anchor-bitch is trying to end-run me.

JEREMY — *(hearing Jim)* Oh, man.

GEORGE — *(getting back to rundown)* Okay, next.

MARK — We have the story on the two Canadian golfers hit by lightning in Florida.

GEORGE — Did they die?

JEREMY — Yes, they died.

GEORGE — Good. Done. That's our lead.

MARK — Okay.

GEORGE — That's it for today.

JIM — *(walking out)* Sorry, I gotta run.

They all watch Jim leave.

Jim is sitting at a workstation, facing a bank of monitors, each of which is showing a different channel. George is standing in front of Jim, his back to the monitors. Jim is playing with his earpiece.

JIM — She's all comfy cosy in a, in a production meeting that I'm not even invited to.

GEORGE — You're usually at home asleep at that hour.

JIM — *(watching monitors)* First I get nailed by a piece-of-shit testosterone test, then some chick from Edmonton pushes me out of my job.

(pointing to monitors) Oh, there's the new Pathfinder. I test-drove that.

GEORGE — You're not out of your job. I want you to do something for me. Here, here. *(hands him some pills)* Take these and calm down. Be careful with those, all right? They're hard to get.

Audrey sits on George's couch and watches George on the phone, pacing.

GEORGE — What kind of pills did he get into? Demerol? And Valium? God, where'd he get that? *(he gives Audrey a who-knows-where-he-got-pills look and shrugs)*

And testosterone pills, Jesus. Tell him to rest. Yup, he's our number-one guy. We love him and get better. *(hangs up)*

Tell Lindsay she's on her own tonight and through the week.

AUDREY — *(getting up)* Oh, she'll hate that. *(she pauses before heading out the door)* Do you still want a muffin?

GEORGE — Yes, the dark bran.

AUDREY — What if he only has cranberry left?

GEORGE Oh, God. This muffin thing again. Why, when I always ask for bran, you come back with cranberry?

AUDREY Because he's usually out of bran by now, and cranberry happens to be all he has left.

GEORGE Oh, and you know why? I'll tell you why. Because he can't make five more bran muffins so by eleven o'clock in the morning, there's something besides a thousand cranberry muffins. And you know why they're sitting there? 'Cause everybody hates them.

AUDREY How about apple-cinnamon?

GEORGE How about most of the commercial apple products that are made are not made with real apple. They're made with turnips and apple flavour.

AUDREY Really?

GEORGE The entire muffin industry in this country is a joke.

AUDREY Yup. *(she leaves)*

Mark and Jeremy watch Lindsay solo on the monitor. Tears roll down Lindsay's cheeks.

LINDSAY And when, nineteen years later, mother and daughter were finally reunited this week, the final chapter in a long and painful saga turned out to have a very happy ending.

JEREMY She's crying, she's crying on the news?

MARK Jeez. You know, it works, though.

Lindsay, George, and Rani are in the make-up room. Lindsay and George each have a glass of wine. Rani reads the Globe and Mail. *Lindsay paces, self-satisfied and excited.*

RANI — Listen to the *Globe and Mail.*

(reading paper) John Haslett Cuff: "Lindsay Warren is a breath of fresh air blowing through a stagnant institution paralysed by tired ideas and an old-regime mentality." Nice. "Watch for her last solo performance tonight before Jim Walcott returns and you'll see the corp's news administration doing something right for once."

Lindsay laughs, satisfied.

GEORGE — *(to Lindsay)* How do you feel?

LINDSAY — That's great. That's great. I don't want this to sound self-serving, I really don't, but you throw the ball to me in the end zone, and I'm gonna catch it. No, that's a game-winner. I love Jim Walcott, I really do, and I respect his work, but run with him, you're heading for a loss.

GEORGE — I love you. But this guy took a ton of pills and almost killed himself. I'm not going to kick him while he's down.

LINDSAY — *(taking a drink of wine)* Well, you're a good person.

George stands over Audrey and reads off her computer screen as she types.

GEORGE — ". . . and we say good-bye to a talented anchor and a loyal co-worker," um, "with a heavy heart and a sense of great loss."

Okay, fax it to Sid Adilman and don't put any name on it, okay? Good, good, good. *(he walks away)*

Jim comes through the newsroom, Toronto Star *in hand, past Mark and straight to George's office. He looks rough, he's just come out of the rain, his hair all wet and matted, his coat soaked.*

JIM *(to Audrey, pointing at George's door)* Is he in there?

AUDREY Yeah. Can you give him this muffin?

She holds out a bagged muffin, but Jim doesn't take it. He marches into George's office, slamming the door. George is on the phone.

GEORGE *(unfazed by Jim's entrance)* Yeah, well, five more bran muffins are not gonna kill . . . they're not gonna kill you. Yeah, well, screw *you*! *(he hangs up, but doesn't look up at Jim)*

JIM You know, you know, George, I have given seven years to this corporation and I find out in Sid Adilman's column I'm out on my ass. Um . . . *(he opens the* Toronto Star *onto George's desk)*

It's that bitch-anchor, isn't it. She got her claw into you, right?

GEORGE Oh, I saw that this morning. I, I, um . . . myself, I have no idea how that was leaked.

A security guard knocks and pokes his head in.

GEORGE Yeah?

SECURITY I'm sorry, sir, I didn't see Mr. Walcott come in here.

GEORGE I'm sorry. Why are you here again?

SECURITY Yesterday you told us to keep him out of the building.

GEORGE *(looking up at Jim)* Um, you know, I wanted to tell you about this at lunch.

JIM — You, sir, are a coward.

(walking out past the security guard) I can see myself out, thank you.

SECURITY — I never could really understand why he was a risk to security, sir.

GEORGE — He's got a bit of a drug problem and you never know what they might do.

SECURITY — Really. Yeah, I know what you mean. I put a couple guys down on angel dust once. I'll take care of it, sir.

Lindsay, Rani, and George are in the make-up room. Lindsay, seated in the make-up chair, is in a red suit. She has a glass of red wine. Rani is leaning on the counter. George is pacing, tense.

GEORGE — Red doesn't read news to me. Yellow, I like yellow. Yellow's fine.

LINDSAY — Red is my favourite colour.

(to Rani) What do you think?

RANI — Red is energy.

GEORGE — I'm the news director. I love you in yellow, I love you in blue. I hate red. I'm sorry.

Dernhoff shows up.

DERNHOFF — Hey, hey, hey!

LINDSAY — *(about to take a drink)* Hey!

DERNHOFF — You seen the ratings, you guys? I just saw . . . they're fabulous. They're fabulous.

GEORGE — She's brilliant.

DERNHOFF — She's fabulous.

GEORGE — Is she great?

DERNHOFF — She's the best.

GEORGE — She's fantastic.

DERNHOFF (*to Lindsay and Rani*) Uh, seven-thirty tonight, Centro?

RANI Yeah, uh . . . (*to Lindsay*) Do you want to drive together?

LINDSAY Sure.

RANI (*with Lindsay*) Okay, great.

DERNHOFF (*to Lindsay*) I love you in red. I *love* that colour on you. Red is energy. It's great.

A few moments later, George is being restrained by Security at the elevator bank.

GEORGE Look, this is crazy, okay. This is insane.

SECURITY I'm sorry, Mr. Findlay, but we have orders to keep you off this floor.

GEORGE Wait, listen. This is my floor, this is my show! This is crazy, okay.

SECURITY Those are my orders.

The elevator doors also open. Jeremy and Mark come out with food from the cafeteria. Mark also has a newspaper. The security guard holds the door open, waiting for George to get in.

JEREMY Hey, buddy, we just read Sid Adilman. You were screwed.

MARK Hey, sorry. It's so unexpected.

GEORGE What, what are you talking about, Sid Adilman? What does he say?

JEREMY (*eating potato chips*) Read him the thing.

MARK (*reads*) Brass shake-up at "Toronto News." Lindsay Warren, who replaced anchor Jim Walcott, is rumoured to have orchestrated the move of reporter Rani Sandu into the news director job formerly held by George Findlay. Sandu said today that the "tired ideas and old-regime mentality" are a thing of the past. Findlay moves into a middle-management position, where, in the words of one industry insider, "he can do no more harm."

JEREMY Bum deal. You were screwed, man. *(he and Mark edge away)*

MARK Sorry, you got a bad deal.

GEORGE Hey, you guys didn't talk to anyone about this?

MARK Well . . .

GEORGE You didn't mention this?

JEREMY/MARK *(talking over one another as they walk away)* No. We couldn't. We tried. We're going to mention this. This is a travesty. This is crap, man.

SECURITY Sir? *(he points to the elevator)*

Lindsay and Rani are walking down the hallway towards the newsroom studio.

LINDSAY *(holding the* Star*)* This is a joke, right? It's impossible. Sid Adilman says they're shipping me out to an anchor job in Winnipeg and you're back on the air. Did you know about this?

RANI Well, I've already been assigned a story. Can you believe it? But Winnipeg's supposed to have a great symphony.

LINDSAY How did this happen?

RANI *(opening studio door)* Know what? It happens.

Um, I gotta get my crew, but it was really good meeting you.

Mark and Jeremy are walking past.

JEREMY Hey, we just read Sid Adilman. Tough break. You were screwed.

MARK That was a shocker.

LINDSAY Did you know about this!?

JEREMY Us? No, no.

MARK We were just as shocked as you were, really. That's . . . *(he pretends to shudder)*

JEREMY Hear Winnipeg's got a great ballet. Have a good time, I swear to God. *(he and Mark are about to enter the studio when Audrey approaches)*

AUDREY *(to Jeremy)* Hey, are you gonna go see George?

JEREMY Yeah.

AUDREY Give him this muffin?

Jeremy takes the bagged muffin and enters the studio.

AUDREY *(walking past Lindsay)* Bye. *(Lindsay mouths "bye?" and shakes her head)*

George, Mark, and Jeremy watch a tape in George's office of a documentary shot for "Witness" showing Lindsay drinking wine.

GEORGE I got these clips from the documentary they shot of her. I cut them together like this and shipped it upstairs.

JEREMY They way you assembled it, she, she looks like a drunk.

GEORGE Yeah, it's a less stressful market. It'll be good for her problem.

JEREMY So, you used that tired-old-regime mentality.

GEORGE Tired and old wins the race.

MARK You know, she was okay, though. I mean, you look at her.

GEORGE — No, she was fantastic. She was brilliant. Okay, this whole game of musical chairs we played together the last couple of weeks? It gave us all pause, you guys. We need changes around here.

MARK — Change. Yeah.

GEORGE — Change.

MARK — Yeah, we'll change the way –

GEORGE — New ideas, new ideas, new ideas.

JEREMY — Yeah, yeah, yeah. We'll get some new ideas, different ideas.

GEORGE — New ideas.

JEREMY — New ideas, right.

GEORGE — Okay, change.

Jeremy picks up the bagged muffin.

JEREMY — Here's your bran muffin from Audrey.

Jeremy and Mark get up to leave. George looks down at his muffin.

GEORGE — Hey, wait a second. This is cranberry. *(yelling after Jeremy and Mark as they head out the door)* You know I hate cranberry.

George and Jim look at ties spread out on the anchor table.

JIM — You know, um, your philosophy of change I think is good. I think it's important, I think it's overdue. But I think these ties are new, and they're in keeping with that change.

GEORGE — This one here, I hate that one.

JIM — Yeah?

GEORGE Yeah, okay? Okay?

JIM What about that one?

GEORGE No, pass on that. I don't like that one. And, uh, these two, these two I don't like. And, uh, this one I hate, and I don't like that one either.

Anyway, so how's, um, how's your drug, uh, thing, problem, now?

JIM Yeah. No, that's over. That's done. Yeah, that was a scare.

GEORGE Oh, good.

JIM Clean as a whistle now.

GEORGE And the testosterone thing . . .

JIM Yeah, well, the pills seem to be working.

GEORGE Really? So your sex drive is back?

JIM Oh, big time.

GEORGE Really? Good.

Audrey enters with a newspaper in hand.

AUDREY *(while glancing at Jim)* George, can I talk to you when you get a sec?

GEORGE Uh, you can talk now.

AUDREY No, when you get a sec.

GEORGE *(sternly)* You can talk now.

AUDREY It's private.

GEORGE Look, all this sort of private, these private conversations, these little political groups and stuff, that's what's been causing the problems around here lately. If you have anything to say, say it now, 'cause I don't want to read about it tomorrow in Sid Adilman's column.

(smiling to Jim) Know what I mean?

JIM Thank you.

GEORGE You can talk.

JIM Tell us.

AUDREY Okay. We won't have to wait 'til tomorrow to read it in Sid Adilman. It's in his column today. Jim's being charged with sexually harassing two of the wardrobe girls.

George and Jim look at each other.

THE END

EPISODE 3

"Deeper Deeper"

First Aired: November 4, 1996

Mark and Jim are walking down the hallway.

JIM	. . . I was thinking not so much in editorial as such, but more an Andy Rooney-type observation.
MARK	You know, I'm not sure George'd go for that.
JIM	Why? Why wouldn't he? Observational humour is huge. Seinfeld, Andy Rooney. Try this. Toilet paper. Have you noticed how it's impossible to start a new roll without shredding the first sheet? Why is that?
MARK	I have no idea.
JIM	No, see, that's the rhetorical observation. "Why is that?" sets it off.
MARK	Oh, okay. I'm sorry.
JIM	They all say that, right?
MARK	Yeah, okay. Go ahead.
JIM	So, I figure we use two rolls a week. So that's two lost sheets a week. About three hundred sheets per roll after three years, you've lost a whole roll. Now that doesn't sound like a big deal, but multiply that by a lifetime of seventy-five years, you've wasted twenty-five rolls per person. Multiply *that* by 30 million Canadians and you're talking about 750 million rolls. That's a huge toilet paper rip-off. See, last line, rip-off?
MARK	Yeah, yeah. I get it. *(he walks into the newsroom while Jim stands at the door)*
JIM	Yeah, that's the Andy Rooney thing. Huh, it's Andy Rooney but it's Seinfeld.

(*noticing Mark is now way inside the newsroom*)
Asshole.

Everyone is watching the TV set in the boardroom. It's tuned to the internal broadcast from the president about budget cuts. There are annoyed and exasperated faces.

PRESIDENT These cuts will be painful, but I know that at the end of the day we can be an even stronger, more competitive broadcaster. Public broadcasting is part of what defines us as Canadians. And we can ensure our future if we make this sacrifice now, together.

GEORGE (*turns off the set to moans and jeers of "Oh Jeez"*) Well, you wonder why he didn't come down in person. I'm not going to let a bunch of free-market idiots in Ottawa destroy perhaps the best public news service in North America. (*people clap in agreement*)

I'm going to fight for every single dollar in our budget and I'm gonna go to the wall for every job on this floor. (*more applause*)

JEREMY (*to Mark*) What does he mean by that?

MARK He's gonna fuck us.

GEORGE If we let them create fear, they will beat us. But if we stand together and we trust each other, I think we can win this.

George and his boss, Dernhoff, are in Dernhoff's office.

GEORGE So what you're saying is that, that my job is secure.

DERNHOFF I'm saying we have no plans to cut executive producers.

GEORGE — Well, then, then I'm basically secure, then, because, um . . . *(Dernhoff stonewalls)* I'm an executive producer. We're not cutting executive producers, so . . .

DERNHOFF — If you can cut 20 per cent from your show budget, I don't think you have a problem.

GEORGE — Twenty per cent means jobs.

DERNHOFF — That's a reality here.

GEORGE — So what you're saying is that, that my job is secure.

Jeremy is at his workstation in the newsroom, talking on the phone.

JEREMY — Yeah, so you know if any producing spots come up, keep me in mind . . . This show? The truth? *(he looks behind him, talks quieter)* He'd be in the toilet without me.

MARK — *(on the phone at his workstation)* I just thought if anything opens up over there I'd love a shot, that's all. Well, virtually I produce the show.

JEREMY — *(on the phone)* Oh yeah, George?

MARK — *(on the phone)* George is a hack, okay?

JEREMY — *(on the phone)* He's an unethical, untalented, weak, self-serving ass-kisser.

MARK — *(on the phone)* He's an idiot who's got a talent for kissing butt. Oh, I make him look good. Okay, well, keep me in mind.

Jim and Stan Kozack, his agent, walk down the hallway and along the atrium walkway.

STAN — You know, phoning me this morning was probably the smartest call you'll ever make in your fuckin' life. This place is going down the tubes. Now, I wanna be in the Jim Walcott business. I can sell Jim

Walcott out there in the private sector with one hand up my ass!

JIM — Jeez, the private sector. Jeez.

STAN — Did I say private sector? I meant the money sector. I meant the career sector. This is your fuckin' life we're talkin' about, Jimmy.

JIM — It's just, you know, after fourteen years in here, out there seems very scary.

STAN — Yeah, well, there's nothing out there that can hurt you, except maybe falling money.

JIM — Falling money, that I like.

STAN — And the fact is that this corporation has given you a real credibility as a thinking anchor. I can leverage that, you know.

JIM — Yeah. Not like those shit-for-brains private network assholes.

STAN — *(laughs)* No, exactly. I mean, you've got something that those private guys don't have, which is intelligence, class, honesty, you know?

JIM — Well don't stop now. I got an erection.

STAN — *(laughs)* I'm a big Jim Walcott fan. You know that.

JIM — Let me, let me try something on you. *(they stop to talk at the railing of the atrium)*

STAN — Yeah.

JIM — This'll be something of a signature editorial.

STAN — Yeah.

JIM — Toilet paper. Have you ever noticed how it's impossible to start a new roll without shredding the first sheet? Why is that?

STAN — I don't know.

JIM — Yeah, no. You're not supposed to. See, that's, that's, that's the rhetorical observation. It's an Andy Rooney bit, you know?

STAN	Oh, fuck, yeah.
JIM	Yeah.
STAN	Yeah, oh, I love Andy Rooney shit.
JIM	Yeah.
STAN	Yeah, yeah. I . . .
JIM	I figure we use two rolls a week. So that's two lost sheets a week.
STAN	You know, I have a meeting to go to, but, um, keep it up.
JIM	Yeah? Well, I'll fax you the end of it.

George, Jeremy, Mark, and Rani are in the boardroom viewing a grainy black-and-white camera tape of a hooker leaning into the passenger window of a car. The driver cannot be seen at this point.

MARK	Our camera was across the street in a van.
JEREMY	That's one of our hookers in the short shorts talking to the guy in the Acura.
GEORGE	She's cute.
RANI	She's bent over with her head stuck in a window. How can you tell she's cute?
MARK	She moves out of the way. She's done. Camera goes right in and look who it is. Our own award-winning anchor, Jim Walcott.
RANI	He knows we're doing a story on hookers. How could he get caught like this?
JEREMY	I don't know. Shit for brains?
MARK	Look, like it or not, we've a story here. George, what do you want to do with this?
GEORGE	Okay, we're journalists, right?
JEREMY	Yeah.
GEORGE	And sometimes you're faced with these tough ethical choices.

JEREMY Yeah.

MARK What are we gonna do?

GEORGE Burn the tape. *(Mark nods)*

George, Jeremy, and Mark are in George's office. George is on his couch with the TV *remote in his hand. Mark is leaning on George's desk.*

GEORGE You can't find it.

MARK It was on his desk and now it's gone.

JEREMY Oh, this is great.

GEORGE If the budget cuts don't kill us, this will sink us for sure, okay? This is my number-one priority. I want this story killed. If this story gets out, we're dead. *(Mark nods)*

George, Mark, and Jeremy are walking through the newsroom.

GEORGE Listen, these cuts have to be made. That's the reality.

JEREMY Right.

GEORGE Everybody has to share the pain.

KRIS *(spotting George)* George? Um, BMW on line four?

George, Mark, and Jeremy are back in George's office. George has taken the phone call. Mark and Jeremy are seated on the couch listening to George's conversation.

GEORGE *(on phone)* Peter, did Henry bring you up to speed on the wipers, I couldn't see where I was going. It flipped off. Yeah, well, the rain was . . . well I'm, I'm sure that Hitler could see where he was going when he went into Poland. I'm, I'm sorry. Okay. I, I, that, I apol– that was in bad tas– I'm sure you were born – well, listen, I want to know about the warranty. Are the wipers covered by warranty? Well, then, talk to your supervisor and call me back. Thank you. *(he hangs up)*

God, a forty-thousand-dollar car. Okay, where were we?

JEREMY We were sharing the pain.

GEORGE Who do we cut?

Mark and Jeremy look out the window at the two assistants at their workstations. Kris is reading the newspaper and Sandra is playing solitaire on her computer.

George and Kris are seated at a table in the atrium walkway. Kris is eating.

GEORGE You know, this isn't easy for me, and that's why I wanted to talk to you away from the office.

KRIS Wait, is this about that lesbian thing between me and Sandra I told you about last week?

GEORGE No, no. I have no problem with that.

KRIS Well, I did. It just didn't work out. Basically, I really, really like sex with men.

GEORGE Really?

KRIS Yeah. *(she takes a drink of pop)*

GEORGE Really.

KRIS Yeah. But that's not a come-on or anything. I just –

GEORGE No.

KRIS It's just, although I find you quite, um . . .

GEORGE Quite . . . ?

KRIS . . . attractive. Is this what you, what you wanted to talk about?

GEORGE No, no. Actually, um, you're doing a very good job.

KRIS Really?

GEORGE Oh, yes, you are. When you poked your head in this morning and you said, "BMW on line five," you know, that was great.

KRIS That was line four, I think.

GEORGE Line four. That's great.

George and Sandra, who is seated, are talking at Sandra's workstation.

GEORGE This isn't easy for me. In fact, you know, I take this very personally.

SANDRA Is this about your mother?

GEORGE My mother?

SANDRA Yeah, if it's about your mother. Um, you know, she's called a couple of times on this number, so I understand that, you know, you're kind of uncomfortable talking to her. So I talk to her now about three or four times a day and –

GEORGE You talk to my mother three or four times a day?

SANDRA Yeah, it's not, it's like she's great to talk to. I mean, I really enjoy talking to her, so. And she seems to enjoy it. So, is that what you wanted to talk to me about?

GEORGE Yeah, no, that's fine. That's fine. Uh, well, you're doing a very good job.

SANDRA Thank you. Thank you.

GEORGE Great.

George and Jeremy are at the coffee station in the newsroom. Jeremy opens a bottle of water. George rifles through the cupboards.

JEREMY Hey, how're the cuts coming?

GEORGE Don't worry about it. They're coming, they're coming, they're happening. Where's the popcorn?

Jeremy opens another cupboard door. George takes out a popcorn bag and puts it into the microwave.

JEREMY So, uh, you talk to Bill today?

GEORGE No. *(he pushes buttons on the microwave)*

JEREMY He's running the ballet story again. You think we got more than six viewers that actually give a shit? You're lookin' for a cut, arts and entertainment . . . there's your cut.

George stands looking over Bill's shoulder as he types at his workstation.

GEORGE How ya doin', Bill?

BILL *(typing)* Fine.

GEORGE Is this the ballet stuff?

BILL Yeah.

GEORGE *(reading)* The line from Martha Graham to Merce Cunningham is evident . . .

Bill stops typing and gives George's shoulder a push to keep him from reading his work.

BILL Can I help you? *(he resumes typing)*

GEORGE No, no. I was just, you know, wondering how you're doing. And I love the ballet myself, but I was just curious, you know, as to how much of our audience, you know, relates to the dance.

BILL If this is about staff cuts, George, I am a personal friend of the heritage minister. And if it comes down to me or you, it'll be you.

GEORGE No, look. I love that ballet.

BILL Tonight is the world premiere.

GEORGE You know, I'm mistaking it for something else.

Maybe for, you know, Swan Lake with Karen Kain. Is Karen Kain still alive? Karen Kain is alive, what am I thinking. It's Margaret Laurence who's dead. You know, we should do something on Margaret Laurence. Maybe a tribute. Okay?

George, Mark, and Jeremy are in the boardroom. George paces.

GEORGE Can't do this, you guys. I can't look these people in the face and tell them they're fired. I think the reason is because basically, deep down, you know, I feel too much.

JEREMY *(not convinced)* Oh, yeah. I don't think so.

GEORGE Oh, you don't think so? Well explain it, then.

JEREMY You're just one of those passive-aggressive guys.

GEORGE Oh, passive-aggressive. You know, people use this all the time, this expression. I have no idea what that means. What does that mean?

MARK You're weak and vicious. That's basically what it means.

GEORGE And how do the strong and gentle ones do this?

JEREMY The human way. Do it fast. Middle of the night, you pack their desk into a cardboard box. Send it down to the front door with a couple of security cops. They tell them they're fired and if they come back, they'll arrest them for trespassing.

GEORGE These are people with lives and families, okay?

MARK You can send fruit with a card?

GEORGE What, fruit in the winter?

JEREMY You make up a basket with capers, anchovies, smoked oysters.

GEORGE No anchovies.

MARK Then a tin of lobster. Whatever.

GEORGE How much is lobster a can?

JEREMY	Crab meat's cheaper.
GEORGE	I can live with crab meat. Done.

Sandra, mad, is collecting her coat and basket of gourmet food at her former workstation with Rani.

RANI	I thought they couldn't fire you?
SANDRA	I wasn't fired. I'm a casualty. I'm a casualty of downsizing. *(they begin to walk through the newsroom)*
RANI	So sue them again.
SANDRA	Oh, what's the point.
RANI	You sued them once. Sue them again. What's the difference?
SANDRA	What an asshole. You know, he couldn't even face me?
RANI	That's typical.

George, Mark, Jeremy, and Audrey are in George's office. George is seated at this desk, Jeremy is on a table, Mark and Audrey are on the couch. Audrey stays out of the conversation.

GEORGE	Do you think we're too white?
JEREMY	White. Us?
GEORGE	No, the show.
MARK	We have a lot of white people.
JEREMY	Yeah.
GEORGE	We have women.
MARK/JEREMY	Oh, yeah. Yeah. We have plenty of women.
GEORGE	Do you think this looks bad? Should we deal with this black issue?
MARK	I think we should . . .
JEREMY	. . . deal with this. Yeah, we should deal with this.
GEORGE	Good. You know, maybe a review.

JEREMY/MARK Review. Review. Yeah, we'll review it.

GEORGE Okay? Review.

Jeremy gets up and leaves.

MARK *(standing)* 'Cause the great thing about reviews is that –

GEORGE A review doesn't hurt.

MARK A review doesn't hurt anything. It's a review.

GEORGE *(as Mark leaves)* Thank you.
(to Audrey) I want you to remind me to deal with this. All right?

AUDREY Okay.

GEORGE Thank you. After lunch?

AUDREY *(getting up)* Yep.

GEORGE Remind me?

AUDREY After lunch today?

GEORGE Good point. Um, after lunch tomorrow. Thank you.

Rani is at her computer. Jim hovers at a workstation in front of her.

JIM You know, with these budget cuts there is more than one way to screw a cat. There's probably a hundred, two hundred, three hundred pretty-boy anchors out there who would do my job at half my salary. And you, you know, you played the affirmative action card. The Indian thing.

RANI I did not play the affirmative action card.

JIM No, no. I'm saying all power to you. I'm saying whatever gets the puck in the net, you know. But I'm telling you that's also on the chopping block.

RANI No, I worked my way! Forget it. I gotta go. *(she gets up and collects her papers)*

JIM	I won't put it past them if they brought in some little blonde chick to do your job at half your salary.
RANI	George and I already talked about this. And, uh, you should know that *I'm* not the one on the chopping block.

Jim and George are in George's office. Jim stands in front of George's desk, hands on his hips.

JIM	You useless piece of crap. Seven years together, and you fire me just to save your own goddamn ass. Huh?
GEORGE	You're not gone.
JIM	I'm not?
GEORGE	No.
JIM	*(relaxes)* I'm sorry. I didn't mean that. You know, there's a lot of paranoia going on around here.
GEORGE	Yes, there is. I've noticed that. I have no idea where, where this is coming from, though. But there's a loyalty that builds up over seven years.
JIM	Oh, absolutely. Yeah. Seven years. Has it been seven years?
GEORGE	Seven years. Unbelievable.
JIM	Jeez, that's a long time. Yeah.
GEORGE	You and me. Seven years.
JIM	*(shaking George's hand)* You're the best, you know that? Really.
GEORGE	Hey!
JIM	You're the best.
GEORGE	No, no. You're the best, really.
JIM	Really?
GEORGE	No, you're great.
JIM	Really?

GEORGE — You are great. You are great.

Audrey has just walked in, and Jim turns and gives her a loose hug. She doesn't respond.

JIM — Okay. See you later. *(he leaves)*

AUDREY — You wanted me to remind you today to deal with the black-white balance on the show.

GEORGE — I thought that was tomorrow.

AUDREY — Yesterday you said tomorrow, which is today.

GEORGE — Uh, can you remind me tomorrow?

AUDREY — Tomorrow morning?

GEORGE — Afternoon.

AUDREY — Should we just drop it?

GEORGE — No, I don't want to drop it. I can't think about the black thing. It's important to me, the black thing, but I can't think about that right now. I've got too much stuff on my mind. Okay, thanks.

Kris pops in.

GEORGE — *(to Kris)* Yes?

KRIS — Your BMW dealer on four.

GEORGE — *(picks up the phone)* Henry.

Audrey leaves.

GEORGE — Okay, these wipers. I know they have to come from Germany. Okay, listen, Rommel had ten thousand tanks in North Africa. He didn't have a big problem getting parts from Germany. I, I'm sorry. I'm sorry.

JEREMY — *(poking his head in the door)* Bad news.

GEORGE — Henry, one sec.

JEREMY	I just heard the hooker tape was slipped to an MPP at Queen's Park. One of those fanatical Christian, conservative, privatize-the-universe, no-sex-before-death types. Evidently, she's out for your ass.

George and Jim are in the hallway.

GEORGE	Okay, I'm gonna ask you point-blank. Have you ever been with a hooker?
JIM	No, no. My philosophy's always been, if you have to pay for sex you're a fuck-up.
GEORGE	That's a philosophy?
JIM	No, no it's not. It's, well . . .
GEORGE	Forget that, okay? The point is, we have you on tape with a hooker in your car in the Lansdowne area. We had a hidden camera across the street. We were shooting the street hooker stuff at night.
	Jim sees someone coming down the hall and signals for George to stop talking. George continues once the person has passed.
GEORGE	That tape has fallen into the hands of a woman who's a member of this legislature, who happens to believe that the earth was created in seven days. Now that doesn't make me feel very comfortable. Now, we have to figure out a way to deal with this.
JIM	Oh, Jesus Christ. *(buries his head in his hands)* This is Hugh Grant time, isn't it?
GEORGE	No, unfortunately this is you.

George, Jeremy, and Mark are walking down the hallway towards the studio.

GEORGE I'm not the bad guy, here.

JEREMY No, no.

GEORGE Cuts are a reality.

JEREMY A reality.

MARK You're the best.

JEREMY Yeah.

GEORGE Thank you very much. You know, I could very easily quit myself, play the martyr, fall on my own sword. *(Jeremy and Mark nod in agreement)* Possibly get some very good press for it. Walk into some big section job at twice the salary, you know, but I'm not gonna do that.

MARK Well, there are no private sector jobs.

JEREMY Yeah, he's right actually.

GEORGE Wait. What, what? Have you guys, have you guys been out there?

JEREMY/MARK No, no.

They walk into the newsroom.

GEORGE Have you guys been checking it out?

JEREMY/MARK No.

GEORGE Okay, 'cause if you are, you can just forget it.

JEREMY No, we wouldn't do that.

GEORGE *(stopping at the reception desk and picking up messages)* Okay, have you not heard of the concept of loyalty? Of not dealing behind someone's back?

George and Jeremy are talking in the stairwell. Jeremy is eating a sucker.

GEORGE You know, I don't want to give the impression, you know, that I'm talking about Mark behind his back, here.

JEREMY	No, no.
GEORGE	I just want an opinion, you know. What do you think of him as a producer?
JEREMY	Mark's a great guy, I mean . . .
GEORGE	Yeah, he's a great guy.
JEREMY	Yeah, no, Mark's a great guy. But, you know. You know a guy for years, you, uh, well, you get to see flaws.
GEORGE	He is weak. I, you know, I mean, we know this.
JEREMY	Yeah, you take the weakness, right? And you combine it with the laziness . . . No, laziness is not the right word. It's more, uh . . .
GEORGE	Complacency?
JEREMY	Complacency, exactly.
GEORGE	Yeah, yeah.
JEREMY	He's, uh, burnt. This has no effect on, on, on his job or anything. This is just a . . .
GEORGE	No.
JEREMY	. . . a chat.
GEORGE	Absolutely.

George and Mark are standing in the atrium walkway, leaning against the rail.

GEORGE	So, what do you think of Jeremy?
MARK	As a producer?
GEORGE	Yeah.
MARK	Oh, he's great! Yeah!
GEORGE	He is great, right?
MARK	He's terrific.
GEORGE	No, he is terrific.
MARK	Yeah.
GEORGE	He's terrific, he's great. Um, how, how good?
MARK	How . . . ?

GEORGE How great?

MARK Off the record.

GEORGE Absolutely off the record.

MARK This won't affect his job.

GEORGE No.

MARK I think he's expendable.

GEORGE And his news instincts, what do you think?

MARK Not the greatest.

GEORGE No, I was a little surprised when he hadn't heard that Sue Rodriguez was dead. Sooo, you think he's great, but you do think he's expendable.

MARK This is off the record, right?

GEORGE Yes, this will not affect his job.

MARK I think he's completely redundant.

George, Rani, Jeremy, Audrey, Bill, Jim, and Mark are in the boardroom. Everyone sits depressed and silent. No one trusts anyone.

GEORGE So, how's everyone this morning? Good? Okay, great, great. The Siamese twins piece worked very well. It was quite brilliant. In fact, the twins stories always work very well. Evidently, because of our piece, people send money and flowers to the hospital and suggested names for the kids. I suggested the Menendez brothers. *(silence)* It was a joke! I'm just trying to lighten things up, all right?

JEREMY *(hand over his mouth)* You fucked everyone up.

GEORGE I didn't hear that.

JEREMY I didn't *say* anything.

GEORGE Look, we've got a show to get out, okay? Do you have the film on the derailment?

JEREMY Hey, ask Mark. He's the king of city news. I'm *expendable.*

MARK (*pointing at Jeremy*) You said *I* was expendable! You said . . .

GEORGE No one's expendable.

JEREMY (*pointing at Mark*) Did you go behind my back and talk to . . .

MARK Wait a second, you said I was expendable.

JEREMY Yes, you did. Yes, you did.

Everyone starts yelling at once about backstabbing, except for Audrey.

RANI (*to Jim*) I heard what you said about me.

JIM What?!

JEREMY (*to George*) The only job safe around here is yours.

MARK (*pointing at George*) You go to Jeremy and you say . . .

JEREMY (*to George*) You go behind my back and talk to Mark about me.

Bill gets up and leaves.

MARK (*walking out*) This is bullshit.

RANI (*to Jim, while walking out*) The race card thing? Bullshit.

JIM (*getting up and following Rani out*) Oh, run away!

GEORGE That's my job. My job is to talk, is to talk to people. To evaluate.

Audrey is the only one left at the table. George puts his head in his hands.

AUDREY You wanted me to remind you today to deal with the black-white thing?

GEORGE (*looks up at Audrey*) Tomorrow, tomorrow.

AUDREY Before or after lunch?

GEORGE After. After lunch, okay?

AUDREY I think you should just rehire Sandra. I think that she doesn't cost you very much and it's obviously causing you grief.

GEORGE Well, actually, I could end up looking all right, if I, you know, on the black . . .

AUDREY Yes.

GEORGE . . . if we hire her. Good point.

AUDREY BMW called again and the supervisor checked out your wiper system and says BMW is not responsible.

GEORGE Oh, I suppose they were only following orders.

AUDREY And the MPP from hell is going to be here at four with Jim's hooker tape.

Mark walks into the newsroom with the female MPP, who is blonde, in her late thirties, and looks uptight. They head towards the boardroom. The MPP has the videotape in her hand.

MARK I know you MPPs are busy. We appreciate you coming down. This is going to be good for Jim, for public broadcasting, for the entire province.

MPP This tape that was sent to me is very disturbing, given that you are supported by a lot of Christian taxpayers.

MARK I know, you don't see a lot of lions paying taxes, huh? (*they stop outside the boardroom door*)

MPP Excuse me?

MARK Oh, I was kidding there. Christians and the lions . . . ? listen, why don't, uh, you go in here (*opening the door for her*) and when we . . . (*she walks into the boardroom*)

Jim, Mark, Jeremy, and the MPP *are sitting in the boardroom.*

JIM Well, I mean, you know, my sin is obvious. It's right there, *(points to the tape on the table)* right there on the tape. I wanted, I wanted to talk to you before we went out there. I mean, this, this whole thing with the prostitute getting on tape, you . . . This whole thing was a huge wake-up call for me. And do you know who was knocking at the door? The Lord Jesus Christ.

MPP Seems like an awfully quick conversion.

JIM No!

MARK It probably seems convenient.

MPP Yeah, it does look a little convenient.

MARK Well, that's not the case. Jim came to us, and he had this revelation, and we said, Jim, what would you like to do?

JEREMY And he said, I want to meet this woman. Get her on the air. Bring some balance to TV news.

JIM I mean, where are family values. This whole sexual need of mine had me by the . . . *(makes his hand curl up)*

JEREMY *(leaping in)* . . . throat.

JIM I couldn't resist. I literally could not resist until I found Jesus.

MARK If you resist the devil, he will flee from you.

JIM Hallelujah.

MARK I think that's James 4:7. I'm not sure.

MPP I don't know.

JIM Blessed is he who endureth temptation. For when he has tried, he shall receive the crown of life. That's James 1:12.

JEREMY Amen.

Audrey comes in.

AUDREY — They're ready for the interview. Are you finished with my *Bartlett's Quotations?*

JEREMY — I don't have your *Bartlett's Quotations.*

AUDREY — I thought you needed some biblical quotes.

MARK — Oh, bi, biographical. Yeah.

JEREMY — Right.

JIM — Yeah, the biographical.

Audrey frowns at them.

MARK — We're doing something on, uh, we're going to do a piece on Mother Teresa.

MPP — Oh, you're going to do something on Mother Teresa.

JEREMY/MARK — Yeah.

JIM — She's marvellous. Is she still alive?

JEREMY — Yes, she is, and she's a wonderful woman.

JIM — Yeah.

The hooker from the tape wanders the corridor beside the studio looking for someone. She stops Audrey, who's walking by.

HOOKER — Excuse me. Hi, I'm looking for Jim Walcott.

AUDREY — I think he's on the air right now. Can I help you?

HOOKER — Oh, he told me if ever I was in the area, I could just pop up and watch a taping.

AUDREY — Pop up? Maybe you should wait for him in make-up. Come with me.

Jim and the MPP *are on the interview set and are being watched on a monitor by George, Mark, and Jeremy at a workstation.*

MPP For me, family values are Christian values.

JIM So what about homosexuality, then?

MPP Homosexuality not only breaks nature's laws, it also undermines the whole foundation of family life.

MARK Man, this is just like the 700 Club.

GEORGE You gotta bend a little, you guys.

JEREMY Yeah, like right over and take . . .

GEORGE Hey, hey, family values. So I assume that the offending tape was destroyed.

MARK Incinerated in a fiery hell of eternal damnation.

JIM . . . with homosexuality you mean?

MPP Yes! I think, I think it's like the devil's disease.

JIM Very interesting.

MARK Oh, this black issue. Are we still going to review it?

GEORGE I reviewed it and I rehired her.

JEREMY You *rehired* her?

GEORGE Yes, I rehired her based on the conclusion of the results of my review.

JEREMY So, who you gonna cut?

GEORGE A lot of management people have been having problems with these cuts, so we're all going off to Banff for a week for a conference on the psychology of corporate downsizing.

JEREMY Get a little skiing in?

GEORGE That's why I'm going.

JIM Well, thank you very much for joining us. That was very enlightening. And now one final thought before we go . . .

Toilet paper. Have you ever noticed how it's impossible to start a new roll without shredding the first sheet? Why is that?

Mark and the MPP *walk out of the newsroom studio and down the corridor.*

MPP Well, I think you're trying to produce a balanced program and I respect that.

MARK Well, we all love Christ.

MPP I have to make a call. Is there a phone I use could before I leave?

MARK Yeah, actually, in the make-up room, if you just wanna come . . .

Mark opens the door to the make-up room. Jim is sitting in the make-up chair, with his back to the door, getting a blow job from the hooker.

JIM Jesus Christ!

THE END

EPISODE 4

"The Kevorkian Joke"

First Aired: November 11, 1996

Jeremy is at his workstation in the newsroom. He's on the phone.

JEREMY Yeah, we were just wondering whether Premier Harris will be marching in the Gay Pride Parade this year? No? We were just wonderin'.

Mark, at his workstation, is also on the phone.

MARK No, I, I, I know, it's horrible, I know, but no one died. I can't get a crew out. Okay, look, I'll make you a deal. If someone dies in the next, *(looks at his watch)* hour, then, uh, this could be a great story. Uh-huh. Well, you have to call me back. No, no. We can still make the six o'clock. Okay.

Jeremy, Mark, and George are in the boardroom watching a bad suicide tape made by Shane Pollack, in his mid-twenties, who works in the tape library. Shane talks to the camera from a chair.

SHANE Hi, Nicole. Hello, Nicole. This is my tape. I'm gonna, I'm gonna kill myself on tape. Thought I'd tape it. I guess everybody wants their fifteen minutes of fame, huh? Hi, I'm going to blow myself away on tape.

MARK He works in tape archives. So, uh, he locks himself in a library, he makes this video. Then he slashes his wrists. *(laughs)*

JEREMY He's a failed screenwriter and his girlfriend dumped him.

SHANE It's my time. It's my moment.

JEREMY Yeah, your moment.

GEORGE Where'd you guys get this?

JEREMY Uh, Mark dubbed it, then he gave it to me . . . and I had a party on Tuesday night and everyone from the station watched it.

GEORGE Except me. And you dubbed it. You didn't tell me you were dubbing this tape. And there's a party, and I'm out of the dubbing loop, and I'm out of the, uh, party.

JEREMY Uh, the party was nothing. Just a couple cases of beer. Nobody had a good time.

GEORGE But I wasn't invited.

JEREMY/MARK No, no.

GEORGE I'm not uptight about this. I'm just saying I was not invited to this, okay? Thank you.

MARK Look, one of these times he'll succeed, and then we'll invite you.

GEORGE Thank you. You know what we have here?

MARK What, what, what?

GEORGE We put this on television, we'll kill with this. This is our ratings week.

JEREMY It's one week. How're you gonna stretch it over five nights?

GEORGE You bring him back. He'll do four more. He talks about suicide Monday through Thursday. Friday, he blows his brains out.

JEREMY Blows his brains out. Where does the gun come in?

GEORGE Yeah, yeah, no. Well, that was metaphorically speaking. He can kill himself, he can shoot himself, he can overdose on pills *(Jeremy and Mark look at George like he's crazy)*, he can slash his wrists. You know, I mean these are production details. The point is, this is not unprecedented. We've seen suicide videos on TV before. This is great. This can work. Let's just make sure it's legal.

On the newsroom set at the anchor desk, Jim is interviewing Daniel Richler.

LYNN In five, four, three . . .

JIM My guest today is Daniel Richler. Writer, critic, and one of the few intellectual voices to be heard regularly on Canadian television. He's also of course the son of the popular and prolific writer, Mordechai Richler. I think I got the Mordechai right. The "*ch*" in Morde*ch*ai. It is Morde*ch*ai as opposed to Morde*k*ai . . .

George and Kris are off to the side of the newsroom. George tries to concentrate on what Kris is saying.

KRIS Quebec is a distinct society but, but so is Newfoundland. I mean, you can't have . . .

GEORGE Wait, wait one second. Are we on for tonight, or is your roommate going to be there?

KRIS You don't want to hear my thoughts on Quebec, do you.

GEORGE Oh, I do, I do. Except the last time her dog was there. He was watching us.

KRIS What?

GEORGE The dog?

KRIS You're not listening at all to my thoughts on Quebec.

GEORGE Okay, what were you saying about it.

Back to the anchor desk.

JIM ... and has taken a shot at fiction himself with a new book, which I haven't read yet but I hear is terrific. *(flips through book)*

What is it? Three hundred and seventy ... three hundred and seventy-six pages. Almost four hundred pages.

Back to George and Kris.

KRIS I don't think English Canada knows how to talk to Quebec.

GEORGE Is she gonna be there? That's all I want to know.

KRIS The dog?

GEORGE Tonight, yes.

The interview now over, Daniel, pissed, comes out of George's office and walks through the newsroom with George.

DANIEL First, I said I would come on his show on the condition that my father's not mentioned. Not only does he mention my father, but he obsesses over this Morde*k*ai, Morde*ch*ai shit. I mean, he's a fucking idiot, okay?

GEORGE I know he's an idiot.

DANIEL And the only thing he knows about my novel is the amount of pages that are in it. Did he count that himself or does somebody do that for him? Then, then he goes on about, uh, I took a shot at fiction. I did not take a fucking shot at fiction. I wrote a fucking novel, for which I received a substantial fucking advance. *(he opens the studio door and they walk out into the office corridor)*

I mean, listen, there's a reason why I did my own book show on television, so I could talk to sensible human beings and not some brain-dead anchor who's more interested in his appearance in front of a camera than any of the pressing issues in English literature.

Kris comes out of an office doorway. She has her coat in her hand.

KRIS Daniel! Hey! Your hair looked great, all right? You were silly to be worried about it. *(she puts on her coat. It's a leather jacket, identical to the one Daniel's wearing)*

DANIEL When my hair gets fucked up, I find people don't really listen to the things that I have to say.

GEORGE I understand. I understand.

KRIS Yeah, well, they spent an hour looking for the right kind of gel.

GEORGE *(together with Daniel)* An hour?

KRIS Yeah, well, it looked great.

GEORGE The man has the best hair on TV.

DANIEL Shall we, are we . . .?

KRIS Oh, yeah. I'm ready.

(to George) So, um, we're going out for a bite. So, um, I left your Fibre First on your desk. Metamucil they ran out of –

GEORGE *(interrupting)* Uh, this is for my mother, this stuff. Okay, it's not . . . um, can we talk . . .

KRIS Yeah.

George take Kris a few steps back to have a private moment in the corner of the hall.

GEORGE Is this a sexual thing here?

KRIS No, no. He's written a novel.

GEORGE Oh, what does that do, make him impotent? I thought we were going to talk about Quebec.

KRIS Oh, can we do that maybe next week?

GEORGE *(whispering intensely)* Look, the country's coming apart. You spent an hour looking for gel for this man's hair. He's most likely going to try to get you into bed. If that's the kind of Canada you want, then fine!

KRIS Fine, fine. *(she walks away from George)*

DANIEL You ready?

KRIS Yeah.

They leave George standing. Jim, seeing Daniel go, approaches George.

JIM Daniel Richler, he's a smart man. It's a good spot, I thought.

GEORGE It was a shitty spot. A shitty spot.

Mark, Jeremy, and George are in the boardroom. Mark consults a book. Jeremy works on a crossword puzzle in a newspaper.

MARK *(reading)* Okay, it's not a crime to, uh, commit suicide or to even attempt suicide. But what is a crime is if you counsel a person to commit suicide or you aid and abet a person to commit suicide.

GEORGE We're not aiding and abetting.

MARK Well, what are we doing?

GEORGE We're . . . going to wrap this, uh, around a social issue, okay? We'll bring in some experts. And, uh, what we're doing is, we're, we're enlightening the public.

MARK *(consulting his book)* Okay, well, there's nothing about enlightening in here, so maybe we're okay.

GEORGE You know, uh, he's going to kill himself anyway. Let him end it with a little dignity. We could win the week with this thing, okay? Let him end it with the dignity of being a winner.

JEREMY Yeah, we win. He just . . . dies.

GEORGE Well, I did not invent the market economy, okay? I think this thing could work.

Jim is seated in his chair at the anchor desk in the newsroom. Lynn, the floor director, is putting on his mike.

LYNN Okay, we're going to pick it up with your last line. And then we're going to roll with the suicide tape.

JIM Yeah. Is my hair too high on top?

LYNN No, it's good. In four, three, two . . .

JIM What you are about to see is real. And, we must warn you, potentially very disturbing. Mr. Pollack is a chronically depressed failed screenwriter who's attempted suicide three times before. Am I correct there, Shane?

Shane is linked up to Jim. He's sitting in a room. There is a caption on the screen: "Wants to commit suicide." George, Jeremy, and Mark watch a monitor in the newsroom.

SHANE Uh, yes. Uh, three, three times. You are correct, Jim. But, uh, you know, I'm not a failed screenwriter. If I am, that's only by Hollywood's bullshit standards.

GEORGE He said "bullshit" on TV.

MARK Well, he is killing himself.

GEORGE Yeah, well, he wants to say "bullshit," he can kill himself in late night.

SHANE It's meaningless. You, you, you look into your own soul. You look into your own soul, and it's just, uh, you realize that . . .

JIM Nothing's there?

SHANE That's right. It's empty. It's a void. It's a spiritual void. There's . . .

GEORGE This is too philosophical for television.

MARK Well, he's killing himself. Give him a break.

GEORGE Know what I want? Tomorrow night I want this punched up.

JEREMY Punch up a suicide?

The next night, Jim is about to start the evening newscast.

JIM How's my hair?

LYNN Too high on top.

JIM *(yelling)* Where the hell's Hair!

LYNN Here we go. In five, four, three, two . . .

JIM Once again, what you are about to see is real and potentially very disturbing. How're you feeling Shane?

George, Jeremy, and Mark are watching again in the newsroom. The caption on the screen reads, "Suicide TV – Day 2."

SHANE: Everyone has the right to die, right? No one, no one, has the right to win though, right? You have to earn, earn the victories. What do we lose? We have a right to be treated with just a little respect, you know . . .

GEORGE: I think we should punch this up.

JEREMY: No, no. It's just a set-up. Wait for it.

SHANE: . . . respect. Yeah, my agents haven't called me back in a year and a half because I'm a loser. Even Dr. Kevorkian, you know, the suicide doctor. I phoned him to help assist me, and, uh, he hasn't returned my calls.

Mark laughs softly, Jeremy smiles.

GEORGE: That was funny.

JEREMY: I wrote that. That's my joke.

George, Mark, Jeremy, Audrey, Rani, Bill, and Jim are seated around the table in the boardroom.

MARK: Okay, our lead is the latest killer virus from Zaire.

GEORGE: Did we get the tape on that?

MARK: Not yet.

GEORGE: We can't do a lead without the tape.

MARK: Well, you know, we do have that stuff from the Ebola virus last year, and I thought maybe we could just, you know, run that.

GEORGE: I like that. Run it, run it.

BILL: Whoa. Year-old tape of a totally different plague? Isn't that going to give us a major credibility gap?

RANI: Slightly.

GEORGE: Listen, I, I just don't think we have to paint ourselves into a factual corner over some footage from Africa.

JIM What country are we talking about here?

GEORGE He already said. Zaire.

JIM Zaire.

AUDREY What, what is a factual corner? This is a term I haven't heard.

GEORGE If it's one village or another in Africa, I mean, who's gonna, you know, these people are dying, right? And who's gonna recognize . . .

AUDREY A bunch of black people.

JIM What country is this again?

MARK/JEREMY Zaire.

MARK Okay, how's this. *(reading)* The International Health Organization warns that this disease kills 90 per cent of its victims, and sources speculate that it's airborne. If one infected person gets on a 747, we have the potential for worldwide death.

AUDREY So, so you're saying we could all die?

GEORGE Yeah, I think that's a good lead.

MARK Yeah.

RANI Is the International Health Organization saying that this thing is airborne or not?

JEREMY No, they didn't say it. Mark said it.

MARK I didn't say it. Uh, George told me to say it.

AUDREY The fact is, we're lying.

GEORGE The fact is, there's a big difference between saying sources speculate and lying.

AUDREY Like?

GEORGE Like, like, you know . . . *(he looks around the room for help)*

JEREMY Well, there's, uh . . .

GEORGE Like one is journalism.

MARK And one is fact.

Audrey doesn't look impressed.

GEORGE Okay, now can we move on? Movies.

BILL The superb retrospective on Fellini at the AGO.

GEORGE Bill, okay, I know Fellini. But our audience doesn't know who Fellini is. Okay, I know that *Wild Strawberries* was a brilliant movie.

BILL That was Ingmar Bergman.

GEORGE Bergman?

BILL Bergman.

GEORGE Next.

George and Mark are in George's office. George is holding a steno pad.

GEORGE Okay, *The Seventh Seal.*

MARK Bergman.

GEORGE *Satyricon.*

MARK Fellini.

GEORGE *Yojimbo.*

MARK Kurosawa.

GEORGE Oh, forget it. *(he throws the pad on his desk)*

George, Mark, and Jeremy are seated among the workstations in the newsroom.

GEORGE Okay, this is the material for the suicide?

JEREMY Yeah.

GEORGE Hit me, hit me.

JEREMY Okay, okay.

GEORGE Just give me the stuff.

JEREMY So Shane's off, he's doing his thing, right? And then in the middle he stops and he goes, you know, I called the suicide hotline today and it was busy. I was gonna try again, but I didn't wanna leave 'em hangin'. *(Mark starts to laugh)* Hangin'. It's like a double . . .

GEORGE I hate that.

MARK Okay.

JEREMY Okay, uh . . .

GEORGE I hate that. It's stupid. You guys, he told one joke.

JEREMY Right.

GEORGE Kevorkian joke.

JEREMY Yeah, I wrote that.

GEORGE The Kevorkian joke, there was a relationship. Kevorkian, he, he helps people commit suicide. The guy . . . but he's real. This . . .

JEREMY It's got to be something that really happened, right?

GEORGE Yes.

JEREMY Okay, I got one. Uh, did you hear Hervé Villechaize committed suicide? Yeah, he jumped off a footstool.

MARK He was Tattoo? Tattoo in "Fantasy Island"?

GEORGE How many years ago was that?

MARK Well, when he died or when he was on the show?

GEORGE How many years ago was that show on?

MARK Oh, I don't know. A while ago.

GEORGE This is a joke.

JEREMY I don't see why we can't go for full belly laughs.

GEORGE This is terrible. This is absurd. Okay, forget it, forget it, forget it.

AUDREY *(interrupting them)* Excuse me, George. Shane Pollack's girlfriend's here.

GEORGE The one that dumped him?

AUDREY I guess so.

MARK Wow.

GEORGE This is good. No, we could put her on. I mean, we could sort of investigate, look at the, you know, what caused this, this suicide. It could have been a sexual, you know, problem, relationship problem. This makes it more poignant. I think. I think it's a good idea. I mean, she's cute. Is she cute?

AUDREY If she's cute?

GEORGE Yeah, if she's cute.

AUDREY Jesus. *(she walks away)*

GEORGE *(calling her back)* Audrey, Audrey, Audrey. *(she stops and turns around)* Welcome to the real world, okay? Okay, cute works in the market place. Am I right? *(looks at Jeremy and Mark)*

JEREMY/MARK Yeah, no, you're right.

Nicole, twenty-four, beautiful, blonde, sits across from George in his office.

GEORGE Uh, so are you and Shane still, um, living together?

NICOLE No, no.

GEORGE You're not, you're not.

NICOLE No.

GEORGE And you want to be kept out of this, uh, this television thing.

NICOLE Please.

GEORGE It's done.

NICOLE Really?

GEORGE No, no, it's done. It's done.

NICOLE Really? Well, I expected that you would want to . . .

GEORGE What? What, bleed every ounce of blood from this story?

NICOLE Yeah, something like that. I've heard a few stories anyway. *(she laughs)*

GEORGE About newspeople?

NICOLE Yeah.

GEORGE Well, I have to admit, I mean, that's the nature of news. And I, I, I sometimes . . . and I'm party to that, you know, that kind of exploitation. *(he leans over to her, she looks at him intensely)*

But, you know, when I saw you, I said, Okay, she's, she's cute. And I could put her on television and I can exploit that. But I looked at you, close up, and I saw some kind of humanity. And every so often you see that. The last time I saw that was in the eyes. The Kennedys had that thing, that humanity. You could see it in their eyes. And, and, uh, when I saw you, the image that went through my head was John-John and Caroline standing by the coffin. *(she nods)* So, I don't want you to get involved in this, okay?

NICOLE Thank you.

GEORGE I, I don't want you to let anyone exploit the pain that I bet you're going through right now with this whole suicide thing. Okay?

George and Nicole leave the studio and walk down the corridor. They have their coats on.

GEORGE This sushi place is great. I mean, sushi's okay?

NICOLE Yeah, sushi's fine.

GEORGE Okay, good.

NICOLE I don't know. I just feel a little weird about Shane. I mean . . .

GEORGE Oh, the suicide thing. Now listen, you have to stand back from these things. They'll tear you apart. I couldn't do this job day in and day out without a sense of humour. Like the Kevorkian joke.

NICOLE Oh, yeah. I saw that. That was funny.

GEORGE You liked that?

NICOLE Yeah.

GEORGE I wrote that joke.

AUDREY — *(walking down the corridor towards George)* I got you muffins. *(she hands him a small carton of muffins)*

GEORGE — Bran?

AUDREY — No, they didn't have any bran. They only had blueberry.

GEORGE — I wanted bran. I wanted bran.

AUDREY — They only had blueberry.

GEORGE — *(taking a muffin out)* What are these on top? These are not blueberries. These are cranberries.

AUDREY — Oh, they told me they were blueberries.

GEORGE — I can't eat cranberries.

AUDREY — That's all that they had left.

GEORGE — Oh, God.

A black man in a suit is walking towards them, looking on the doors for the right nameplate.

GEORGE — Okay, fine. I'll eat it. Thank you. Thank you.

AUDREY — No, thank you.

GEORGE — No, I'll eat it, okay? Good.

Audrey walks away. The man, Dr. Mbsoya, approaches George.

DR. MBSOYA — *(African accent)* Excuse me.

GEORGE — Yeah.

DR. MBSOYA — I'm looking for Mr. Jamieson, about the virus story.

GEORGE — Oh, yeah. The virus story. Uh, down there to your right, okay?

Dr. Mbsoya coughs hard on George's muffin and walks off. George looks at the muffin.

George and Jeremy are in George's office.

JEREMY — If he coughed on your muffin, why'd you eat it?

GEORGE — I don't know, I ate it, okay? Big deal. What're you gonna get? They're speculating that this virus is airborne.

JEREMY — Yeah, *we* speculated that, remember?

GEORGE — I don't care who speculated.

They leave George's office and walk towards the studio entrance.

JEREMY — He wasn't anywhere near Zaire. He's black, so you think Africa, from Africa. You think virus. It's just your racist stereotyping.

GEORGE — Oh, thanks. Now I'm a racist.

JEREMY — Yeah, but you're alive.

GEORGE — Okay, so why was the guy coughing, huh?

JEREMY — A cold. He had a cold.

GEORGE — You know, I read that you can actually touch a surface and if there's a cold on that, you get it on your hands. You rub your eyes, you can get a cold.

JEREMY — Well, there you go. He coughed on your muffin. He didn't spit in your eye.

GEORGE — Fine. Oh, Christ. Here he comes again.

Mark approaches with Dr. Mbsoya. The doctor is coughing.

MARK — *(pointing at George)* George, this is Dr. Mbsoya from Doctors Without Borders. He's doing an interview with Jim on the, uh, virus.

GEORGE — *(shaking his hand)* Actually, we met outside. How're you doing, doctor? Have you got a bit of a cold there?

DR. MBSOYA Actually, I'm not exactly sure what it is.

GEORGE *(rubbing his eye)* Uh-huh. Anyway, uh . . .

JEREMY You're rubbing your eye. You're rubbing your eye. No, I saw.

GEORGE Would you just shut up. Excuse me, doctor. This is from a previous conversation. Anyway, doctor, it's good to have someone on the show who's been in phone contact with sources in Zaire.

MARK Actually, Dr. Mbsoya just came back from Zaire, so it's even better.

Jeremy looks worried. Dr. Mbsoya coughs.

GEORGE *(putting his hand to his mouth)* Uh-huh. Okay, uh, excuse me. Excuse me.

George, Mark, and Jeremy are in the men's washroom.

JEREMY The guy from Zaire coughed. You shook his hand. You rubbed your eye.

GEORGE I didn't rub my eye, and I'm washing my hands now, anyway.

MARK Well, it doesn't matter if you wash your hands now. The whole point is that if you stuck your finger in your eye when you were infected, washing your hands now isn't gonna make any difference.

JEREMY Too late. It's over.

GEORGE What do you mean, when I was infected!? I wasn't infected, okay? So let's just drop it.

MARK Okay, all right.

JEREMY I don't think that's the important thing anyway.

MARK Why, what happened?

JEREMY Well, the guy from Zaire coughed right on his muffin and then he ate it. I saw.

George takes a towel from the dispenser.

MARK Is that true? He coughed on your muffin?

JEREMY Yeah.

MARK He coughed on his muffin?

JEREMY Yes, and then he ate it.

MARK And then you ate it?

GEORGE Okay, stop it.

JEREMY Yes.

GEORGE I, I, I know what you guys are doing, okay? Can we just drop this?

MARK All right.

GEORGE Thank you. Thank you.

JEREMY All right.

GEORGE Okay, thank you.

JEREMY All right.

Jim and Dr. Mbsoya are in the newsroom, near the anchor desk.

JIM So a couple of hundred people have died from this virus already, haven't they?

DR. MBSOYA Yes.

JIM Yeah, with a potential for thousands more. Millions. What's the flight from Zaire? It's like fifteen hours, is that right?

DR. MBSOYA Yes, fifteen hours.

JIM Yeah. I just got back from Mexico, and that was a six-hour flight. About my maximum on an airplane. Um, but I also got a virus down there. Uh, terrible. I

was on the can for a week with the thing. *(Dr. Mbsoya stares at him)*
Well, excuse me. I have to . . .

George, Mark, and Jeremy are seated around the boardroom table.

GEORGE We're number one with this thing. Okay, the suicide thing. I want to move the item to the top of the show.
MARK Okay.
JEREMY We'll have the Kevorkian joke. It's, like, my joke.
GEORGE They love the idea that the guy is committing suicide on TV, which is my idea.
MARK We have a problem with that, though.
GEORGE What's the problem?
MARK Well, the jokes worked.
JEREMY Yeah, my Kevorkian joke.
MARK Right and, uh, he doesn't want to die any more.
GEORGE He doesn't want to die? What does he want to do?
MARK Live. It's not a real nutty idea. He wants to live now.
GEORGE Well, the suicide, you know, has made him a star. You know, a local star.
MARK Sure.
GEORGE So what the hell is he gonna do if he doesn't die?

Mark, Jeremy, Jim, and Audrey are gathered around a monitor at a workstation, watching George with Shane.

SHANE I think I can do stand-up, you know? Really.
GEORGE Shane, be realistic, okay? You did five jokes. You didn't even write them.
SHANE I wrote the Holocaust joke.

JEREMY I wrote the Holocaust joke. The guy steals my joke! It's pathetic.

GEORGE The Holocaust joke I happen to think was in very bad taste, even for somebody who's committing suicide. Five jokes don't make a routine, okay?

SHANE Oh, they worked and, you know, with the right material I know, I know I can make it.

GEORGE *(getting impatient)* You keep saying that. You keep saying that. Okay, stop with that already! Okay, I'm sorry. I don't want to sound too harsh here. The fact is, you're virtually a cultural phenomenon. The next guy that tries to come out and commit suicide on television, what's he doing, what's he doing? He's doing a Shane Pollack.

SHANE Gotten great numbers. The numbers . . .

GEORGE Oh, stop with the numbers!

SHANE . . . were there.

GEORGE Stop with the numbers! The reason they're watching is they're waiting for you to blow your brains out! Not because of the jokes! All right, I'm sorry. That's ugly, but there's an ugly audience out there. Okay? Now I'm not counselling suicide. That would be illegal. Understand? Illegal. But what I'm saying is, this is your moment. It's your choice. Go for it.

George is walking with Audrey along the atrium walkway.

AUDREY *(handing George some papers)* It's the memo on Jim's hair, they love it upstairs. The wire service on the virus – 385 confirmed dead.

GEORGE It's getting up there. That's good.

AUDREY — And Shane Pollack's agent is in your office.

GEORGE — What, he got an agent to kill himself? Do you think they get 10 per cent of the ashes or something?

Anything more on whether the virus is airborne?

AUDREY — No, but people are saying not to rub your eyes.

George is at Jeremy's workstation.

GEORGE — You've been walking around the office telling people I rubbed my eye.

JEREMY — Yeah, well, I mentioned . . .

GEORGE — Okay, why? Why?

JEREMY — You don't have the disease. You don't have it. You don't have the disease. If you had the disease, you'd be dead. You'd be dead by now. You don't have it. You'd be dead.

Shane Pollack's agent and George are in George's office. The agent is sitting on the couch with a tape beside him.

AGENT — I'm not here to play the heavy, George. I just want to do what's best for Shane. He's always been one of our most important clients.

GEORGE — How long have you represented him?

AGENT — Actually, just about an hour and a half. *(he picks up the tape and goes to the VCR)* But I want you to have a look at this. It's a segment of last night's show . . . *(puts the tape in the VCR)*

GEORGE — No, no. Why am I looking at this?

AGENT — Just bear with me for a second, okay? It's a segment of last night's show.

GEORGE — I saw the show last night.

AGENT — Can we just watch this, where Shane actually pitched one of his unsold movie ideas? Just bear with me for a second.

Shane appears on the screen. A caption reads, "Suicide TV – Day 3."

SHANE — *(has a gun in his hand)* All right. Here's another idea that didn't sell. Okay, all right? The loser. Right. Let me lay it out for you. Two male comics, who's routine is trashing woman, can't get a gig. Can't get a gig, right? They run into some trouble with these hoods and, uh, they dress up as women in order to escape. They disguise themselves to escape. They dress as women. They find themselves on stage, in drag, and on the spot improvise a routine as men-hating women, when really they're women-hating men, right?

GEORGE — I can see why this idea didn't sell.

AGENT — Just, just . . .

SHANE — By the end of the movie, they learn to be better men, as women.

AGENT — It's beautiful, George. It's beautiful. It's *Tootsie* meets *Pulp Fiction* meets *Some Like It Hot.*

GEORGE — Where did this meet *Pulp Fiction*?

AGENT — He'll work that out. George, it really doesn't matter. The point is, a major studio in L.A. saw that last night and I made a deal on it this morning.

GEORGE — What, they picked this up in L.A.?

AGENT — Of course! CNN picks it up. They love this kid out there, George. He's the guy that's gonna kill himself on TV. Some creative guy called that quirky. What does this mean to you? That's what you want to

	know, right? Basically, uh, we're going to ask for fifty thousand for day five.
GEORGE	From us? Fifty thousand?
AGENT	Yep.
GEORGE	This is public broadcasting.
AGENT	I know, I know. Well, that's why you'll be glad to know we're only asking for ten more for each appearance he makes after that. Till he either kills himself or changes his mind.
GEORGE	Changes his mind? I made a deal! He's gotta kill himself on television or I end up with egg on my face.
AGENT	Look, George, George. You took advantage of a very weak, not too bright, potentially brilliant screenwriter, and now the kid is hot, George. You are number one. All I'm sayin' is, share the wealth.
GEORGE	If he doesn't go through with this, I'll get an injunction to stop him.
AGENT	To stop him from what? Living?

Mark, Jeremy, and George are sitting around at a workstation.

JEREMY	So, you just blew him out.
GEORGE	Yeah, he wanted fifty thousand for the fifth day. And, uh, you know, this is a Canadian local news show.
MARK	I mean, we'd already won the week. What's the point?
GEORGE	Yeah. And his studio deal in L.A.?
JEREMY	Yeah.
GEORGE	Totally collapsed, right. He was no longer committing suicide, so he was no longer high concept and quirky, so they killed him.

JEREMY Tough town.

Jeremy and Mark leave, and Audrey walks up with a fax.

AUDREY *(handing fax to George)* Fax from Dernhoff. She sends her congratulations on the ratings. And a bran muffin. *(she gives him the muffin)*

GEORGE Wait, wait, wait. What's this on top?

AUDREY A slice of apple?

GEORGE So this is an apple-bran. I mean, it's no big deal. I'm just saying that this is an apple-bran. It's not a bran muffin.

George and Nicole are in George's office. George is flipping through a newspaper.

GEORGE Uh, there's a Fellini retrospect at the AGO tonight, and, uh, let me see what's on. Yeah, it's *Satyricon* tonight.

NICOLE I always thought that was Bergman.

GEORGE No, no. Fellini is the one who did *Satyricon.*

NICOLE Oh, I feel like an idiot.

GEORGE Oh, no, no, no. Actually, I find that mistake to be, uh, very sexual.

Shane and Mark are walking through the newsroom.

SHANE You know, if George hadn't said, like, no to my agent, I'd seriously be dead now.

MARK It's possible, yeah.

SHANE In a sick kind of way, I have George to thank, you know?

MARK Oh, Audrey. Is George in right now?

AUDREY Yep.

MARK *(to Shane)* You can thank him right now.

Mark knocks and opens George's door before getting an answer.

SHANE Hey, George. I just . . .

George and Nicole are kissing. Both look up, then George leans his head in his hand.

THE END

EPISODE 5

"A Bad Day"

First Aired: November 18, 1996

George walks into the lobby at the same time as an attractive woman. She is twenty-one years old.

GEORGE	You know, I've seen you around the building, and I was just wondering what department you're in?
WOMAN	Children's Programming.
GEORGE	Oh, Children's. You know, some of the best shows this place puts out are the kid shows. Like, "The Friendly Giant" is great.
WOMAN	They cancelled "The Friendly Giant" years ago.
GEORGE	They cancelled Friendly, really? God!
WOMAN	It was due to budget cuts, I'm not sure.
GEORGE	What'd they replace it with, "The Common Sense Giant"?

She just looks at him.

GEORGE	Anyway, um, you know, I was wondering, uh, you gonna be free for, for a drink after work?
WOMAN	Oh, I don't think that would be, uh . . . I'm only twenty-one. Get it?

They stop walking.

GEORGE	Yes. Um, anyway, say hello to Mr. Dressup for me, okay?

WOMAN	He's off the air too.
GEORGE	Oh, right. That incident where they caught him in a dress.

Audrey and Mark are in the cafeteria, standing at the food counter.

AUDREY	*(to the woman at the counter)* Can I get a bran muffin, please?
WOMAN	No bran left.
AUDREY	What's that? That looks like bran.
WOMAN	That's carrot.
AUDREY	Well, is it really carroty? I mean, does it have a really strong carroty taste to it?
WOMAN	It's a *carrot* muffin.
AUDREY	Never mind.
MARK	Audrey, just give him the muffin. Tell him it's carrot-bran.
AUDREY	No, you do that. I'm not doing that.
MARK	Fine, I'll do it. It's just a muffin. George is not going to freak out.
MARK	*(to woman at the counter)* I'll have a carrot muffin.
WOMAN	To go?
MARK	Yeah.

George and Mark are in George's office watching George's TV. George is eating the carrot muffin. Mark is sitting on the couch with the remote. Shane's suicide tape is playing on the TV.

GEORGE	Is this bran?
MARK	Yeah. The documentary they're making on the history of news needs a couple things from us. First they need this, uh, tape of the suicide attempt we aired in October.

GEORGE Yeah, this was good. Does he still work here?

MARK He was in the hospital for a while, but he's back.

GEORGE We really got inside the head of a guy who was attempting suicide. And I think that contributed a lot to our understanding of the human condition. Now, this is a very carroty muffin.

MARK Oh, it's carrot-bran.

GEORGE Carrot-bran?

MARK It's new. Uh, that's the one that followed Jim around with a camera for a couple days. You know, sort of get-that-guy-behind-the-anchor-desk kind of thing, you know.

GEORGE Do we really want the public to see the real Jim Walcott? You know, I mean, here's a basically ignorant, self-obsessed, um, very small-minded guy, okay? You know something? This is very carroty. You sure this isn't all carrot?

MARK It's all carrot-bran.

GEORGE So, it's carrot-bran, carrot first. Meaning mostly carrot, less bran. I'm just saying that, that's all.

MARK You win, you win. *(he stands)*

GEORGE It's not about winning, okay. I'm just saying this is a very carroty muffin. That's all.

MARK Can they just shoot Jim for the documentary? Can they shoot?

GEORGE Yes, fine.

Mark, George, Audrey, Bill, Jeremy, and Rani are seated around the boardroom table having a production meeting.

MARK Okay, segment three is the interview with Linda McQuaig on her new book, *Shooting the Hippo.*

RANI Um, good book.

GEORGE Yeah, I've heard Linda McQuaig speak. She's got a nice body, doesn't she?

RANI *(eating cereal)* What does her body have to do with her book, for Christ's sake?

GEORGE I'm sorry. I noticed, okay. I'm only human and you're right; her body has nothing to do with what we're talking about here. We're talking about the ideas and her book, which is on the, uh . . .

BILL The deficit.

GEORGE On the deficit, good, good.

MARK She basically believes that the deficit can be cut without throwing people off welfare.

GEORGE Well, that's the extreme left, isn't it?

MARK I wouldn't call it extreme.

GEORGE No, *I'm* not calling it extreme. But there's a huge number of jerks out there who would love to just attack us for a left-wing bias. And I just don't think we can put Linda McQuaig out there alone and let her use our show as a platform for her ideas. I think we need some balance here.

JEREMY *(doing a crossword)* David Frum?

GEORGE I like David Frum. David's, he's smart. He's got good ideas. Um, but it's funny. On TV there's something I find odd about his hair, you know?

JEREMY Yeah, what is that? What is that? Is that just a hairline? Or is it some freaky transplant? What is that thing there?

GEORGE I'm sure it's just his hairline.

MARK It could be a transplant. It could be a weave. It could be a rug. It could be his hairline. This has nothing to do with David Frum's free-market economic analysis.

JEREMY You think it's a rug?

MARK It could be a rug or a weave. I don't know.

GEORGE Or plugs.

JEREMY Plugs.

MARK I don't see someone of David Frum's intellect having plugs.

Audrey flips through a magazine, not interested in this conversation.

JEREMY What are you saying? You've got to be an idiot to have plugs? It's not like that spray-in-the-can stuff. I mean, you can't jog with that. Your hair drips down the side of your face.

MARK Look, plug guys have the jewellery, they have the tan, they have a hairy chest. These are people that don't have the background or intellect of a David Frum.

GEORGE I agree with him. David Frum's in bed with the Christian Right. They are pro-life, anti-abortion, let-God's-will-take-its-course. I just don't see inserting a plug in your head being consistent with that ideology.

JEREMY Anti-abortion, anti-plug, pro-life, pro- . . .

GEORGE Pro-weave. Pro-rug. Pro-life.

MARK So, he's not plugged.

AUDREY Why don't we just move on to someone else until this issue's resolved.

JEREMY Preston Manning.

GEORGE Yeah, Preston's smart. He's got good ideas. But, um, again I have this problem when I see him on television, um, I try to listen to him, my eye goes right, you know, to . . . *(he puts his pencil to his chin)*

MARK The chin.

JEREMY Yeah, the chin thing.

GEORGE You've got to hand it to him. He didn't have it fixed, which I guess is consistent with his, uh, anti-abortion . . .

MARK Pro-chin.

JEREMY Chin.

GEORGE . . . chin ideology.

RANI How about Diane Francis against Linda McQuaig?

GEORGE Diane's an intelligent woman, and I have nothing in theory against putting Diane Francis and Linda McQuaig on the air together. One right, one left, two intelligent women. But I'm afraid that this is going to end up looking a bit like a political wet T-shirt contest.

RANI Come on!

JEREMY You shouldn't have said that, because that's going to set her off. *(pointing to Rani)*

RANI Oh, excuse me!

GEORGE Let's just round up our usual right-wing suspects. Okay, you've got Andrew Coyne in the *Globe*, you've got Peter Worthington. There's a hundred guys out there on the right, that will do any show like this for a buck, okay?

Jim enters followed by a documentary film crew (camera and audio guys) shooting him.

JIM Excuse me. Sorry I'm late. *(to the crew)* Come in, please. These people will be, uh, shooting me during a normal day. Just ignore me.

GEORGE Okay, let's go.

MARK Uh, segment four. Cats bred for short legs.

JEREMY Munchkins.

MARK The munchkins, exactly.

GEORGE — Okay, wait a second. I think I should explain this.

(to the documentary camera) Uh, this munchkin piece is what we call a "Hey, Martha" piece. It's a fluffy item. We do one a show. Um, a "Hey, Martha" is, um, "Hey, Martha, look at the cats with short legs."

JIM — However, um, I think you could say that there is a continuum between a lighter munchkin "Hey Martha," right there to, uh, wait here, uh, "Hey Martha, look, it's ethnic cleansing!"

GEORGE — Okay, let's have our lead.

JIM — On this munchkin thing, *(Mark, Jeremy, and George can't believe Jim is going on)* my feeling on this trend in genetic engineering, if I may. Um, I think the more they force this stuff on us, right – from the genetically altered tomato right through to cats with shorter legs – I think in the end we are bound to see legislation on this.

JEREMY — The cats are cross-bred, Jim. They're not genetically engineered.

GEORGE — Okay, let's have our lead.

JIM — Uh, but the tomatoes are.

MARK — Thanks for that, Jim.

JIM — Yep.

Jim, the documentary producer, and a cameraman are in a lounge room. It is surrounded by windows.

JIM — *(to the camera)* You know, dog-bites-man isn't news. But man-bites-dog is news. And if we look at the war in Bosnia, we definitely had Croat-bites-dog or Serb-bites-dog, depending on how you looked at it.

PRODUCER — Cut, cut.

JIM	What?
PRODUCER	*(getting up and sitting beside Jim)* Okay. What I'm looking for here is something real. I'm not interested in your theory of the news. Even though, you know, your theory is . . . What I'm looking for is the real Jim Walcott.
JIM	Okay, yeah. Yeah, yeah. You want, you want to know what I think makes the news work.
PRODUCER	No.
JIM	Okay, all right.
PRODUCER	Okay? What makes the news work, what makes anything work, what makes this documentary work, is that, that spin. Okay, that hook. It'll make the audience just sit back and say, "Jim Walcott."
JIM	Yeah, holy shit.
PRODUCER	Holy shit.
JIM	Yeah.
PRODUCER	Holy shit!
JIM	Right.
PRODUCER	Holy shit, yes!
JIM	All right.
PRODUCER	Okay.

The documentary producer goes back behind the camera.

JIM	Holy shit, yeah.
PRODUCER	Are you ready?
JIM	Yeah, gimme a second.
PRODUCER	Sure, yeah. Go ahead.

Shane Pollack is walking fast down the corridor behind the studio, looking for George. He has a tape in this hand.

SHANE *(under his breath)* Fucking asshole.

GEORGE *(on the phone in his office)* Yeah, well, I wanted to apologize for this morning in the lobby, what I said about Mr. Dressup. You know, I have tremendous respect for any man who could dress up for thirty years, five days a week on television.

Shane enters without knocking. He is distressed.

SHANE *(loudly)* I want to talk to you, I want to talk to you, man! I want to talk to you about my suicide tape. I thought it was over!

GEORGE Hold on one second. Um, listen, that's out of my hands now. That's in the documentary division.

SHANE I thought this was over!

GEORGE I'm just talking to a woman in Children's Programming, trying to set a lunch date.

SHANE I just can't believe you're gonna, you're gonna, you're gonna broadcast my suicide tape again, man!

Audrey enters.

AUDREY Excuse me. *(she puts a bottle on his desk)*

GEORGE What?

AUDREY That's the fibre you wanted.

GEORGE Can a person not make a phone call here? What is going on?

AUDREY I thought it was an emergency.

Shane gets impatient.

GEORGE No, no, no. That's not the emergency stuff, okay? That stuff takes forty-eight hours to go through your system.

SHANE Are you gonna deal with this?

GEORGE I'm gonna deal with this.

SHANE Are you gonna deal with this or not?

GEORGE I'm taking this seriously. I'm taking that very seriously.

AUDREY And BMW called again. Your new muffler system's gonna cost thirty-two hundred. *(she leaves)*

GEORGE *(to Shane)* Can you believe that?! Thirty-two hundred dollars, for a muffler! For a five-year-old BMW?

SHANE I don't give a shit about your BMW, okay? I'm healthy now. See, I'm healthy.

GEORGE I understand.

SHANE You know?

GEORGE I understand.

SHANE I mean, if I hadn't dug down into my soul and discovered some kind of spiritual strength, man, I wouldn't be here, you know, talking to you at this time.

GEORGE Wait a second. *(looking at the bottle on his desk)* Oh my God. Audrey! You know what she did? She got the natural stuff. The natural tastes like wood chips. I wanted the orange flavour with NutraSweet.

SHANE *(yelling)* Are you gonna deal with this??!!

George, Dernhoff, and an attractive Public Relations woman are seated in the boardroom around the table. The PR woman is wearing sunglasses.

GEORGE He's on the roof right now?

DERNHOFF We don't think he's gonna jump.

GEORGE He was just in my office. We were talking about the suicide tapes.

PR WOMAN We're hoping that it's just a gesture.

GEORGE Are you a psychiatrist?

PR WOMAN Public Relations. Uh, we want to be prepared with a press release if he happens to jump.

GEORGE A press release if he jumps? Wouldn't a net be softer? *(no reaction)* Um, we haven't actually met, have we?

PR WOMAN I need to know what went on in your office. He claims that you were insensitive to his problem with the tape and that when he tried to talk to you about it, you seemed more interested in, um, trying to date a twenty-two-year-old woman from Children's Programming, fix the muffler on your BMW, and get an orange-flavoured laxative powder.

GEORGE Okay. This is, this is crazy. And this is madness, okay? First of all, that stuff is not a laxative, okay? It's a fibre supplement. *(Dernhoff, looking unimpressed, glances at the PR woman)* It takes, like, forty-eight hours to go through your sys . . . *(he sees they are not giving in to him)*

Okay, thirty-two hundred dollars. I'm gonna pay thirty-two hundred dollars for a BMW muffler?

PR WOMAN We checked out the story and found the woman in Children's who says you've been sexually harassing her.

GEORGE Me? Sexually harassing?

DERNHOFF You're old enough to be her father.

GEORGE What does this have to do with the guy on the roof who's gonna jump?

PR WOMAN There's also some comment about Mr. Dressup wearing a dress?

GEORGE That was this morning in the lobby. I, I, it was a joke. I mentioned it to this . . . I still don't see how this is relevant to the guy committing suicide.

DERNHOFF It's only relevant if people are talking about it. That's why we have Public Relations.

PR WOMAN Someone mentioned the comment to him. He was pretty upset.

GEORGE Someone mentioned the dress line to the guy on the roof?

DERNHOFF To Mr. Dressup in retirement!

GEORGE Someone mentioned the dress line to Mr. Dressup? How did Mr. Dressup get into this?

PR WOMAN When he was at lunch this afternoon commemorating his thirty years on the air. And he happened to mention it to the president of the corporation.

GEORGE Someone mentioned the dress line that I mentioned to the girl in the lobby? To Mr. Dressup? And Mr. Dressup mentioned it to the president of the corporation?

PR WOMAN Yes.

Back to Jim and the documentary crew in the lounge.

JIM If we take a Bosnia. A Gulf War. Um, Vietnam War. O.J. Simpson, Nicole Simpson. A Ron Goldman. Rosa Lopez. Uh, . . .

PRODUCER Cut.

JIM What's wrong?

PRODUCER You're not getting it.

JIM Right. The holy-shit hook. Yeah, I'm not getting that, right? No.

PRODUCER Yeah, that personal angle.

JIM Right. The, the heat, the hook, the . . . holy-shit hook.

PRODUCER	Holy shit. You coined it.
JIM	Now, that's basically the essence of the modern electronic news hook is, is holy shit. Uh, holy shit, it's ethnic cleansing. Holy shit, Jim Carrey made twenty million on his last feature. Holy shit, uh, Jim Walcott, whatever.
PRODUCER	That's it! There, you got it, you got it! Okay.

Jeremy and George are walking down the hallway.

JEREMY	Yeah, yeah, I just got off the phone with the guy. He said he can get me an Italian muffler, five hundred bucks, labour included.
GEORGE	Five hundred? Really?
JEREMY	That's great, man. You can't beat that. So, uh, the problem?
GEORGE	Yeah, I ran into this woman in Children's Programming, and I asked her out for a drink and she was kind of young.
JEREMY	What do you mean, young? Like, she ordered Nestlé Quik?
GEORGE	No, she was twenty-two years old.
JEREMY	So, you were too old for her?
GEORGE	Anyway, I made a comment about Mr. Dressup wearing a dress and, the comment got up to the president of the corporation in about three hours.
JEREMY	Really? Wonder what took so long.

Back to Jim and the documentary crew in the lounge. One of the crew guys is asleep in a chair. Jim is looking out the window.

JIM	*(turning around)* Okay, okay. Here's something we might be able to use. Last summer, I was out doing a story on a strike. It was a hot summer day and, uh, I

	was wearing this beige Brooks Brothers suit. And off I go to the bathroom and I come back and unbeknownst to me there's a big stain. And I looked down and I thought, holy shit, right?
PRODUCER	Is anything I'm saying making any sense to you? Am I getting through to you?
JIM	Oh, no, no, no. We'll get this. We'll get this. Don't worry. Don't worry. Is there any gum? Do you have any gum?
PRODUCER	Uh, yeah. Can we get some gum for Jim?

George and Jeremy are at a workstation in the newsroom. Jeremy is on the phone.

JEREMY	Yep, bye.
GEORGE	So, what'd he say? What'd he say?
JEREMY	He can't get you the Italian muffler . . .
GEORGE	Ohhh.
JEREMY	. . . until tomorrow!
GEORGE	Oh, he can get it tomorrow?
JEREMY	Yeah, yeah!
GEORGE	Okay, great.
JEREMY	Yeah, no, it's fine. And, and they were having a party over there just now, drinking. You know the way bikers are, right?
GEORGE	Wait a second. You said your guy wasn't a biker.
JEREMY	No, he's not a biker, but he hangs out with a predominantly biker crowd. And they were partying and having some pizza and somebody threw up in the back seat of your car.
GEORGE	Someone threw up in my BMW?
JEREMY	Yeah, it's just, you know, barf. They'll, they'll clean it up. But, uh, five hundred bucks, man. What a deal!

Back to Jim and documentary crew in the lounge. The crew is shooting again.

JIM I was a very young reporter. I was staying out at a farm. We had to stay out there for a few days. And there were a few guys staying there who lived there. I mean, one of them was an agricultural college grad, I think. You know, we had a few beers. We got pretty loaded. And there was this cow. And, um, you know, I'm sure you know, what . . . It was apparently something they did quite often. I'm sure you know what cultural relativism means, you know. When in Rome . . .

(thinking about what he just said) It's actually not quite as odd as you might think. Holy shit.

Mark and George are at Mark's workstation.

MARK *(looking at his notebook)* Okay, on the Linda McQuaig front, I've got calls into Conrad Black, to Peter Worthington, to the *Financial Times*, to the *Globe and Mail* business section, to the Fraser Institute, to the Mike Harris office. I'm looking for that, uh, blonde chick with the business suits and the mean face? She's always on TV touting the Common Sense Revolution? Worst comes to worst, we can always get Hugh Segal.

Mark and Hugh Segal are walking down the office corridor.

MARK It's great you could do this on such short notice, Mr. Segal.

HUGH Not a problem. I have to be down for a ball game anyways, so it's no hassle at all.

MARK Oh, great. We have Linda McQuaig, and we thought, who could we have up against Linda McQuaig? And it was unanimous, Hugh Segal, right? I mean, I don't think another name came up.

They stop outside of a dressing room. There is a sign on the door: "David Frum."

HUGH Are we in here?

MARK *(taking down the sign)* Yeah, that's your dressing room.

HUGH Thanks very much. *(he walks in)*

MARK Okay, thanks.

Jim and the documentary crew have finished and are walking along the atrium walkway towards the elevators.

PRODUCER So, you've never told this to anyone else before?

JIM No. Not a soul.

PRODUCER Holy shit.

JIM *(gets the reference and laughs)* That's right, holy shit.

They stop at the elevators, waiting.

JIM Well, here's one for you. Why did the, uh, newsman do a news story on cows in India?

MAN Why?

JIM Holy shit. *(he laughs)* Will you send me a copy of that?

The crew gets into the elevator.

PRODUCER Yeah.

JIM Great. Take it easy. Hey, why did the chicken cross the Ganges? *(the elevator door closes)* Oh, shit, shit, shit, shit, shit.

George and Dernhoff are walking along the atrium walkway.

GEORGE Oh, come on. She was from Children's Programming. I asked her for lunch. Is this a crime?

DERNHOFF You also showed up at the Gemini Awards last month with some muffin half your age.

GEORGE She was very smart.

DERNHOFF She was wearing a see-through top. The brass could see her tits.

GEORGE Look, she thought the Geminis were like the Oscars. *(they stop walking)*

DERNHOFF Look, the optics on this are killing us and I can't defend you. Why don't you, just *try* dating someone closer to your own age or you could have a problem here.

Audrey and Linda McQuaig are walking through the newsroom. Audrey has a package and some paperwork. She is taking Linda to meet George.

LINDA I just heard some gossip about your news director? Some sexual harassment charge?

AUDREY Oh, that. That's with young girls. He won't hit on you. You're too old. I mean, you're too young, they're too young. Forget it. Um, George, Linda McQuaig?

GEORGE *(standing at a workstation)* Oh, Linda. *(they shake hands)*

LINDA Hi, George.

GEORGE It's nice to meet you.

LINDA Nice to meet you.

GEORGE *Shooting the Hippo*. I love that book.

LINDA Oh, did you read it?

GEORGE Yes, it was brilliant. You know, I'm curious. Uh, *Shooting the Hippo*, what does that mean?

LINDA Oh, I actually explain that in the opening line of the book.

GEORGE Yeah, listen. I want to ask you a question. *(they start to walk)*

Now, this is not about the book. This weekend there's a news symposium up at Mont Tremblant. And people are bringing their skis. And I was just wondering, I mean, separate rooms, whether you'd be interested in coming? *(they stop walking)*

LINDA I don't think so, thanks.

GEORGE Well, anyway, I guess that having a best-seller changes a person's life.

LINDA Yeah, it means that I get hit on a lot more by middle-aged men who love my book but haven't read it.

GEORGE Yeah, I've got to do the rundown. Um, make-up's through there. *(points to studio door)* We're gonna have a good show, okay?

Linda is walking down the corridor, looking for the make-up room. Jim walks past.

JIM Can I, um, help you?

LINDA I'm just looking for make-up?

JIM Oh, are you Linda McQuaig?

LINDA Yes, yes.

JIM The deficit?

LINDA Right, right.

JIM I'm Jim Walcott. I'm hosting this spot. *(they shake hands)*

LINDA Oh, well, nice to meet you.

JIM Nice to meet you, too. Yeah, it's right down this way.

JIM I love the title of your book by the way, *Shooting the Hippo.*

LINDA Oh, thanks.

JIM Yeah, but I was wondering. Don't you think you would have actually sold more copies if you had put a picture of a dead hippo on the cover.

LINDA *(small laugh)* Maybe.

JIM I, I wanted to ask you a question, and it's obviously not something I'd ask you on air. You'll see why. But, you are an incredibly tough woman. I mean, you've attacked some pretty powerful men in your day. *(they stop walking)* I remember what Conrad Black once said about you. "Linda McQuaig should be horse-whipped." *(they chuckle)*

LINDA Oh, right. Right.

JIM But here's what I wanted to ask. And please don't take it personally, I'm really just curious. Do you think an average man could be attracted sexually to a woman of your, you know, self-assuredness?

LINDA *(avoiding the question)* Make-up?

JIM It's right here.

The reason I ask is that I dated some woman from Western some time back. And these women definitely have feminist leanings. You know, these chicks really, really had their heads screwed on straight, you know. But I found I couldn't get into it.

LINDA Really?

JIM	Sexually, yeah. But the deficit is our biggest problem right now, isn't it?
LINDA	Actually, my biggest problem right now is finding make-up.
JIM	Yeah, it's right in there. *(he points to the room)*
LINDA	Thanks. *(she leaves him standing there)*
JIM	Yep.

George and Linda are in the make-up room.

GEORGE	You should talk about *Shooting the Hippo*. Whatever has happened, it's still a great book.
LINDA	You haven't even read it!

They walk out and down the corridor.

GEORGE	I'm getting it today.
LINDA	First you insist on putting me on with Hugh Segal, as if by myself I'm gonna corrupt the minds of your viewers. I mean, that was really gutless. Second, I barely meet you and already you're hitting on me about some sex-and-ski weekend.
GEORGE	News-and-ski weekend, okay? News-and-ski. I said separate rooms.
LINDA	Oh, yeah, right. And third, third, that news anchor of yours is a brain-dead moron.
GEORGE	That's very perceptive, because Jim is a complete idiot, okay? He wasn't even my choice as anchor for this show. The man hasn't even read your book.
LINDA	Neither have you!
GEORGE	He's still an idiot, okay? Hugh Segal loves you. Do the show, I'll read your book tonight, okay?
LINDA	Forget it. *(she walks away)*

Mark, Jeremy, and George watch a monitor showing Jim interview Hugh Segal alone.

HUGH	My sense is that Bob Rae's New Democrats helped kill it. I think the Liberals in Ottawa have helped to kill it. And I think the Mike Harris Conservatives in Ontario have killed it.
JIM	Well, I don't have a comeback to that.
GEORGE	It works without Linda McQuaig.
HUGH	... They have to do the tough stuff first. That's always how it works.
JIM	Well, thank you, Hugh Segal. Munchkins. Characters out of a Disney cartoon? No. They're actually genetically altered cats. Do you need lower cat boxes? Rani Sandu reports.

Jeremy and George are standing in the corridor.

JEREMY	These bikers, usually they're really good guys. But right now, they're embroiled in a bit of a gang war.
GEORGE	What happen to my car?
JEREMY	Relax. No one else threw up in it. I mean, they cleaned that up. But it seems a rival gang put about fifty pounds of dynamite in the trunk of a car and blew my guy in his garage.
GEORGE	Where's my car?
JEREMY	Well, that's the coincidence. The bomb? It was in the trunk of your car. But the basic deal on the muffler was still a great deal, theoretically. And I think we should probably lead with the biker bomb thing on tomorrow night's show.

Mark and George are in the boardroom, watching the tape of Jim's story for the documentary.

JIM	. . . and, uh, they had this cow . . .
MARK	We let the documentary crew in here, and this is the story Jim tells them.
GEORGE	Holy shit.

Heading home after a long day, George stands behind two young female staffers in the elevator.

STAFFER #1	Shane, you know, the guy from the tape library?
STAFFER #2	Yeah, yeah, on the roof?
STAFFER #1	Totally. All afternoon threatening to jump.
STAFFER #2	Really, why?
STAFFER #1	Well, this girl from Children's Programming, like a researcher, called the cops on him for sexual harassment, and he snapped. First he tried to overdose on some orange laxatives. Then he tried to jump.
STAFFER #2	Unbelievable.
STAFFER #1	Yeah, that's what I heard. Evidently, he just flipped out and started eating the stuff.
STAFFER #2	Laxatives? God.
STAFFER #1	I know, sick. What triggers something like that?

The elevator doors open and they exit.

STAFFER #1	'Night.
STAFFER #2	'Night.
GEORGE	Excuse me. *(to Staffer 1)* You know, I've seen you around the building. I was just wondering. What department are you in?
STAFFER #2	Sports, why?

THE END

EPISODE 6

“Petty Tyranny”

First Aired: November 25, 1996

Jeremy on the phone at his workstation in the newsroom. George is seated beside him.

JEREMY Yeah, heavy-water spill in Pickering. Is it a nuclear accident or an incident? What are they calling it? Incident? Okay. Have they stopped the leak? Yes, I'll hold.

(to George) So, you were saying?

GEORGE So, my point is this. By eleven in the morning, the cafeteria has nothing but cranberry muffins left, right?

JEREMY Yeah.

GEORGE So, I get pissed off at the guy, right? So he calls me petty. Here's a guy in a chef's hat calling me petty. Here's what happens. I pick up a cranberry muffin, just to take a look. I put it back on the rack. It rolls off onto the floor.

JEREMY It rolls off?

GEORGE The guy freaks out and charges me for the muffin, right? So I take another cranberry and I crumble it on the floor.

JEREMY Hang on.

(back to his phone) There's containment, so, so, they shut the reactor down? No, I'm just wondering. It's just like twenty miles from Toronto. Yeah, I'm here.

(to George) Go ahead.

GEORGE Okay, so the guy calls me a rich asshole. Which is clearly anti-white racism.

JEREMY Yeah.

GEORGE So I say to him, What, in Mexico they don't know the difference between cranberry and bran?

JEREMY Actually, he's from Turkey. He's, uh, Turkish.

GEORGE Yeah, well, that's not the point.

JEREMY No, it's a big difference. Different country, different culture.

GEORGE Can we get by that? Can we get by that?

JEREMY Okay, yeah.

(to the phone) A statement on camera? Yeah, yeah. We'll take that. Good. *(hangs up the phone)*

Look, I don't know what you want from me. I, I gotta go. I gotta get a camera crew to Pickering, I mean . . .

GEORGE I want your support, okay?

JEREMY Okay, uh-huh.

GEORGE 'Cause I know that you have that situation with a suit. This guy's got an attitude, right? Remember the time you asked the guy to ladle the soup from underneath 'cause there was scum on top and he still ladled the scum into your bowl?

JEREMY Oh, Jesus. That was two years ago, the soup thing. I can't believe you could possibly remember something so . . . petty.

George walks with Rani into the newsroom. She has her coat on her arm.

GEORGE The muffins are just the subtext here, okay? The guy calls me petty and he virtually calls me a racist. I mean, I mean, you think I'm petty?

They stop at her workstation.

RANI — I wouldn't say "petty."

Veejay, Rani's twenty-year-old brother, approaches her desk. He is dressed in a leather jacket and sunglasses.

RANI — *(to Veejay)* I thought you were gonna wait downstairs?

VEEJAY — Yeah, well.
(to George) Hi.

RANI — It's my brother.

VEEJAY — I'm Veejay.

George and Veejay shake hands.

GEORGE — Oh, how you doin', man. How you doing?

VEEJAY — All right, all right.

RANI — Well, we should get going, eh?

VEEJAY — I saw you speak last month at Ryerson on the evils of chequebook journalism. You were really good.

RANI — He's in Journalism at Ryerson.

GEORGE — I remember those lectures. You know, I don't think they paid me for those lectures. I spoke there in September, October, November . . .

RANI — You know what? We, we gotta go. You should get on that.

GEORGE — I am sure they didn't pay me for October and November. Anyway, I'm sorry. Uh, hey, good luck with it, man. What is it, a restaurant, right?

VEEJAY — Journalism.

GEORGE Oh, right. Well, take it easy then. Good luck, okay? Bye-bye.

George is on the phone. Audrey sits across from him.

GEORGE A hundred and sixty dollars for the lecture and, um, four dollars for the, um, yeah, that's right, for the donut and the coffee at the break. Okay, I'll hold. Thank you. Okay.

(to Audrey) My point is, at the end of the day, the guy ends up with nothing but cranberry muffins in the cafeteria. Now why is that?

AUDREY I don't mean to over-intellectualize this, but there does have to be a last muffin. Your mail. *(she hands him a stack of mail)*

GEORGE *(stares at her a beat, then goes to his mail)* Amnesty International. How'd they get my address? *(puts it in the garbage)*

Greenpeace. *(puts it in the garbage)*

God, why don't these people leave me alone?

AUDREY You could give them a few dollars.

GEORGE Okay, let me tell you then. There's Amnesty International, there's Greenpeace, there's single mothers, there are animal rights groups, there are clean air groups. Have you ever heard of the concept of sympathy fatigue?

AUDREY Yes. But George, you never give. How can you be so fatigued?

RANI *(poking her head in)* Excuse me.

GEORGE Yeah.

RANI Can I ask you a personal favour?

GEORGE I'm actually right in the middle of –

RANI I'm reluctant to have to ask you this, okay? Uh, but my mom and dad threw my brother out of the house last night. And, um, my brother, uh, drives a limo for my uncle who owns a fleet of limos at night? And, uh, anyway, he got caught driving hookers around with their tricks. And I thought it would be a good idea if you talked to him. He admires you, he looks up to you so –

GEORGE Wait a second. Is this like a mobile brothel type of thing? This is . . . *(he thinks for a second; it's a rather inventive idea)*

RANI Would you talk to him?

GEORGE No, I can't, I can't. I couldn't do that, because, you know, if he gets involved with the police and then the media and then I have to keep my objectivity. I'm a news director . . .

RANI Say no more.

GEORGE You know, personally, I would do it.

RANI Forget it.

GEORGE No, no, but personally, I would do it. It's the principle, believe me. It's the principle.

RANI Yeah, yeah. Yeah, yeah. *(she leaves)*

GEORGE *(to Audrey)* It's the principle. I just can't do it.

Mother Teresa. *(puts envelope in garbage)*

Karen Hall's one-woman show. "An evening of satire by one of Canada's leading feminist comics." *(he stretches out his arm with envelope in hand and lets it drop into the garbage)*

AUDREY I'll go check on your bran muffins.

Jeremy is at his workstation, flipping through a Vanity Fair *magazine.*

JEREMY Hey, Sharon Stone. Check it out. *(he shows the guy at the workstation behind him)*

We should rename *Vanity Fair* "We're All Winners – You're All Losers."

Mark walks up to his workstation.

MARK	Hey, you know Cynthia Dale's coming here?
JEREMY	Yeah, she's following George around for a week. Watch him work.
MARK	Why?
JEREMY	Uh, researching a movie.
MARK	What movie?
JEREMY	*Dumb and Dumber Two.*

George is walking from the elevator bank, along the atrium walkway with a talent agent.

AGENT	I've represented Cynthia for over five years, and I can tell you, not only is she a terrific actress, but she's a terrific and down-to-earth girl.
GEORGE	Right. She dates Peter Mansbridge, doesn't she?
AGENT	Uh, now listen. *(they stop walking)* I'm glad you brought that up, actually, because it's something I meant to discuss, you know. That's her personal life, and she really doesn't like to get into that, okay?
GEORGE	Right.
AGENT	Okay?
GEORGE	Okay.
AGENT	Now, she's got this part in this feature film, and she's playing a news director like yourself. *(they start to walk)* And what she'd kind of like to do is just hang around with you, you know? Observe how you work. For about a week. Be like a little fly on the wall.
GEORGE	No, I understand. That's great.

George and the talent agent are in George's office. George is seated at his desk, the agent is on the couch.

GEORGE You know, is, is there a stipend, you know, money that the studio pays that I can get? You know, I mean, it's my time, and I'm not trying to, you know . . .

AGENT Uh, you know, I, I *(stumbles)*, I mean, I don't usually get involved in these petty, you know, little . . .

GEORGE Petty? What do you mean, petty?

AGENT *(laughs)* No! I didn't mean you are petty! I didn't mean you're petty.

GEORGE No. I'm just asking. You know, I mean . . .

AGENT I don't get involved in these little, you know, these little amounts.

GEORGE You keep saying "little," I mean, so there's nothing, is there?

AGENT Maybe, maybe they'll throw a few dollars your way. I don't know. You know?

GEORGE They'll "throw," I mean, is that how they do it? I mean, they don't . . . They just throw in money. *(agent laughs)*

Do they write a cheque or . . . I don't, I don't want to make, let's not make a deal of this. It's, it's a privilege to have Cynthia here.

AGENT It's a, you know, it's a legitimate question you have there. But, uh, you know, like I said, I mean, I don't usually get involved in this kind of stuff.

GEORGE Okay! Forget it then. Forget I asked. I'm just, you know, wondering, you know, would it be more than, you know, a hundred?

George walks with Cynthia down the corridor towards the newsroom. George has his coat on.

CYNTHIA So, I don't want people making a big deal about me being here, okay?

GEORGE No, that's been taken care of. I've told everyone why you're here, and nobody's going to bother you.

CYNTHIA Thanks.

Jim approaches and stops them.

JIM Cynthia Dale. My God, you look different in public.

GEORGE Jim, I mentioned Cynthia doesn't want to be bothered, okay?

JIM No, no, no. I mean, smaller.

I'm Jim Walcott, by the way. *(they shake hands)* Peter might have mentioned me to you.

CYNTHIA No.

JIM You know, I just wanted to say with "Street Legal," I, I honestly didn't think it was the greatest, but I thought you were fantastic.

Cynthia gives him a look.

GEORGE Well, thanks, Jim.

CYNTHIA Thank you.

GEORGE Thank you for that.

George and Cynthia continue to walk. Jim follows.

JIM I know you're here to research *News Break*, the feature film, and I got the script and made some notes. *(Cynthia looks back at Jim)* Not, not, not so much on character and plot development. I think those work kind of well. But, uh, they are similar to . . .

GEORGE Jim?

JIM . . . the real news game.

GEORGE Jim. I told you she didn't want to be bothered, okay? Thank you.

JIM No, no, no. I don't mean that. I think the script works okay. It's not that. But I have some ideas about the news stuff that you might be . . .

GEORGE Jim, for Christ's sake! Cynthia doesn't want to hear your ideas!

(to Cynthia) I'm sorry. I just . . .

JIM Yeah, I know, I know. I know what time's like. I gotta run too.

GEORGE Okay, good.

JIM I just, I just want to say with, with "Street Legal." You know, you were five years on the air.

CYNTHIA Seven, actually.

JIM There's nothing to be ashamed of there, no matter what the vehicle, right?

GEORGE Okay. Thank you, Jim.

JIM Right.

GEORGE Thank you.

JIM I'll see you later.

Jim walks away and Audrey approaches.

GEORGE Sorry, sorry.

AUDREY Hi, George. I reached the film production office, but they said they thought it was ridiculous showing Cynthia Dale around.

GEORGE Uh, why would you do that?

AUDREY 'Cause you asked me to.

GEORGE No, I wouldn't ask you to do that. This is Ms. Dale.

AUDREY Oh, shit. Hi.

CYNTHIA Hi.

AUDREY Uh, I've never seen you on TV before, but I hear you're a really talented actress.

CYNTHIA Thank you.

Audrey takes off, aware that she has screwed up.

GEORGE Sorry for that.

They walk. George and Cynthia have reached the newsroom and are heading towards the boardroom.

GEORGE Now, look. This is gonna work. It's really good having you here, and I think if you just stay focused, you know . . . Right this way here.

CYNTHIA I should have listened to people when they warned me about you.

They walk into the boardroom. They don't sit; they pace around the room.

GEORGE Warned you about me? What are they saying? I mean . . .

CYNTHIA *(laughing)* It's just, you know, gossip. People dish.

GEORGE Well, who are these people?

CYNTHIA I don't know. People you talk to. I don't know.

GEORGE I mean, do I have no right to know what's being said about me?

CYNTHIA Uh, that you're weak, two-faced, you treat your staff badly, and you're a company man. But it's meaningless gossip, okay? People dish! It's just people dishing. Don't worry about it. Well, I should never have opened this up.

GEORGE	Well, you did. You brought it up, I mean.
CYNTHIA	Peter and I were talking and it just came up, you know?
GEORGE	What, Peter who . . . Mansbridge?
CYNTHIA	Well, yeah.
GEORGE	What, you and Peter Mansbridge sit around talking about me?
CYNTHIA	Excuse me? Peter doesn't even know who the hell you are, okay? He'd heard some gossip.
GEORGE	What do you mean he doesn't know who I am. I'm a news director.
CYNTHIA	Well, okay, he thought he recognized your name. But, you know, he'd heard you were . . . I'd like my private life to stay private, okay?
GEORGE	He heard that I was what?
CYNTHIA	A liar.
GEORGE	Well, you know, at least I have my hair, you know.

Cynthia emits a huff.

Dernhoff, George, and the talent agent are in George's office. George is on the couch, Dernhoff is leaning on a table, and the agent is seated in an office chair.

DERNHOFF	I set this up for Cynthia as a favour to Peter Mansbridge.
GEORGE	Hey, hey. He said I was weak. He said I was two-faced.
AGENT	I think you're being petty.
GEORGE	What is this "petty"? What do you mean, "petty"? Where are you getting this?
AGENT	Look, Cynthia just wanted to get her research done.

GEORGE Wait, wait, no. Let's go back to the petty. Is this a line on me?

AGENT This has nothing to do with you. This is about Cynthia trying to get some work done here. You're being childish. Let the woman do her research.

GEORGE Let her do her research? Fine. You know, she should research around for a new boyfriend. One with hair.

AGENT *(to Dernhoff)* See, it's shit like that.

GEORGE I'm sorry. I'm sorry.

AGENT He's trying to squeeze money from the production company for this, too.

DERNHOFF Can we make this work?

Cynthia is with everyone in the boardroom, sitting in on their production meeting.

GEORGE Okay, before we start this morning, uh, I'd just like to bring attention to the new face in the room. Uh, very attractive face. Cynthia's, you know, one of our best and biggest stars.

Mark waves at Cynthia. She waves back.

GEORGE Cynthia is doing some research on a film. She's playing a news director, and she has come here to watch me at work. That's part of her research. But she has specifically asked me to, uh, tell everyone that she should be completely ignored. Make like she doesn't exist and go on about our work as we normally would. So, I'd just like to say that we should respect that, uh, request. So Mark, what's the rundown?

JIM Well, uh, I discovered a little secret about Cynthia this morning on Cable News . . .

GEORGE Jim, Jim. Cynthia has just asked us to respect her –

JIM This isn't about the movie. I discovered a little secret about Cynthia this morning on Cable News that I don't think anybody knows. Uh, today is Cynthia's birthday.

(starts singing) Happy birthday to you . . .

Kris and a few staff enter singing "Happy Birthday" with a birthday cake lit with candles.

George and Cynthia are outside the boardroom. Through the glass wall we see the others waiting, watching them.

CYNTHIA This is exactly want I didn't want.

GEORGE Cynthia, Jim is a moron. He's an idiot. He wasn't even my choice as an anchor for this show.

CYNTHIA Do you think you should be trashing your news anchor in front of me like this?

GEORGE I thought you were pissed off about the cake thing.

CYNTHIA Shouldn't you be standing up for your people?

GEORGE I have a tremendous amount of respect for Jim. He's resourceful, he's talented. You know, I love and respect the man. Peter Mansbridge, really, I'm sorry about that. You know, I love and respect Peter as a newsman as well.

CYNTHIA That was a childish thing to say.

GEORGE Okay, I'm sorry. I'm sorry. I was a little overwhelmed by your coming in here, okay? I admit that. You know, you're a big Canadian star.

CYNTHIA No, no, no. I really don't want to talk about being a Canadian star. Please.

GEORGE Okay, I'm sorry about that, okay?

CYNTHIA Okay, okay.

GEORGE — I know you never cracked the American market, but you're about as big as it gets here.

Cynthia glares at him.

George, the talent agent, and Dernhoff are in the boardroom. George sits at the table, eating a piece of the birthday cake. Dernhoff stands, leaning on a chair. The agent paces.

AGENT — And this guy! What's this dig about Canadian? What the fuck is that?!

GEORGE — I said she was a big Canadian star.

AGENT — You said . . . No, I know what you said. She told me what you said. She said that you said that she was a star in Canada, but that she was nothing in the U.S.

GEORGE — I didn't say "nothing."

AGENT — You know, if you would stop being such a petty little asshole, I can make this work.

GEORGE — Oh, there. "Petty."

DERNHOFF — You've done yourself a lot of damage. Now, I'm not saying that Cynthia hasn't even mentioned this to Peter. But if you don't do something about her perception of you, you've got a serious problem on your hands.

Dernhoff leaves. George and the agent watch her go. George waits a moment, then . . .

GEORGE — One second. The stipend, from the studio? Did that money come through?

The agent just looks at George then walks out.

Rani and Kris are in the coffee area. Kris has a coffee, and Rani is making herself a cup. George and Cynthia walk up.

GEORGE Okay, there's coffee here and there's mugs up there if you want one, okay?

CYNTHIA Thanks. *(she stands to the side, looking on)*

GEORGE Okay? Okay, good. Look, you know, now that we're all here, there's just something that I want to say. You know, I get a lot of credit for this show. But the truth is, without your intelligence *(Kris and Rani are looking at George like he's speaking a foreign language)* and without your, you know, really amazing and selfless energy, this wouldn't get done, this show. And I really appreciate that.

Kris smiles. Rani just stares at George.

GEORGE Is there a problem?

RANI No.

GEORGE Good, because if you have a work problem or a personal problem, you know that my door is always open. Okay?

RANI Okay. Excuse me.

She leaves. Kris raises her hand tentatively.

GEORGE Okay, but I have to run right now, okay?

KRIS Can I just say something? Do you mind if I just, I mean, I don't mean to interrupt or anything.

GEORGE Okay.

KRIS I mean, I know you always tell me to shut up, you know, but I just . . .

GEORGE — *(to Cynthia)* No, no, I don't . . . She's a fantastic skier, really. Just one of the best I've ever seen on a mountain.

KRIS — Okay, well, I just wanted to say, um, what you just said, right, about problems and stuff? That was great. *(she walks off)*

GEORGE — Well, thank you.

Jim walks in, script in hand.

JIM — Mmmm . . . is that grilled cheese I smell?

Cynthia looks uncomfortable.

GEORGE — No, Jim. We were just grabbing a coffee, and Cynthia and I are just running.

JIM — Yeah? Cynthia, I just wanted . . .

GEORGE — Yeah, Jim. One second.

JIM — Thirty seconds.

GEORGE — No, I asked you not to.

JIM — Thirty seconds, please, for the lady? Thanks a lot.

George leaves and Jim stands in close to Cynthia.

JIM — Cynthia, I just wanted to apologize for reading your film script. I know that it was none of my business. Um, but to be honest, I did have it. So I read it again, and I now think the verisimilitude of the newsroom was actually done quite well. I'm still not clear on what motivates your character to sleep with the accused killer. Um, as a newsman, I do know what it's like to get too close to a story. Interesting, here's something to note. Use it, don't use it . . . We, a little while ago, we were doing a story on prostitution.

And, uh, I got involved with this young prostitute in the car. Uh, really, really young, sexy woman. A lot of make-up and really short skirt. And it was, I really, something I really dug. Really cheap, really dug that. And, uh, we were in the car and, you know, it was fellatio, it was oral sex. It got on tape. Uh . . . anyway, use it, don't use it. Um, here's, uh, here's my notes on the script. Um, I'm a big fan. Read them, burn them, throw them away, whatever. I'll still be a fan. I'll just leave them here, okay?

George, Rani, and Cynthia are in George's office. Cynthia stands leaning against a table, taking notes.

RANI — You know what you said about any personal problem of ours being –

GEORGE — Yes, that's a policy.

RANI — I know, yeah. My mom and dad threw my brother out of the house last night. My brother works for my uncle who owns a fleet of limos. Airport limos. Anyway, he got caught driving hookers around in the back with their tricks. You know, sort of like a mobile brothel?

GEORGE — Right, right?

RANI — Anyway, uh, they would like to set up a big family meeting and my brother insists on having a neutral territory. And, uh, your offer and everything, I told them they can meet here?

GEORGE — The family, here?

RANI — Yeah, well, he would feel trapped anywhere else. And, uh, you know, it's neutral, it's safe.

GEORGE — Wait a second, wait a second. No, no, no. Wait, wait, wait. The personal thing stands, but aren't we pushing the edge of the personal envelope?

CYNTHIA	I don't know, but it seems to me like he's reaching out for help.
RANI	Yeah, yeah, he is.
GEORGE	I think you're right. It's done. It's done.
RANI	But what you said earlier . . .
GEORGE	No, you don't have to say any more. You don't have to say any more. No, no, that's fine. You've said enough. *(he gets up from his chair to show Rani out)*
RANI	You sure?
GEORGE	Done, done. Done, done, done.
RANI	I really, really appreciate it.

Rani leaves. Cynthia is sitting in George's chair, going through his garbage.

GEORGE	Done, done. No problem. It's done, okay? Um, that's my chair.
CYNTHIA	Oh, this Karen Hall one-woman show, it's really good. You should go see it.
GEORGE	Yes, well, actually, I was going to get to that. Where'd you get this?
CYNTHIA	In the garbage.
GEORGE	You went through my garbage? Is this part of your research?
CYNTHIA	You know, I just wanted to see what kind of mail, um, a TV news director gets.
GEORGE	Junk mail, junk mail. Mostly junk mail, Canadian Tire . . . You know, I have no idea how this got in there.
CYNTHIA	Amnesty International? Greenpeace?
GEORGE	Yes, yes.
CYNTHIA	You call this junk mail? Oh, okay. *(she's making notes)*

GEORGE — No, I, this must have gotten into the wrong pile. I have to send cheques out to these.

AUDREY — *(poking her head in)* Excuse me.

GEORGE — Yes?

AUDREY — Sorry, uh, the cafeteria manager is now claiming that you made a racist comment to the counter guy after you crumpled a cranberry muffin on the floor. But he's willing to make a dozen more bran if you stop complaining about the muffins and apologize to the worker.

GEORGE — I don't know what you're talking about.

George looks first at Audrey and then at Cynthia.

Rani's entire family are in the boardroom: an uncle, an aunt, cousins, her mother, father, grandfather, sister, and brother, Veejay. A mix of traditional and western dress. The family fight rages. Jim and Jeremy are at a workstation in the newsroom, watching the boardroom.

JIM — Do you know, they make more movies in India every year than in all other countries combined? It's true.

George walks into the newsroom as Rani's family comes out of the boardroom. Cynthia stands at a workstation, looking on and taking notes.

GEORGE — Well, I hope that everything turned out all right.

FATHER — Well, it's not quite all right.

SISTER — Yeah, nothing's resolved.

FATHER — It's caused a real rift in the family.

SISTER — He's not ready to come home.

FATHER — Yeah, it's a big problem. He has no place to stay. It's terrible. Nobody will take him in.

SISTER He doesn't want to come with Mom and Dad.

GEORGE Well, I wish, I wish I could help. You know . . .

FATHER Do you think that you possibly could?

CYNTHIA Maybe he could stay at your place?

SISTER That would be great! I mean, if you have the room. Just for a couple nights till he finds his place.

FATHER Do you think that maybe, as a possibility, he might?

GEORGE Well, my place is small.

SISTER Oh, he doesn't take up a lot of room.

GEORGE Well, I'm renovating.

MOTHER Well, he's not going to be a bother to you.

GEORGE Excuse me, can you give me a second.

FATHER *(together with mother)* One second? Sure, sure.

GEORGE Can I talk to you for a second?

CYNTHIA Yeah, sure. What's up?

GEORGE *(turning Cynthia away and whispers intensely)* What's up is that you're supposed to be a fly on the wall. You're getting into the food, Cynthia.

CYNTHIA It was just a suggestion, George.

GEORGE You're testing my character in this, aren't you? You really are. I can tell what you're doing, you know. Listen, I've been tested on very big ethical issues on very big stories. I don't have to prove anything about my character on a couple of nights at my apartment.

CYNTHIA Well, maybe the real test of character isn't the big ethical issue where you get credited in print for taking a stand, but a little thing like this, where there's nothing at stake.

George stares at her. She leaves. After a moment's pause, he turns to the family with a smile.

GEORGE Maybe a couple of nights.

FATHER — *(together with mother and sister)* Oh, thank you so much. Very kind.

GEORGE — Okay. No, no, it's no problem for me, really.

MOTHER — Come for dinner on Friday night.

FATHER — Friday night, will you come?

GEORGE — Dinner? Uh, actually, this Friday I'm doing a show.

MOTHER — Maybe Thursday?

GEORGE — Thursday is also bad. You know, it's a news show.

MOTHER — Maybe another time.

GEORGE — The world turns twenty-four hours a day. I have to be there.

FATHER — How about some tea?

GEORGE — Tea is a great idea. That's a great idea.

SISTER — Thank you so much for . . .

GEORGE — Okay. Okay, bye-bye. Thank you.

He turns and bumps into Jeremy and Mark. Without looking back, George asks:

GEORGE — Are they going, are they going, are they going?

JEREMY — They're going, they're going. They're gone, they're gone.

George and Cynthia are walking through the newsroom and out into the corridor.

GEORGE — Wait a second. You're leaving now? You were supposed to be here until Friday.

CYNTHIA — I don't think you're the right character for me.

GEORGE — Right character? What does that mean?

CYNTHIA — I don't want to get into it again.

GEORGE — Listen, you raised it. You brought it up. Come on.

CYNTHIA — I just think you're too, um . . . No, forget it, really.

GEORGE — Too what? Too petty?

CYNTHIA Too predictable, too on the nose, too TV.

GEORGE What, did you see me with that family in there? You call that TV?

CYNTHIA Yeah, but that's a perfect example. You're too Lou Grant. All that father-figure stuff with Rani's brother, you know. You give to Amnesty International, you give to Greenpeace. All the obvious liberal moves. You're too hackneyed and predictable to be interesting. You lack edge. I guess there's no contradiction. No internal conflict between the different dimensions of your character. Uh, and I think you're too one-dimensional. And there's no depth, no dark side. And none of that sexuality that generally flows from all that stuff. You just lack edge. But I appreciate your time. Thanks.

Audrey is with George and the manager in the cafeteria.

MANAGER You threw that muffin on the floor, man.

GEORGE Yeah, well, I paid for that muffin.

AUDREY George?

GEORGE Just a second. I paid for that muffin, okay?

AUDREY I think we should go.

GEORGE And I don't even like banana muffins. And you know why? 'Cause you take five shitty little black slices of banana, you put them inside, and you put your one nice slice of banana on top. I know that game.

MANAGER You got him crazy, you know that? My guy is right. You're a racist, obsessive asshole.

GEORGE Oh, your guy, your muffin guy's calling me obsessive? What is he, a shrink at night when he's not pushing shitty muffins by day? You can stuff your muffins.

George and Audrey leave the cafeteria and walk across the atrium.

GEORGE I tell ya, Cynthia Dale should have seen that. You know what I had in there?

AUDREY A childish tantrum?

GEORGE No, that was edge. I had edge in there. That was my dark side. I should have had that much edge when it came to that stipend.

AUDREY Oh, the film production company sent you a cheque. Two hundred dollars. Should cover your Greenpeace and Amnesty International donations.

GEORGE You're very good. *(they walk up to the elevators)*

AUDREY *(pushing the button)* Thank you. Is there anything else?

GEORGE Yes. That family that was up here? They phoned. I was forced to accept an invitation to tea. I'd like you to cancel it, okay?

AUDREY What lie should I tell them?

GEORGE I don't want you to lie. Just tell them that, uh, my mother's sick and that she could die at any moment.

George is in the back of a limo with a woman who might be a hooker. She is holding a glass of wine.

GEORGE You know, I was really surprised at how many NBA players you know personally.

HOOKER Well, I do work the sports teams.

GEORGE Yeah, I appreciate the Dennis Rodman autograph. God, how'd you get that?

HOOKER — You don't want to know. You're very different from my usual clients. I mean, they wouldn't give up a dime to something like Amnesty International or Greenpeace, but, I mean, two thousand dollars apiece?

GEORGE — Well, you know, the health of the planet and human rights, that's all-important, right?

HOOKER — Oh, I guess in my line of work, you really don't meet people as honest and down-to-earth as yourself. Do you mind if I ask you what you do for a living?

GEORGE — Oh, uh, industrial freezers. Freezers. Industrial.

Veejay is driving the limo. He looks back and smiles.

THE END

EPISODE 7

"Dis 'n' Dat"

First Aired: February 10, 1997

Mark and Bruce, the weatherman, are at Mark's workstation in the newsroom. Mark is collecting messages off his computer.

MARK I got Shayna Campbell from, uh, "Newsworld" to do your weather spot for you on Friday. When you do that, uh, celebrity AIDS golf tournament thing? So, she's gonna be doing it.

They start to walk towards the coffee area.

BRUCE What do you mean, AIDS? I signed up for a haemophilia tournament.

MARK Yeah, it's haemophilia and AIDS research, so . . .

BRUCE Is this a gay thing?

MARK No, it's an AIDS thing. I mean, there could be some gay players.

They stop at the coffee area. Mark opens the fridge and takes out a juice.

BRUCE Okay, wait, wait, wait. I'm not prejudiced, but, uh, golf is not a homosexual sport.

MARK Well, what sports do homosexuals play?

BRUCE I don't know, they play . . . I don't know! They swim laps. I mean, the point is I signed up for this tournament because I support haemophilia research. And now all of a sudden it's, you know, it's AIDS stuff.

MARK So what's the problem?

They walk out of the coffee area, back to Mark's workstation.

BRUCE Well, look, I, I hosted two heart-disease events last year and a kidney telethon. I mean, I'll get in there and bust my balls for any disease. I mean, there's a half a dozen dialysis machines in this town that would be toaster ovens if it wasn't for the money I helped raise. *(Mark sits down at his workstation)* But, you know, I heard this story of a guy coming on to the trees with a five iron. His club hits this tree trunk, snaps, comes right back in his neck, severs his jugular. Somebody's gotta get down with a towel and stop the bleeding. I got kids at home, and I draw the line at my family . . . so you get me out of this!

MARK *(phone in hand)* No, you signed up. You get out of it. Excuse me.

He turns away to make a call.

Audrey and George are in George's office.

AUDREY All of the indoor parking spaces are taken.

GEORGE The parking guy told me he'd meet with me.

AUDREY He'll squeeze you in tomorrow on his break, but he can't promise anything.

GEORGE If all the spots are gone, how busy can he be? What does he mean, he'll squeeze me in?

AUDREY Well, apparently he has to re-stencil names on spaces all day.

GEORGE They get their names stencilled on spaces? I'm a news director. I don't even get a space. I have to park across the street for seven bucks a day, fifteen when there's a ballgame. The guy that parks my car is an Ethiopian doctor. That's the truth. That's not what they're trained to do. This is what's wrong with our immigration policy. *(Audrey looks at him)* They should let these guys practise medicine. I'd rather have them operate on my heart than park my car. Do you know the three scariest words an Ethiopian doctor can say to a BMW owner? Huh, do you? "Leave the keys."

George is standing at the secretary's desk outside Doddie Graham's office.

SECRETARY She'll just be a moment.

GEORGE Okay, that's good.

A young woman walks up and puts some papers on the secretary's desk.

GEORGE *(to young woman)* Oh, excuse me. Can you grab me a coffee with milk, 1 per cent if you've got it?

The young woman looks at him and walks away. Doddie Graham (in her fifties, smart, a smoker, doesn't suffer fools gladly and can kiss ass with the best of them) walks up to the secretary's desk and drops off some paperwork.

GRAHAM I want to introduce you to the new head of Regional Programming.

GEORGE Do I know him?

GRAHAM Her? No.
(to the secretary) Can you do that? Thank you.

(to George) No, she's from outside. *(they start to walk down the hall)* She wants to work closely with local news, but I think you two can get along. She's smart, she's got good ideas.

GEORGE Did she get indoor parking?

GRAHAM She did.

GEORGE I thought all the spots were gone.

GRAHAM Spot came up last Thursday when Jack McPherson died.

GEORGE Jack McPherson died? Nobody told me that. And she got his spot?

GRAHAM Massive brain haemorrhage. He woke up next to his wife – which was unusual for Jack – grabbed his head, screamed "Oh my God," and dropped down dead. Evidently he woke up exactly the same way four years ago when he had the brilliant idea of moving the ten o'clock news to nine. This time it killed only him.

Graham walks George to the office of the new head of Regional Programming. It's the young woman George asked to get his coffee. She's seated at her desk.

GRAHAM Gillian Soros . . . George Findlay. I gotta run. I'll let you two get acquainted. *(she leaves)*

GEORGE I guess there was no more coffee.

GILLIAN You can have a seat.

GEORGE Oh, okay.

GILLIAN Can we talk about your show? You have to get a Website.

GEORGE Oh, the Internet. I don't completely get that.

GILLIAN It's generational.

GEORGE No, I mean in a news capacity.

GILLIAN	Information is power; power is freedom. The Net is the ultimate window into true democracy.
GEORGE	You got indoor parking, didn't you?
GILLIAN	Yeah. Can we talk about your show?
GEORGE	No, I was just, I was just interested, because, you know, you got Jack McPherson's spot, and he just died on Thursday. I thought . . .
GILLIAN	I don't know who's spot I got. I'm not here for the parking.
GEORGE	No, I, I just thought that was a little fast. I mean, the oil stain under his car hasn't even dried yet.
GILLIAN	I would love to see the tone and pace of the show tweaked a bit.
GEORGE	Tweaked? What does that mean?
GILLIAN	The show's a little tight-assed. I'd love an ex-pro athlete to anchor a sports desk. High profile. A character. Someone you don't expect to see on TV.
GEORGE	Like O.J.?
GILLIAN	Boxer, Canadian heavyweight. God, what's his name?
GEORGE	Oh, not George Chuvalo?
GILLIAN	Yes. I love George Chuvalo.
GEORGE	Well, you know, Chuvalo can be, I guess, okay.
GILLIAN	I'm not actually sure if he can do it, but if you think he can, he's your call.
GEORGE	I thought Chuvalo was your call.
GILLIAN	It's your call. It's your show.

George and Audrey are walking down the corridor to the atrium walkway. Audrey's clearly in a foul mood.

AUDREY	Gillian Soros? Well, she went to Ryerson. She was in the TV program there. She quit when she

was nineteen to be Teen Accessories editor at *Flare* magazine. After that, she organized some monster rock-festival thing in Ottawa for Canada Day.

GEORGE Right.

AUDREY And up until she took this regional head thing, she was Marketing Director for Polly Pocket Canada.

GEORGE Do you have a problem with this woman?

AUDREY No.

GEORGE You sound like you have a problem with her.

AUDREY You wanted her bio; I gave you her bio. If I had a problem with her, I would have mentioned the people she screwed to get a brilliant bio.

Angelo Mosca comes from the elevator bank and stops Audrey.

ANGELO Excuse me? Have you seen a news director?

Audrey points to George and leaves.

ANGELO Hi. Angelo Mosca . . . Hamilton Ti-Cats. Happened to be in the building. I hear you're lookin' for a sports anchor.

GEORGE Angelo Mosca the wrestler?

ANGELO Correct.

GEORGE You know what? Uh, Angelo, this is not against your record or anything, okay? But we kind of need a more recognizable face. You played football, you had the face guard. And in wrestling you wore the mask and . . .

ANGELO I never wore a mask in wrestling.

GEORGE That was your face?

ANGELO Yes, sir.

GEORGE Oh, well.

ANGELO I heard you wanted to go with George Chuvalo.

GEORGE Nobody has mentioned George Chuvalo to me.

ANGELO Come on, it's all over the building. I have nothing against George. But he's not a great speaker. But if you're lookin' for a "dis-'n'-dat" kinda guy, you've got your man.

GEORGE Well, wait a second. Chuvalo's a smart guy. He doesn't talk "dis 'n' dat." Look, they wanted George Chuvalo upstairs. My hands are tied, really, really Angelo. It was nice meeting you. I love you. I would have you. But they want George upstairs.

Bruce is on the phone at his workstation. Karen, the new segment producer, sits at her workstation in front of him. She is listening to his conversation.

BRUCE Yeah, I'm, I'm really sorry I have to cancel, since both the game of golf and the disease of AIDS are very important to me. You know, golf is my game, and AIDS is a terrible tragedy which has hit so many people in my industry from, uh, Rock Hudson all the way down. But, uh, you know, I threw out my back. And, uh, my doctor is telling me that, uh, a golf swing is just about the worse thing you could do for it right now. Thank you. Take care. Bye-bye. *(hangs up)*
What?!

KAREN Your nutty definitions. George doesn't think they've been working that well, and he suggested that if you insist on doing a bit, that I write them for you.

BRUCE Oh *(laughs)*. Oh, my material is shit, is that it?

KAREN Yeah, basically that's it.

BRUCE Oh, yeah, well, Jeremy never had a problem with that, and he was a *good* producer.

KAREN Maybe this kind of abuse is why Jeremy quit.

BRUCE All right, all right. What have you got?

KAREN "Dogmatic. What is a dog without a clutch?"

BRUCE No, that, that sucks. No, hold on, hold on. Okay, okay, uh, What's a bull terrier?

KAREN What?

BRUCE A dog without a clutch.

KAREN That makes no sense.

BRUCE A bull terrier doesn't have a clutch.

KAREN Yeah, but that's not a joke. That's not *nutty*.

BRUCE Yeah, well, neither is "dogmatic."

KAREN Look, this routine was your stupid idea, all right? You don't know what dogmatic means, do you? That's why you don't want it.

BRUCE Oh, yeah, yeah. You think you know everything 'cause you graduated from the University of goddamn Toronto and I sold outboard motors.

KAREN I don't happen to know the full range of Evinrudes on the market, if that's your point.

BRUCE Look, sweetheart. I've sold more outboard motors than you've read books. All right. Gimme that. I'll do your shitty dogmatic joke.

Karen slaps the paper in his hand and he snatches it away. She walks away mad.

George and the parking guy are in the basement parking lot. The parking guy is smoking.

PARKING I assign the spots. I'm told to assign.

GEORGE So you have absolutely no discretion, none?

PARKING Well, I wouldn't say "none." I mean, I know when the spots come up.

Now, this is between you and me, all right?

GEORGE Okay.

PARKING Fred Jamieson from Northern Services?

GEORGE Yeah?

PARKING Had a heart attack this morning.

GEORGE Really.

PARKING Yeah, he's in intensive care.

GEORGE Really. What's it look like?

PARKING Oh, it's a beautiful spot. Pillars on both sides.

GEORGE No, no. I meant . . . What, pillars? That's good?

PARKING Yeah, 'cause no one can open the car door into you.

He might not make it, but I can't guarantee you anything.

GEORGE Well, if he lives, he lives.

PARKING I mean, I can't guarantee you'll get the spot.

GEORGE Right. If it goes, it goes. We're all rooting for Fred, right?

PARKING Yeah, yeah.

George is in his office on the phone.

GEORGE Yeah, is this Fred Jamieson's office? Yeah, this . . . this is George Findlay in, in local news, and we'd heard that, uh, Fred had a heart attack? Uh-huh . . . oh, he, he lived. Uh-huh . . . oh, that's great. That's good.

Audrey is in the coffee area when Mark walks in and checks the microwave timer.

MARK Nine minutes? What are you cooking in there, a rib roast?

AUDREY	My lunch. Interns are allowed to eat.
MARK	Ouch. Someone's got PMS.
AUDREY	I don't need this right now, Mark.
MARK	You know Ilsa the She-wolf Nazi? Do you know what her problem was?
AUDREY	She was also an intern?
MARK	No, uh, PMSS. The SS? Do you want to talk about it?
AUDREY	Gillian Soros is my problem. Our new executive in charge of Regional Programming.
MARK	She was the one who got Jack McPherson's parking spot?
AUDREY	Yes. We were in the TV program together at Ryerson. Now, she's an executive. I'm an intern making less than minimum wage. *And* she's the bitch queen of the universe.
MARK	Well, I guess you just have to decide what you want from life. Be a successful bitch or, uh, a decent human being.
AUDREY	A successful bitch.
MARK	I'll, I'll find another microwave.

Jim and Bruce are at a workstation. Bruce stands and reads a multi-page list of names.

JIM	You know, I'm playing in that tournament too, and they just faxed me that list of T-off times. Your name is crossed off.
BRUCE	Yeah, yeah, you know I had to cancel. Aw, shit, you're right! Shit, shit, shit! They had me playing with Cito Gaston and Joe Carter.
JIM	Yeah, I was jealous as hell.
BRUCE	Aw, shit! This is that AIDS thing, right?

JIM — Yeah, through the Haemophilia Association. They say they can beat this disease. Every eighteen holes helps.

BRUCE — This is, this is, a gay thing, too. Right?

JIM — Jeez, I don't know. I never thought of golf as a gay sport. Except the LPGA. Most of those chicks are lesbians, aren't they?

BRUCE — Goddamn it! I didn't know I was playing with Gaston and Carter.

Well, screw that. I'm back in, man.

JIM — Anyway, I thought I'd drive out with you. But, uh, if you're out, I'll have to go it alone.

Bruce is on the phone at his workstation.

BRUCE — Well, the doctors have cleared me to play, and I figured, you know, since I, uh, got my swing back and, uh, it's for AIDS and everything . . . Excellent. Well, Friday's going to be a great day for golf. Uh, sunny with a high near twenty-three. Yeah, that's right. I'm the weather man. Well, let's beat this AIDS thing, all right? I know we won't be able to do it in eighteen holes, but, uh, every hole gets us that much closer to a cure.

Eddie Shack is sitting across the desk from George in George's office.

EDDIE — I think the problem with a lot of ex-pros is the fans don't know what their thing was.

GEORGE — Yeah, yeah, that's right.

Eddie Shack was the, uh . . . What were you, Eddie? You were, uh, scoring?

EDDIE — No *(laughs)*. I was the entertainer.

GEORGE Crazy Eddie Shack, right?

EDDIE We gave the game that dimension.

GEORGE We?

EDDIE Ed Shack.

GEORGE Right. I'm sorry.

EDDIE This is why I think I'd work in your sports spot. With Chuvalo, it's "dis" or "dat."

GEORGE You're great, Eddie, but they want Chuvalo upstairs. I can't do anything about it.

MARK *(poking his head in)* Chuvalo passed.

Eddie looks at George.

George, Mark, and Gillian are in the boardroom. Gillian is on the phone. George and Mark talk in whispers.

GEORGE Okay, if I give you a look, say Angelo Mosca.

MARK Angelo Mosca? He's wrong. Why would you think Angelo Mosca?

GEORGE Because we can get him.

GILLIAN Thank you. Bye-bye. *(she hangs up)* Okay, Mats Sundin.

MARK Uh, we, we couldn't get him. We tried. And the accent, too, we thought . . .

GEORGE He has an accent.

GILLIAN Oh, okay.

GEORGE We tried, though.

GILLIAN All right. Okay. Doug Flutie.

GEORGE Couldn't get him.

MARK We couldn't get him.

GEORGE He's American.

MARK Yeah.

GILLIAN Right . . . ?

GEORGE Well, they had heavy schedules and, um, we tried, and he doesn't live here, and we couldn't get him.

GILLIAN *(clears her throat)* Roberto Alomar.

GEORGE Well, Alomar spit in the face of an umpire.

MARK Plus the accent. We did try.

GEORGE We tried. But we couldn't get him.

MARK He doesn't even play in, in Toronto any more. He plays for Baltimore.

GILLIAN Okay, okay. All right, all right.

GEORGE But we tried to get him.

GILLIAN Okay, okay.

MARK We did try, but we couldn't get him.

GILLIAN *(clears her throat)* Eric Lindros.

MARK We tried to get him, but we couldn't get past his agent, actually.

GILLIAN You tried? So you didn't speak to him.

GEORGE No. We couldn't get him. Uh, we couldn't get *to* him.

MARK But, I mean, he's, he's, he's very busy and . . .

GILLIAN Silken Laumann.

Mark and George both look at her.

GILLIAN The rower?

MARK Oh, um . . .

GILLIAN Okay, um, this is the list that I have. Have you guys even made an effort to come up with anything yourselves? Am I, am I working alone here?

MARK No.

GEORGE No, no. We tried a number of, uh . . .

MARK Oh, well, I mean, uh, well, one guy we didn't try was, uh, Angelo Mosca. But, I mean . . .

GEORGE We would never get him.

GILLIAN Sorry. Who is he?

MARK Oh, well, he's a football player. Kind of high profile, cross-generational, kind of a media guy.

GEORGE Yeah, but I don't think we would ever get him.

GILLIAN Well, did you try?

MARK *(laughing)* Well, we didn't try. I mean . . .

GEORGE We can try. If you want us to try, we can try, but I don't think we'll get him.

GILLIAN Well, don't you think you should?

MARK Okay, okay. We'll try.

GEORGE We'll try.

MARK We'll try.

GILLIAN Thank you.

Gillian, George, Graham, Mark, Karen, and Angelo are sitting in the network brass boardroom.

ANGELO So, if this is my sports desk, I would have a ref's whistle. And whenever I report a loss or a loser, I'd blow the whistle like dis. *(blows whistle)*

GRAHAM *(whispers to George)* Did he say "dis"?

GEORGE I think so.

ANGELO Dat's the basic idea. I gotta very strong point of view.

MARK Excuse us.
(leans over to Angelo and whispers) Uh, Angelo?

ANGELO Yeah?

MARK You're doin' great. If you could just drop the "dis" and the "dat," we have an educated audience, and it looks kind of . . .

ANGELO I'm sorry. I have a problem with that. Once in a while I slip into dat.

MARK This, that.

ANGELO Okay, okay, I understand, okay.

(to everyone) Okay, now, certain sports, I don't consider legitimate. This is my point of view. For example, a sport I don't give a shit about *(Mark closes his eyes)* . . . sorry, I don't give a *(blows whistle)* about is curling. Any game where you can smoke and drink while you play is not a sport. Hockey, some guy takes a shot that goes between the goalie's legs. Any game you can win by shooting something between another guy's legs is not a sport. *(blows whistle)*. Football, that's a sport.

GILLIAN I . . .

Oh, well.

Audrey is standing in George's office, expressionless.

GEORGE You know, I've noticed the last few days, around the office, you know, you've been, like, depressed or angry, and I just wanted to talk about it. I'd like to help, because I'm under a lot of pressure, and I don't need someone around the office who's pissed off all the time. You know, if this is some kind of, you know, menstrual, you know, thing, woman thing, I think you have a responsibility as a professional woman to, you know, to control, you know, to control it.

AUDREY And how would I do that?

GEORGE I don't know. How do women do that? I don't know. I . . .

AUDREY Is that all you wanted to say?

GEORGE Yeah, basically, yeah. I have to make this call.

AUDREY Okay. Thanks for that, uh, wise advise. *(she leaves)*

GEORGE — *(dials phone and waits a moment)* . . . Yeah, is this Fred Jamieson's office? Yeah. Yeah, this is George Findlay. Again. I talked to you a couple of days ago? . . . Right, right. Um, I was just wondering how Fred's heart . . . He lived? Oh, good. So, he's out of intensive care. That's good. Okay, uh, well, I wanted to know . . . . Okay, thanks. Bye.

(hangs up) Shit.

Bruce is on the phone at his workstation.

BRUCE — Yeah, yeah, you just faxed me the new pairings for the golf tournament? I thought I was back in with Cito Gaston and Joe Carter? . . . Yeah, I know I cancelled and re-booked. But, did you have to shift everything around, I mean . . . I'm sorry if I created a problem, but you've got me paired up with Peter Gzowski, for Christ's sake. I mean, there's got to be some mistake . . . No?

(he suddenly grimaces, faking a back spasm) Aw, oh, no, I, you know, I think my back just went out again . . . Yeah, no, you know what? I, I, I think I'd better cancel. No, it's, it's really bad. I, I'd better cancel. I, I've really gotta go. Okay, bye-bye.

George, Graham, Gillian, and Alex Gonzalez are in the boardroom. Audrey leans against the wall.

GILLIAN — I took the liberty of making a deal with Alex Gonzalez because I knew you'd love him. He's one of the hot new Blue Jays. He's young, and I think very sexy.

(to Alex) Excuse my language, but this is TV, and sex appeal's a big part of the business.

I know it wasn't exactly my call, but I'm a terrible bureaucrat. I get an idea and I get excited and I can't help myself. I have to get on the phone! *(laughs. Audrey looks mad)*

This is a brilliantly simple concept. We get the top active Blue Jays, Raptors, Leafs, and Argonauts to host a weekly sports segment on their game in season. Alex Gonzalez is the perfect baseball personality. I spoke to the baseball commissioner, who loves it. And I spoke to Alex's agent, who loves it. And he loves it at our price.

ALEX — You've got a good salesgirl. I mean, she can play real hardball on the money.

GILLIAN — *(laughs)* The only thing we played hardball over was an indoor parking space that just opened up this morning, and Alex won.

George is walking down the hallway with Graham.

GEORGE — The bastard got Jamieson's spot?

GRAHAM — I think this kid's a great idea.

GEORGE — I didn't know Jamieson died. The last I'd heard, he was coming out of intensive care.

GRAHAM — Well, he had another heart attack. He was sixty-eight, he smoked like a chimney.

GEORGE — Listen, this kid's gonna be here once a week on the sports desk for an hour, taping, and they gave him a permanent spot? How can they do that?

GRAHAM — I'm going for a cigarette. *(she walks in the opposite direction)*

Gillian and Alex are walking through the newsroom. Audrey comes up behind them within earshot.

GILLIAN This is going to work. You're terrific. You've got this star quality. It's amazing. How would you like to grab a dinner tonight, on me?

Audrey catches up to them and walks ahead. Alex notices.

AUDREY *(as she walks by)* Excuse me.

GILLIAN We can discuss the show, or not discuss the show.

ALEX I'm really sorry. I've already got plans tonight.

GILLIAN Cool, another time.

She walks away. Alex turns and runs to catch up to Audrey, who has a depressed look on her face. He hurries up behind her and puts a hand on her shoulder.

ALEX Excuse me?

AUDREY Yes?

ALEX Want to have dinner tonight?

AUDREY Why?

ALEX Well, you're about the only girl I've met up here in Toronto that doesn't care who I am. I'd like to find out why.

AUDREY Well, I thought that you were more interested in that, um . . .

ALEX She's not my type.

Uh, what do you think? I want to take you out to dinner.

AUDREY Okay.

ALEX Yeah?

AUDREY Yeah.

ALEX All right, great.

AUDREY Cool. *(she laughs)*

Bruce runs into Alex at the elevators.

BRUCE Alex Gonzalez, holy shit! Alex Gonzalez. Hey, hey. So are the Jays gonna win the World Series this year? Tell me it's gonna happen. Come on, come on, tell me. Tell me it's gonna happen.

ALEX Yeah, we're gonna win.

BRUCE All right! Excellent, excellent. Thanks a lot. I'm a huge fan, huge fan. Well, actually, I haven't been for a couple years, because, uh, you know, the team sucked. *(Alex presses the "down" button)*

I'm Bruce Moffat, by the way. Channel Six weather?

ALEX Right, right. The weather guy.

BRUCE Yeah, yeah.

ALEX Sorry we couldn't've played golf together.

BRUCE What do you mean?

ALEX Oh, I just ran into that guy, uh, Peter Gzowski? Uh, the radio announcer that works here? Um, he said that we were paired up for the golf tournament, but you dropped out this morning. So take it easy. *(he leaves a stunned Bruce)*

Bruce is on the phone at his workstation. He's standing and pacing.

BRUCE Look, look, I know you're busy. This, this is easy. Just go back to your last list. Yeah, me, Gzowski, and, and, and Alex Gonzalez . . . What? You put our anchor Jim Walcott in with Alex Gonzalez? . . . Okay, fine, fine. Let me tell you something. Okay, sweetheart. AIDS is not the only disease in this town, all right? Heart disease kills a hell of a lot more people than . . . Hello? Hello?

Audrey and George are in George's office. Audrey is upbeat. The newscast plays on George's TV set.

AUDREY Um, Fred Jamieson's office called. They want to thank you for your concern for his health before he died. They'd also like you to speak at his memorial.

GEORGE They want me to speak? I didn't even know the guy. All I knew about him was that he had a great parking spot.

AUDREY Well, if you do speak, I wouldn't say that.

GEORGE You're in a better mood today. Is it that little talk we had, the little . . .

AUDREY Hormonal, woman, professional . . . um, yeah, yes. That was, that was very helpful.

GEORGE Good.

Audrey leaves. Karen enters and looks at George's TV.

KAREN First he's gonna do his nutty definition.

GEORGE Okay, okay, okay, okay. God, thank God she's in a better mood.

KAREN You'd be in a good mood, too, if you were sleeping with Alex Gonzalez. Here it comes.

GEORGE I hope you wrote this.

KAREN Yes. It's funny, it's good. It works.

On the TV set, Bruce and Jim are at the anchor desk.

BRUCE Last word.

JIM All right, hit me.

BRUCE	What's a schnauzer?
JIM	I don't know, but I have a feeling you're gonna tell me.
BRUCE	A dog without a clutch.
JIM	*(laughs)* Dog without a clutch. That's the last word. Very funny. Good night.
BRUCE	Good night.
KAREN	What an asshole.

As the credits roll at the end of the newscast . . .

JIM	What does it mean?
BRUCE	I don't know. Fuckin' asshole writers.

THE END

EPISODE 8

"Unity"

First Aired: February 17, 1997

George walks through the studio door accompanied by an accountant. Together they walk towards the receptionist, who hands George a newspaper. He quickly goes through it as he and the accountant walk through the newsroom.

GEORGE — I've got my receipts and my records for you in a shoebox in my office.

ACCOUNTANT — George, I'm your accountant, not your bookkeeper. A shoebox?

GEORGE — Sorry, I'm sorry.

Mark approaches.

MARK — More welfare cuts at Queen's Park. Five P.M. *(he walks away)*

GEORGE — Okay, good. That's our lead. That's our lead.

ACCOUNTANT — And you're not my only client. It's tax time. I come down here to you, the least you could do is put your expenses on computer.

GEORGE — Next year, I'm sorry.

Karen walks up to George.

KAREN — Okay, so it was a horse. The hooker was charged, but the real estate developer got off.

GEORGE — Great. *That's* our lead. Tell Mark the welfare cuts come second. Lead. Thank you very much. *(Karen leaves)*

GEORGE — Now, can I at least deduct my new VCR and television set?

ACCOUNTANT — Not if they're at home.

George has reached his desk in his office. The accountant sits across from him.

GEORGE — *(going through the newspaper)* My car, what about my car?

ACCOUNTANT — *(investigating the contents of the shoebox)* Now, again, only if you use it for the show. You'd have to set up an independent corporation that owns the vehicle and then leases it back to the network.

GEORGE — *(spotting something in the paper)* Look at this! They published the salaries of public employees making over a hundred thousand dollars a year. They said they would do it, and they did it.

ACCOUNTANT — Yeah, I saw that this morning. It's beyond me why people would want their incomes published, but they seem to love it.

GEORGE — Wait a second. They published "A" to "M" today, and my name's not here. They left my name off.

ACCOUNTANT — Yeah, I noticed that.

GEORGE — I can't believe this! I make a hundred and thirty-seven thousand dollars a year, and they left my name off!

ACCOUNTANT — George, the last thing you want is somebody at the tax department thinking about your income.

GEORGE — What do you mean? We declare it.

ACCOUNTANT — Every cent. The car in '93 was slightly dicey. I wouldn't want them looking into that.

GEORGE — What do you mean "slightly dicey"?

ACCOUNTANT Basically, I feel very comfortable with that deduction.

GEORGE What does "basically comfortable" mean?

ACCOUNTANT You wanted the deduction. I made it work.

GEORGE Wait a second. I said to you, Can we get the car deduction? You said, I can do it.

ACCOUNTANT And that's what I did. Basically it worked.

GEORGE There, you're going "basically" again! Would you quit saying "basically?" It worked or it didn't work. Isn't that what an accountant does? It works or it doesn't work.

ACCOUNTANT "Basically" means it worked back then. Just always avoid an audit. That's all I'm saying.

GEORGE All I want to know is, can I go to sleep tonight?

ACCOUNTANT Oh, basically you can sleep like a baby.

Jim is on the air.

JIM High seas are now threatening the overcrowded vessel, which coastguard officials estimate is carrying more than three hundred starving refugees off the shark-infested South Florida coast.

And Bruce Moffat can tell us exactly what kind of weather they can expect. Bruce?

Bruce, reporting from the roof of the building.

BRUCE Well, those boat people are right in the path of that storm we reported earlier, Jim, with winds gusting up to a hundred kilometres an hour.

And speaking of boat people, you know I'm a sailing fanatic, and we'll be heading up to the Thousand Islands on Saturday, and it looks like we'll have sunny skies right across Ontario for the long weekend.

JIM — Well, I wouldn't mind being a refugee on your boat. Well, of course, we are all hoping for those boat people, and I guess we can be glad we live in a country where we don't have to hop on a boat every time our government changes hands.

BRUCE — Oh, this is a great country, Jim. And I get letters from Canadians of all national origins. Uh, here's a cooking tip today from *(he refers to a letter he's holding)* Heather Laidlaw of Oakville, Ontario, who writes that the best way to avoid the stringy part of the asparagus is *(he puts the letter down and picks up a spear of asparagus)* take the raw spear like so and snap it. *(he snaps it)* There you go. Heather claims that the asparagus naturally breaks at the point between the tender and the stringy part.

JIM — You know, Bruce, I'm wondering if it could be the stringy part that gives your urine that pungent odour that so many people experience after eating asparagus.

(realizing he's gone too far) Well, who knows. It's, uh . . . but it's a good point. Thanks, Bruce, thanks, Heather.

Bruce enters the studio with Mark.

BRUCE — It gives your urine a pungent odour? Who writes that tasteless shit for him?

MARK — He ad-libbed it, okay? We didn't write it. He made it up.

BRUCE — Yeah, well, that's my audience. They love me. And if Miss Piss-ass Ontario writes in with a suggestion on how to snap asparagus spears, then I owe her the common decency not to have that prick kill my bit with the stench of his own urine.

George, Mark, Audrey, Bruce, Jim, Karen, and David, the entertainment reporter, are in the boardroom for a story meeting.

MARK — The Toronto businessman vacationing in Florida? Remember the cop who reported he was shot by two blacks? Well, they didn't do it. The wife confessed.

GEORGE — So, it's a domestic thing?

KAREN — He's still dead.

GEORGE — Yeah, well, so is the story. "Canadian businessman shot by his wife in Florida" doesn't work.

AUDREY — But shot by two black kids worked.

GEORGE — I didn't say that. The story doesn't work, okay? There's no hook.

MARK — By the way. The wife, uh, the wife didn't actually pull the trigger. Allegedly she put the boyfriend up to it.

GEORGE — Was the boyfriend black at least?

MARK — He was white.

GEORGE — Pass on that.

KAREN — Well, there is an amateur video of the body floating in the pool.

GEORGE — Was the body floating face-up or face-down?

KAREN — Face-up.

GEORGE — Are the eyes open?

KAREN — Uh, one eye was open. The other was gone.

GEORGE — Gone?

KAREN — Shot out.

GEORGE — I love that. We've got tape.

MARK — What about the welfare cuts?

KAREN Well, actually, the welfare cuts were bumped to second. We're going to do the horse with the hooker as the lead.

GEORGE Well, I think we've got two leads now. We've got the body in the pool; we've got the horse and the hooker and the developer.

MARK Okay, well, who's, who's for, uh, body in the pool?

Mark holds up his hand, as do George and Jim.

GEORGE/JIM I'm for body in the pool.

MARK Okay, uh, hooker and horse?

Bruce, David, and Karen raise their hands.

MARK Uh, body in the pool.

GEORGE Body in the pool.

MARK Okay.

GEORGE Next.

DAVID Uh, the Toronto Film Festival. The names in town this week I'm trying to line up for an interview. We got De Niro, Sandra Bullock, Pacino, Wynona Ryder, Hugh Grant and Elizabeth Hurley, and, uh, Rob Lowe.

MARK Do you really think you can get Hugh Grant and Elizabeth Hurley?

DAVID I know I can get Rob Lowe.

BRUCE You know, this is just an idea, but, uh, I really love this. I was thinking, every Friday during the summer I could do the weather remote from my boat on Lake Simcoe. Uh, you know, kind of a weekend weather report for cottage country. And we could have a celebrity fishing thing . . .

KAREN That's a tax write-off.

BRUCE (*ignoring Karen*) Oh, it's a beautiful boat. It's a Mark II with two hundred-horsepower Merc engines.

KAREN It's a tax write-off.

BRUCE Up yours!

KAREN (*laughing*) I don't believe it.

Mark and George are in George's office. They are on the speakerphone with George's accountant.

ACCOUNTANT Um, how will the car be used on the show?

MARK In a summer weather segment where Bruce the weatherman will do the weekend forecast on the road from George's car. A different vacation area of the province every week.

ACCOUNTANT Why not use a boat? Summer, cottages . . .

GEORGE 'Cause a boat's a fishing show, Alan. That's why. It's Charles Kuralt on the road, it's intelligent.

ACCOUNTANT But your weather man, from what I've seen, is an idiot.

MARK We know Bruce is an idiot, okay? He'll be just as big an idiot in a boat as he will be in a car.

GEORGE So let him be an idiot in my car and I'll get the deduction, okay? I just want to know, will this deduction work?

ACCOUNTANT Basically it works.

Bruce, Mark, and George are in the boardroom.

BRUCE The whole concept was the boat.

MARK It was a fishing show. You're better than that.

GEORGE Absolutely, you're better than that. Look, you could be a thinking journalist. You know, you remember Charles Kuralt? "On The Road," Charles Kuralt?

BRUCE Yeah, yeah. No, no, I used to watch him all the time. He did very smart shit.

MARK Exactly. And this is your chance to do shit just as smart.

GEORGE Absolutely. This is your chance to go beyond just being, you know, an asshole weatherman. You know what I mean?

Bruce gives George a look.

MARK He, he means that you have a basic understanding of the people of this province. That's what you mean by "asshole."

GEORGE Yeah, that's what I meant. Okay, look. Fifty-three per cent of this province love Mike Harris, right? This is your audience. They love you. These are people who have values that you relate to, right? Golfing, hunting, uh, fishing, family, hard work, church, . . .

MARK Alcohol.

GEORGE Alcohol.

BRUCE Yeah, yeah. Real shit.

MARK Real shit.

GEORGE You know, these guys get out there. They have a couple of drinks, they kill a couple of animals, they blow off some steam, the odd guy comes back and slaps his wife around . . .

BRUCE But they're my audience.

MARK People are sick of hearing about condoms and lesbians.

BRUCE Yeah, yeah. No, I, I, I think this is great. Uh, so who's car will we use?

MARK Well, that's a production detail.

BRUCE	Well, I could use my car.
GEORGE	Oh, I think there's an insurance problem with that. Personal. Uh, you know, anyway, I love this. This gives you an opportunity to, uh, blend the best of, of public broadcasting, which is, um . . .
MARK	Ideas.
GEORGE	Ideas, ideas. With the best of the private sector, which is . . .
MARK	Being a guy?
BRUCE	Being a guy. Being a guy with a motor.
GEORGE	Private sector.
BRUCE	Yeah.
GEORGE	Being a guy with a big motor.
BRUCE	Yeah.
GEORGE	Big motor.
BRUCE	Yeah.

George, Mark, and Karen are in the boardroom. George is eating popcorn. Mark is going through the Globe and Mail. *Karen is writing.*

GEORGE	See, I'm glad they left my name off that. You know, I have no interest in people knowing my salary.
MARK	Right. Frank Devreau makes a hundred and thirty thousand?
KAREN	You're kidding.
MARK	No.
GEORGE	See, this is the problem. People sit around and gossip about how much people make, right? It's just completely counter-productive.
MARK	Margaret Lund makes one forty.
KAREN	*(together with George)* In radio?
GEORGE	You see, this is it. I don't want people sitting around

saying, you know, George Findlay makes a hundred and fifty thousand dollars a year. And my tax dollars pay for that.

KAREN You make one fifty?

GEORGE You see, that's my point. It does nothing but make people jealous. Okay, I make a hundred and fifty thousand. Somebody makes a lousy sixty-seven thousand. They're gonna feel horrible when they see that in the paper.

MARK So, now my sixty-seven is lousy?

GEORGE It was an example, okay? Let's just drop that.

KAREN George is right. In the cafeteria this morning a bunch of them couldn't find your name in the paper. So right away they're gloating over the fact that you make under a hundred grand.

GEORGE And you said nothing?

MARK Well, well, I mean, you're not on the list here. And so, I mean, we assumed . . .

KAREN Well, we said that you must make at least eighty-five.

GEORGE I make under a hundred thousand dollars? I'm a news director. I make under a hundred?

KAREN I thought you didn't . . . care.

GEORGE I don't care whether my salary's published. But power in this place is based on image. When you make a hundred and thirty-seven thousand dollars a year and people think you make eighty-five, your credibility is underminded.

KAREN I thought you said one fifty?

GEORGE Oh, well, I just rounded it off. That's all.

KAREN Okay, but if you were going to round it off, wouldn't you round it down to one thirty-five?

MARK Yeah, or, if you were going to round it up, to one forty?

GEORGE — The point is, I don't care what people think about how much money I make, all right?

George and Bruce are walking down the corridor.

BRUCE — I, I, I just couldn't believe that you didn't make the list.

GEORGE — Lookit. I didn't *not* make the list, okay? Some guy left my name off the list, all right? And I don't care whether my name was left off the list, because I don't need my salary published.

BRUCE — I know, I know. It's just that everyone's going around here saying you make eighty-five and that you're not a member of the hundred-plus club.

GEORGE — *(moans)* Listen, you can take your hundred-plus club and shove it, all right? Between you and me, all right, I happen to make a hundred and thirty-seven thousand dollars a year.

BRUCE — That's only four grand more than me. You only make four grand more than me?

GEORGE — I get a lot of deductions, okay, you don't even know about. All right, okay?

BRUCE — What, what kind of deductions?

GEORGE — I don't care about this.

Audrey is at the window of the Payroll office. A Payroll person flips through files.

AUDREY — He earns a hundred and thirty-seven thousand dollars a year and he really, really wants it published in the *Globe* by Friday.

PAYROLL — He's not on the payroll.

AUDREY — Director of local news? They left his name off the hundred-thousand-a-year list.

PAYROLL This is generated from computer records. Straighten it out with them.

AUDREY But this is really, really important.

PAYROLL Why does he care so much about this anyways?

AUDREY Because . . . um, okay, the truth is that it's his mother's eightieth birthday on Friday. And he thinks it would be nice to get his salary published, and that way she can be proud of him, you know? I think it's a wonderful birthday gift.

George and Mark are in George's office.

GEORGE Goldman's blood on O.J.'s sock, in O.J.'s bedroom, what could be more clear? What could be more definitive? This is insane.

Graham walks in with Gillian.

GRAHAM Hi. Are we busy?

GEORGE Uh, no, we're just actually watching the news.

GRAHAM Lucien Bouchard just announced that he will decide before the weekend about the referendum next year. I want a unity panel Monday. And Gillian suggests that maybe we have some new faces.

GILLIAN Something fresh.

GEORGE Done, it's done. Okay?

GRAHAM Good, thank you.

GEORGE No problem.

GRAHAM *(walking out)* Let's do it.

MARK Well, uh, Brad was saying that Phil Vannatter, the detective, he could have planted the sock in O.J.'s bedroom.

GEORGE Vannatter couldn't have planted the sock. I mean, first of all he has no motive. He was on the force for twenty-five years. They don't do that sort of thing. He doesn't know Fuhrman. Plant it? Where did this come from? Planting the sock? It wasn't in the civil suit. It wasn't in the criminal suit.

The unity thing, okay? We'll do it. You can do it? Take care of it?

MARK Oh, yeah. It's not a problem.

GEORGE Okay, good.

Jim interviews author Linda McQuaig and Lise Léger, a smart, attractive PQ *deputy minister.*

LISE As a member of the PQ and a sovereigntist, I see no contradiction in a deficit-cutting policy for Quebec, especially when starting a new nation. It is like starting a new business. You need to show the bank that you can balance the books. I'm here in Toronto to let Mike Harris know that when we do business together, he's dealing with a fiscally responsible partner.

JIM Well, Linda McQuaig, I think you want the last word.

LINDA I can only imagine that René Lévesque just turned over in his grave.

JIM Okay, we only have a few seconds left, but I'd like to respond to Linda. I guess I have to take exception to that comment about René Lévesque, a Quebec premier who fought to keep Canada together and who died only recently after devoting his life to Quebec politics. I think to say that –

LINDA *(interrupting)* No, no. You're thinking of Bourassa. Bourassa who died recently and fought to keep this country together.

LISE Mr. Lévesque, who fought for separation, um, died in 1987.

JIM (*a pause while he realizes his error*) Yeah, of course. I misspoke. Of course I meant Mr. Bourassa. Um, but here's a man, I think, who's still very much alive in the hearts and minds of Quebeckers and Canadians everywhere. I think to say that Bourassa turned over in his grave does a disservice to his memory, don't you think?

LINDA I said Lévesque.

JIM I'm sorry?

LINDA Lévesque turned over in his grave.

JIM Huh, okay, that's an edit, that's an edit. (*stopping the interview*)

Linda, could you give me that lead-in line again about René Lévesque turning over in his grave, all right? And I'll take it from there.

LINDA Uh, I said that spontaneously. You're goin' to try and script that? That's ridiculous.

JIM Fine, fine. I can do it, I can do it. Ready? Well, in response to Lise Léger, I can only imagine René Lévesque turned over in his grave. That's all the time we have. Lise Léger from Quebec City, Linda McQuaig from Toronto, thank you for being with us.

Linda subtly winces.

Linda and Lise are in make-up chairs in the make-up room. Both have a glass of red wine.

LINDA God, what a moron that guy is.

LISE An incredible idiot. I find him very appealing.

LINDA Really?

LISE Yes. Sexually.

LINDA He's so creepy.

LISE Very creepy. A few weeks ago I saw the film *Belle de Jour*? Do you remember it?

LINDA I don't think I ever saw it, no.

LISE Catherine Deneuve, an upper-class woman with a very orderly life and a rich husband, who she loves, is frigid with him. She can only find sexual excitement in secret as a prostitute, where she has sex with strange men, some perverted, one a violent criminal of the lumpenproletariat. Men who are opposite to her attract her. I have this impulse from time to time. I work with very intelligent, honest men with strong characters and serious ideas. But I find I'm very hot about "la sexualité de surface," to sleep with a false and superficial man . . . a complete idiot.

Jim is walking with Lise down the office corridor.

JIM Dinner tomorrow night? Yeah, that sounds great.

LISE Great. I'm at the Plaza for a week. Call me in the afternoon?

JIM For sure. Yeah, all right.

Um, listen, that mistake I made in there about Lévesque and Bourassa, I had this ridiculous dumb lapse. It was very embarrassing, you know. It happens all the time to newspeople. You know, sometimes you deal with lots of stories and names and people, I just sort of . . .

LISE It was a lapse?

JIM Yeah, you know, I feel really embarrassed about it. I just get mixed up with names, you know? Lévesque was against separation, right?

LISE Wrong. *(laughs)*

JIM Oh! *For*, *for*, right.

LISE — Great, I'll see you tomorrow night. *(she kisses his cheek)*

JIM — Right, okay. Ooh la la!

Audrey is talking with a computer person in the Computer Records Department.

COMPUTER PERSON — One thirty-seven.

AUDREY — Right. Do you think you can get this done by Friday?

COMPUTER PERSON — Well, I can straighten out the record, but the *Globe* stuff must have gone through Public Relations.

Why does he care about this so much?

AUDREY — Well, this is the truth. His mother *(she clears her throat)* is very sick. And she's eighty . . . four years old. And, you know, she, she worries about what's gonna happen to him after she dies. So he just thinks that it'll give her some sense of security to read that he makes a hundred and thirty-seven thousand, you know, right there in the *Globe and Mail.*

COMPUTER PERSON — I don't know.

Jim is on the air. George, Mark, and Graham watch on a monitor in George's office.

JIM — Welcome back. We're now going to go live to the command centre of the Toronto International Film Festival, where David Ross is standing by. David?

David is with Jay Sherrick in the lobby of a hotel.

DAVID Jim, the festival is as star-studded as always, but the deal-makers are also here. With me is Jay Sherrick, one of the Disney executives from L.A. who helped secure all the marketing rights to the Royal Canadian Mounted Police for the Disney company.

Is there a Mountie movie or Mountie TV show in the works? Can we expect to see a Mounted Mickey Mouse, Jay?

JAY Well, we're still lookin' for the right vehicle for the Mounties. We figure this is the perfect police force for Disney. We love the fact that the Mountie always gets his man. We love Canadians, and, frankly, we think that this whole Mountie thing will be great for Canada.

JIM Mind if I jump in here, Jay?

JAY Sure.

JIM You know, unity is a big issue here in Canada with the threat that Quebec could separate with the next referendum. I was just curious, what do Americans think about this whole thing?

JAY Personally, I feel that Quebec belongs in Canada as a unique place, just the way that Disney World belongs in Florida.

JIM Well, I'd like to think so. Quebec as another Magic Kingdom, a place the whole family can enjoy, as it were.

JAY Well, why not, Jim? I see it as a magical place. I mean, I love the culture of the place. I love the whole look. It's so Euro. It's so Old World. I mean, where do you get that – outside of Disney World – where do you get that in North America? You know, I don't know a lot about these political things, but I would just like to say, I would take the Disney model and I would pay to get into Quebec.

JIM — At the border?

JAY — Who knows where provinces are gonna be in the future, Jim. But I'll tell you one thing. I think I could sell Quebec. I love the accent, I love the whole fur-trading thing.

JIM — Well, that's a very interesting proposition. So people could pay to access different areas of the province, uh . . .

JAY — Well, you know, Jim, one thing we've learned at Disney is that Americans feel more comfortable in places that they've payed to get into.

JIM — Interesting. You know, I loved *Hunchback*. I just rented it. Terrific movie. Great animation. Nobody does it better than you people at Disney, Jay.

JAY — Well, thank you very much for saying so. And I'll tell you, no one runs a country better than you people in Canada. We love you.

JIM — Thanks for being with us, Jay.

JAY — Thanks, Jim.

JIM — *(to camera)* Quebec. How do we keep Canada together?

A final thought. A thought from a Disney classic, perhaps. Maybe it would all work if we just wished upon a star. That's the news. I'm Jim Walcott. Goodnight.

George looks at Graham and Mark.

GRAHAM — Quebec as Disney World?

MARK — I mean, obviously Jim picked up on what the guy from Disney was saying.

GRAHAM — And the country will just stay together if we just . . . wish upon a star!

GEORGE — Jim's an idiot. But he gets good numbers.

GRAHAM — Who the hell does he think he is? Jimminy goddamn Cricket!?

MARK — Well, we had the footage of the Toronto businessman, his body in the pool.

GRAHAM — Yeah, that was good. That and the horse and the hooker. That's good. That's news.

GEORGE — It was a good strong segment. The whole thing, the whole opening.

GRAHAM — *(standing)* Yep, which clearly goes to prove the old news adage. With a body in the pool and a horse and a hooker, you can fuck Canadian unity!

MARK — Well said.

GEORGE — And well said by her.

MARK — Yeah.

GEORGE — Thank God we didn't say that.

Audrey sits in the Public Relations office with a PR *woman.*

PR — I can't just phone up the *Globe* and have them publish a salary. There's a process for this.

AUDREY — Okay, here's, uh, the thing. His mother is dying and she thinks he can't afford the nursing care. He tells her, I make a hundred and thirty-seven thousand dollars, but she doesn't believe him. She says that's impossible. How could you make that much money, you know. He wants her to read it in the paper, because she's going senile and and she's at that stage where she'll believe anything that she reads in the *Globe and Mail.*

Jim is walking down the hallway of the hotel. He knocks on Lise Léger's hotel room.

LISE Oh, bonjour.
JIM Bonjour.

Jim leans over to kiss her in the doorway and she pushes him away.

LISE Ça va?
JIM Oui?
LISE Je dois m'expliquer. Est-ce que tu parles français?
JIM No, uh, oui, oui, oui, oui. Un peux, oui.
LISE Oui? Okay. Uh, ce que je veux te dire c'est que les . . . j'ai développé un concept qui s'appelle l'érotisme fausse . . . Ce que je veux te dire en bref, c'est que, uh, j'ai trouvé quelqu'un encore plus superficiel que toi . . . um, je m'excuse.
JIM Huh.
LISE Je suis vraiment desolé mais . . .

Jay Sherrick walks up.

LISE *(to Jay)* I'm sorry, I'm running . . .
JAY That's all right.
JIM Jay Sherrick, right?
JAY Yep, that's right.
JIM Jim Walcott. *(they shake hands)*
LISE You guys know each other?
JAY Do I know you, Jim?
JIM Oh, I'm sorry. It was a one-way feed, so I could see you, but you couldn't see me. I did the interview with you.

JAY Oh, sure. I remember. You were great. That was . . . you're the anchor.

JIM Yeah.

JAY Aw, you were great! Good questions, good questions. It was a real pleasure talking to you. You're good at what you do.

JIM Oh, yeah, thanks very much.

LISE *(to Jay, looking at her watch)* I don't have much time.

JIM I actually wanted to ask you in the interview about this whole Eisner, Ovitz lead-in? What was that all about?

JAY Michael Ovitz was a visionary, and we're sorry to lose him. But we feel that he left many of his best ideas with us. And we wish him the very best in the future.

JIM Yeah. So what's it like working with Michael Eisner now?

JAY Aw, Michael Eisner is Disney, you know. He's a very dear friend of mine. And he's a friend of America's, really, and therefore the world.

JIM Yeah, yeah. Listen, I have this idea for a script, kind of like a *Broadcast News* thing. But an insider's perspective. Do you know what I mean? Like my perspective?

JAY Hey, listen. You get any ideas, you call me. We have a saying at Disney: Some of the best ideas are the derivative ones. I mean, that's between us, but what I'm saying is, you call me.

JIM Oh, great. Okay.

JAY Yeah, call me.

JIM I'll give you a shout.

JAY Always good to hear from Canadians. I love Canadians. What a talented race.

JIM Thanks very much.

LISE *(Lise, speaking to Jay in French, is trying to get him inside the room)*

JAY Yeah. Uh, take care, huh? *(he starts going in)*

JIM You speak French?

JAY Well, when I have to. *(he closes the door on Jim)*

JIM *(to himself) Broadcast News*, hey. *(he snaps his fingers and walks away)*

George and Audrey are in George's office. George looks at the Globe.

GEORGE George Findlay, annual salary: four hundred and eleven thousand dollars. How did that happen?

AUDREY I figure that basically what happened was that four-eleven is a hundred and thirty-seven thousand times three, exactly. I went to three departments. They probably each did their own thing, and that added up to four eleven.

GEORGE Oh, Jesus.

MARK *(poking his head in)* Your accountant's on three.

GEORGE *(hitting the speaker button on his phone)* Alan, did you see the *Globe and Mail?*

ACCOUNTANT Yes, George. And so did the tax people. We've got an audit and a problem with our 1993 car deduction. But I think basically we'll be fine.

THE END

EPISODE 9

"Parking"

First Aired: February 24, 1997

Graham and George are walking out of the elevator and down the atrium corridor.

GRAHAM	So, we're going to Florida to catch the Jays' spring training. Flight's at six-thirty. We want to leave from here. He's bored hanging around the apartment, so I told him he could come down and hang around here for a couple of hours. Maybe watch you package the show. That okay?
GEORGE	Hang around? Is he in the business?
GRAHAM	News? No, uh, he's a comic. Stand-up.
GEORGE	Comic. Did you see this? *(he shows her piece of paper)*
GRAHAM	Oh, yes, I heard. Congratulations.
GEORGE	Yeah, twelve years in this place and they finally acknowledge me.
GRAHAM	What level?
GEORGE	P3. Spot 66, right next to handicapped parking.
GRAHAM	That's my old spot. How'd you finally pull it off?
GEORGE	Oh, I told them that I, um, had a foot problem and I couldn't walk from the outdoor lot. My application was in the system for two years. I finally nailed it.
GRAHAM	Oh, ya. The old so-called-foot-problem-to-get-pain-killers routine.

George and Graham stop outside the studio door.

GEORGE — I had real pain.

GRAHAM — Don't we all. *(she continues to walk down the corridor)*

GEORGE — Wait a second. Why did you give up that spot?

GRAHAM — There was something leaking from the ceiling down onto the hood of my car.

GEORGE — Something leaking?

GRAHAM — Yeah, some kind of white gooey, abrasive guck. You try to wipe it off, it would just take the paint right with it.

GEORGE — It took the paint off?

GRAHAM — Yeah, I'd get that checked if I were you. It just ruined my car.

GEORGE — Oh, shit.

Mark and Bruce are in the coffee area. Mark is watching his food in the microwave. Bruce is waving a piece of paper at him.

BRUCE — You know what this is?

MARK — No.

BRUCE — My bear-hunting licence. This little piece of paper gives me the right to shoot one fully grown black bear. It's such a rush, I can't wait!

MARK — Sounds like fun.

BRUCE — Yeah.

MARK — So you shoot the male, then you rape the female?

BRUCE — Oh, okay, okay. I get it. Oh, hunting is evil, right? Yeah, yeah, yeah. Oh, the big bad hunter with the high-powered rifle against the poor defenceless creature of nature.

MARK — So, you gonna eat the bear? *(The microwave stops. He takes his food out and starts to walk. Bruce follows.)*

BRUCE Look, let me tell you something. If we don't shoot 'em, they overproduce. And, and you could pretty much kiss the balance of nature up there goodbye.

MARK Oh, so you're doing God's work.

BRUCE You got that right, asshole.

George is on the phone in his office.

GEORGE Well, that's the reason she gave up the spot, because the shit was dropping onto her car. *(Graham's boyfriend appears at the door)* . . . Yep. Well, well, fix the ceiling. You're the parking guy. Fix it . . . Well then, yes, then get me Mechanical . . . Yes, I'll hold. Thank you. *(he looks up at Graham's boyfriend)*

The boyfriend, in his early sixties, is dressed for Florida in light-coloured pants, shirt, pale alpaca sweater. He is bald on top with hair at the sides and back. He carries a coat and a suitcase and smokes whenever he can.

BOYFRIEND *(placing his bag in the corner)* I'll just put this down here out of your way.

GEORGE Uh, it's only *(he looks at his watch)* ten-thirty. Uh, she said your flight wasn't leaving until six-thirty. Aren't you here a little early?

BOYFRIEND Oh, yeah. But I can't stay at her place. It drives me crazy. She's got cats. *(he sits on the couch)* I've got friggin' cat hair all over my alpaca sweater. Just ignore me. *(he takes a cigarette pack out of his shirt pocket)* We'll be out of here by five, tops. Mind if I smoke? *(he lights up, not waiting for an answer)*

GEORGE Uh, there's a building regulation against it.

BOYFRIEND Don't worry about it. I'll just get the door. *(he gets up and shuts the door.)* Do you want one?

GEORGE No.

BOYFRIEND *(picking up a newspaper off the TV set on his way back to the couch)* Bosnia, Bosnia. There's one town I'm not in a big rush to see. You know who won the Miss Bosnia beauty pageant?

GEORGE No.

BOYFRIEND Nobody. Are you finished drinking that?

GEORGE Yeah.

BOYFRIEND Good. Thanks. *(he flicks his cigarette ash in George's coffee mug)*

Audrey and George are in the boardroom, using the phone. They listen to George's voice mail on the speaker.

AUDREY This was on your voice mail.

VOICE ... there's been talk among upper management about the way you've handled a number of stories recently on this government, and I think we should ...

GEORGE That's it? That's all?

AUDREY Yeah, that's all. The voice mail's still screwed up. *(George moans)*

Who was it?

GEORGE I have no idea who that voice was. When are they gonna fix this goddamn thing?

AUDREY Today, supposedly. What stories is he talking about?

GEORGE Oh, I have no idea. Listen, ignore this, right? Okay? This is bullshit. If you let these guys bug you with every one of their little complaints, you can never do this job. Just ignore it. Don't think about it. *(he leaves)*

George, Mark, Karen, and Graham's boyfriend are in George's office. The boyfriend sits on the couch, clipping his nails with a noisy nail clipper. The nails fly.

GEORGE — *(punching numbers on his phone)* Here's the voice message I want you to hear. Listen to this.

VOICE — . . . there's been talk among upper management about the way you've handled a number of stories recently on this government, and I think we should . . .

GEORGE — That's all there was.

MARK — What stories is he talking about?

GEORGE — I don't know what stories he's talking about. The voice mail's completely screwed up.

BOYFRIEND — Voice mail. Always something new. *(he clips a nail)*

Karen checks her shoulder for the nail clipping.

MARK — Well, whenever the brass needs its dirty work done, Paul Thomas is the guy with the bad news.

GEORGE — How do you know it's bad news?

BOYFRIEND — When's the last time they called you with good news?

MARK — He's right.

KAREN — He's right.

BOYFRIEND — Good news, bad news.

A quick one: Guy walks into the doctor's office. He says, I've got some good news for you and I've got some bad news for you. Bad news is you've only got one month to live. Good news, did you see that gorgeous receptionist on the way in? I'm banging her twice a week. *(he clips a nail and George flicks it off his shoulder)*

KAREN	They can't face you, so they send voice mail.
MARK	There goes our great tradition of journalistic independence.
KAREN	These gutless messages. It's fucking censorship.
MARK	You know what you do? You call 'em up and you say, Listen, if you don't like the way I'm running the news, you can fire me.
KAREN	Counter-attack and the whole thing will go away.
BOYFRIEND	Best defence is a good offence.
KAREN	He's right.
MARK	He's right.
GEORGE	*(dialling)* Voice mail.

Mark and Karen exchange looks.

GEORGE *(into the phone)* Paul, this is George Findlay returning your call. *(boyfriend smokes)* If someone from upstairs thinks that they can just call up and influence how I do this news, they're playing a very dangerous game. Uh, journalistic independence is an absolutely basic principle of news producing.

Mark and Karen nod.

GEORGE If they can't deal with their own petty little fears, then they can just take those fears and, uh, um . . .

Karen signals "shove 'em."

GEORGE . . . you know, shove 'em up their tight little asses, Paul. And if they have a problem with that, I can just quit, okay? Goodbye. *(hangs up)*

So?

KAREN — I wouldn't have said, "I can quit." But other than that I think it was great.

GEORGE — You said I should threaten to quit.

MARK — No, we said tell them they can fire you.

KAREN — There's a difference. See, they need cause to fire you.

MARK — She's right. I mean, the ball's in their court now. You offered to quit.

GEORGE — So I said I'd quit to this gutless guy Paul Thomas. You said yourselves he's the messenger boy. He has no power.

KAREN — But you left it on his voice mail. Mistake. It's like paper. You never commit this stuff to paper. Never leave voice mail. Rule one.

BOYFRIEND — Never quit. You do the gig, but take the dough.

George and Audrey are at Audrey's workstation.

GEORGE — Can you break into his voice mail and erase my message?

AUDREY — Everyone has a six-number code that accesses their mailbox. Most people pick six fives or six sixs or six sevens, so technically I could dial his extension and run through all nine digits six times each, but I won't. On principle.

GEORGE — Well, there happens to be a higher principle operating here. It's a principle of nature called self-preservation.

AUDREY — Yours or mine?

GEORGE — Yours.

AUDREY — What's the message?

Audrey and George walk into the newsroom and head towards George's office.

AUDREY I got into Paul Thomas's mailbox.

GEORGE Did you erase my message?

AUDREY Your message was gone.

GEORGE Gone? What do you mean, gone?

AUDREY I guess he listened to it and erased it.

GEORGE Oh, God. Could he have dumped it onto somebody else's mailbox before he erased it?

AUDREY Yep.

GEORGE Oh, then it could be out there in the system. It could be in the system.

AUDREY I heard something else on his voice mail.

They enter George's office and see Graham's boyfriend is on couch, talking on the phone.

BOYFRIEND . . . Yeah, and he's got that whole bowel problem.

GEORGE God, he's still here. Ignore him, ignore him. What did you hear?

AUDREY His last message. I took the liberty of putting it on your private-line mailbox. This is totally illegal.

GEORGE Don't worry about it. We're all adults here. This was brilliant. You're perfect. This is fantastic. *(he picks up the phone at his desk and dials)*

BOYFRIEND Uh-huh. Arnie Gordon. It's the prostate thing . . . Yeah, a least he's not as bad off as his brother. They've got to put plastic *everywhere* . . . Yeah, bye. *(hangs up)*

It's my buddy. He's in the hospital. It's a bowel thing. You don't want to know about it.

GEORGE *(hangs up)* That was the message? That was a guy by the name of Bob, thanking Paul Thomas for sending him the message that I sent to Paul Thomas.

KAREN I know.

GEORGE — Who's Bob?

George and Karen are in the boardroom. Karen flips through the corporate structure handbook.

KAREN — I don't know. It could be Vice-President, Business Affairs and Corporate Development, Bob Coleman. Vice-President and Regulatory Affairs, Bob Stoltz. Vice-President, Media Accountability and Regional Broadcasting Operations, Robert Johnstone . . . Robert, Bob. Executive Assistant to the Vice-President of News and Current Affairs, Bob Hubert.

GEORGE — How many Bobs are there for Christ's sake?

KAREN — I found eleven Bobs with enough power to have you fired.

George and Mark at the pop machine in the office corridor. George opens a can.

MARK — Of the eleven Bobs with potentially enough power to fire you, there's only five who would ever exercise that power: Bob Coleman, Bob Hubert, Bob Johnstone, Bob Gaffeny, Bob Seymour.

GEORGE — Oh, God.

George is sitting at a table beside the coffee area in the newsroom. Graham walks up and sits next to him.

GRAHAM — What are you doing here?

GEORGE — I'm here because he's in there, okay?

GRAHAM — Oh.

GEORGE — Sitting in there. You said he was going to come after lunch.

GRAHAM That's typical of Vince. He, he can't just sit in a room. He's a presence.

GEORGE Well, I have no idea what you see in this man.

GRAHAM He makes me laugh.

Oh, I spoke to, uh, Paul Thomas. He claims he never sent you any voice mail.

GEORGE It wasn't Paul Thomas?

GRAHAM No, but he wasn't terribly happy about the message you left him.

GEORGE That was a mistake! Didn't you tell him that was a mistake?

GRAHAM Well, he thought it was. So he passed it on to the person who actually phoned you.

GEORGE Yes, Bob. But Bob who? That's the name I need.

GRAHAM Well, he wouldn't say. Very political up there.

GEORGE You're my boss. Why don't they come to you if they have a problem with me?

GRAHAM Well, when they're out to kill someone, you know, in these downsizing slaughters, they, they're like lions in a herd of wildebeest. They go straight for their prey. They ignore everything else.

GEORGE I'm not a wildebeest, okay? I'm the news director of the show. You got to protect me on this.

GRAHAM Well, I'm afraid I'm gonna have to hide out in the long grasses over this one. I want that, uh, condo in St. Barts, and I, I need a few more well-paying years to get it.

(looks at her watch) Got a meeting, gotta go.

GEORGE One second, one second. Someone's out to kill me. How do I find out who it is?

GRAHAM Maybe your parking spot's a clue.

GEORGE Parking?

GRAHAM Well, why did they give you that leaky spot?

George sits with a Parking woman in her office. She is Chinese and is eating noodles with chopsticks. Karen sits beside George, waiting this out.

WOMAN I finally got through to Parking for you.

GEORGE I'm sorry. I thought *you* were Parking?

WOMAN No, I'm a building services co-ordinating secretary. But I had them move you out of the leaky spot.

GEORGE Great, great. No, I appreciate this. You know, I've, uh, this is not racial or anything, but, you know, um, you know I've worked with Japanese people before, and you want to get something done . . .

WOMAN I'm Chinese.

GEORGE Anyway, um, it's great. You're a genius. I appreciate it.

Where'd they put me.

WOMAN Nowhere, yet.

GEORGE Nowhere?

WOMAN They're reviewing your application before they assign a new spot.

GEORGE Wait a second. You took me out of one spot and you didn't have another spot for me?

WOMAN You gave them a doctor's letter about your foot, right?

GEORGE Yes, yes. What's that got to do with this?

WOMAN There seems to be some confusion over that doctor and your family doctor that's listed in your personnel file.

GEORGE What are you talking about?

WOMAN They called your family doctor to confirm the letter.

GEORGE Those are two different doctors. I didn't get my family doctor to write the letter. I got another doctor to write the letter.

WOMAN Right. After a while they realized that they should have called the other doctor. Something came up and it turns out you're seeing both doctors about the same foot problem and getting painkillers from both of them? Apparently now the two doctors are into it.

GEORGE The doctors are into my parking spot?

WOMAN Your painkillers.

GEORGE How can you sit there and be so cool about this? This is a disaster, okay? And you can just sit there and be that cool, right? Is this some kind of Zen thing that you . . .

WOMAN I think I have to go.

GEORGE No, no, this is . . . this is some kind of Zen thing.

The Parking woman just looks at him.

George and Karen are at Karen's workstation.

GEORGE The whole Zen thing, I just don't buy it. No one has a clue what any of them are thinking. And they've been getting away with it for far too long.

KAREN Well, you're allowed your opinion.

GEORGE Oh, now you're doing it.

KAREN Doing what?

GEORGE You're patronizing me. This is the Western equivalent of Zen. I know what you're doing. But I also know what you're thinking. That's the difference.

KAREN I'm, I'm not actually thinking anything.

GEORGE Yeah, you're thinking, Patronize him, because he's going be fired anyway.

KAREN If anything I was thinking more that you're getting just a little, um, *(whispers)* paranoid.

GEORGE — Yeah, well, you don't know how this corporation works. It's all about parking.

KAREN — Okay, I should, um . . . I've gotta go.

George and Graham's boyfriend are in George's office.

BOYFRIEND — So, the guy goes to the psychiatrist. He says, Doc, my brother thinks he's a chicken. Psychiatrist says, Why don't you take him to therapy. He says, I would, but we need the eggs.
(lights up) Want a cigarette?

GEORGE — No thanks.

Mark and George are walking down the office corridor towards the newsroom studio.

MARK — When they want to push you out of here, it's never bad performance. It's always downsizing. Failure to perform would set a terrible precedent that would threaten 90 per cent of the jobs up top, and they want you out. It always starts with the little signs. And no one can tell you why it's happening . . .

GEORGE — That's right.

MARK — . . . and it definitely . . . no one will take any direct responsibility.

GEORGE — You're telling me.

MARK — Now, a guy I know in Arts Programming? Last week they took away his VCR, right? He couldn't find out why or who gave the order. Just some guy shows up with a piece of paper. It's gone. Right?

GEORGE — Right.

MARK — Then, last Monday, they take away his parking spot.

GEORGE — Yeah?

MARK	Wednesday, they don't invite him to the department meeting? Yesterday, he's gone.
GEORGE	Really?
MARK	Yeah.
GEORGE	God. You know Zen? I've been thinking about this. Very internal, right? They hold it in, they hold it in, they hold it in. Then, boom. Pearl Harbor.

George, with Mark, opens his office door to see Graham's boyfriend on the phone, sitting on a chair where the couch used to be. He's smoking.

BOYFRIEND	They turned something over in a month and they made, like, two hundred thousand dollars. (*he looks up at George and Mark*) They took our couch. I just brought a chair in here.
MARK	Oh, who took your couch?
GEORGE	I don't know.

George and Gillian are walking down the hallway in the executive area.

GEORGE	I just want to know what's going on, okay?
GILLIAN	What's going on? What does that mean?
GEORGE	With me and the show.
GILLIAN	Nothing that I know of.
GEORGE	Nothing that you know of? What does that mean? You're the regional head.
GILLIAN	*(stopping at the secretary's desk)* I'm sorry. I don't get this.
GEORGE	Someone took my couch away.
GILLIAN	I don't handle furniture.
SECRETARY	Gillian, Shelley's on three. She wants to know if the Mercer Street Grill's okay for lunch.
GILLIAN	Yes, but tell her to hold. I have to confirm aerobics. *(to George)* Can I go?

Jim and Bruce stand at the rail in the atrium corridor. Jim is examining Bruce's bear-hunting licence.

BRUCE So, the testicles on that bear, shipped over to China, I figure will fetch me five grand U.S.

JIM Really?

BRUCE Yeah.

JIM That's amazing.

BRUCE Yeah.

JIM *(handing back the licence)* What can they do with them?

BRUCE I don't know. Freeze them and make nutsicles.

Bruce and Jim laugh as George passes. George thinks they're laughing about him.

GEORGE What's so funny?

BRUCE Nothing.

JIM Nothing.

GEORGE Is this about my couch?

BRUCE No.

GEORGE Is this something I should know?

BRUCE No.

JIM No. What?

GEORGE Nothing, nothing. Okay, forget it. Nothing, nothing, nothing.

George leaves, and Bruce and Jim go back to their conversation.

JIM Yeah, so I hear the whale penis is really big in Asia, too.

BRUCE I've heard that. The dicksicle?

Gillian, Audrey, and Karen are having lunch at a table in the atrium corridor. They are laughing. George, hearing them laugh, walks up to the table.

GEORGE What's so funny?

GILLIAN *(together with Audrey)* Nothing.

GEORGE Is this little laugh about my parking spot?

Gillian leans closer to Karen and continues to talk in hushed tones.

AUDREY *(to George)* No, why?

GEORGE No, I was just . . .

AUDREY *(turning back to Gillian)* So, then what did he say?

GILLIAN So, Bob, if you don't like my work, fire me. And he did.

They laugh, then look up at George.

GEORGE Nothing, okay? Nothing.

George leaves and the girls start to laugh again. He turns to look at them and they stop.

Mark is walking with John Haslett Cuff along the dressing-room corridor.

MARK Everyone freaked out when they called you to do the segment on the new TV season. You know, John Haslett-Cuff has made a career of trashing the corporation.

JOHN Well, I think they take it all a little too seriously.

MARK I think you're gonna find there's a new wave of

optimism here after these cuts. The dust has settled, and the people who made the cut are more confident, they're less paranoid. I mean, the sniping has stopped.

George, Mark, and Karen are in George's office.

GEORGE — Assholes up there. They're completely gutless. They fire you with parking, with couches, with voice mail, and no one has the guts to face you.

MARK — Absolutely.

GEORGE — Well, screw 'em. I can bury the entire board of directors with all I know.

MARK — Oh, John Haslett Cuff would love this. He'd run it in the *Globe and Mail* in a second.

George is with John Haslett Cuff in the make-up room. John is getting touched up by a make-up artist. George sits in a make-up chair.

GEORGE — I'm not just kissing ass here, John, because you're a critic, but I think you're great. No, you've written brilliantly about this place. But the thing you've missed, because you don't work here, is the epidemic level of, of, of ass-kissing and back-stabbing and small-minded politicking that leads to that third-rate chicken-shit programming. I have to be honest. I don't think anyone on the inside has ever been really honest about this.

John turns and looks at George.

George and Audrey are in George's office.

AUDREY They have a new policy where they clean all executive couches annually. So they took yours, cleaned it, and it's on its way back.

GEORGE They only took my couch to clean it?

AUDREY Yeah, I saw it in the hallway. It looks a lot better. And as far as the voice messages go, you know the mysterious Bob guy? He copied you and sent his own message. And it turns out that the stories about the government were on our series "Deficit Cutting: Who Wins, Who Loses." And the reason they were discussing it up top is because they thought it was the best series on the provincial government's policies since they came to power.

GEORGE That was the voice mail. That was the whole thing.

AUDREY Yeah.

GEORGE Oh, no.

AUDREY They figured that the voice mail you left in response telling them to shove it up their tight little asses was a joke, but not very funny.

GEORGE Oh, my God. John Haslett Cuff. Where is he?

AUDREY I think they finished. I saw him going towards the elevators.

GEORGE *(getting up from his chair)* Oh, God.

George hurries down the corridor, passing Graham and her boyfriend. She has her coat, her boyfriend has his luggage and coat.

GRAHAM We're off.

GEORGE Have a good time.

GRAHAM Oh, wait a minute.

GEORGE I gotta go.

GRAHAM It'll just take a second, it'll just take a sec. Never reveal your anxieties like that to Gillian again.

GEORGE I didn't reveal anything.

GRAHAM Your job, your couch . . . Now that little girl can smell blood. It just puts ideas in her head. I don't trust her.

GEORGE You don't trust her? You chose her.

GRAHAM Well, I also chose my first husband. He screwed everyone in sight. Now, just, just be more careful what you say and do while I'm gone.

BOYFRIEND Real nice to meet ya.

GEORGE Yeah, it was great.

They shake hands and part, and George continues to the elevators. The elevator doors open and John Haslett Cuff gets inside. Just as the doors are closing, George sticks his hand in.

GEORGE John, I'm glad I caught you. Just one last thing, okay? Just one last thing, please, please? Just one last thing. *(he lures John out of the elevator)*

Um, this whole story about the corporation? I'm not sure this is the best time for this kind of story.

JOHN Why?

GEORGE John, this place has been decimated by budget cuts, okay? These people have families to feed.

JOHN Look, I'm not trying to destroy anybody's life.

GEORGE Okay, look. I had this root canal. The dentist really screwed it up, okay? And I've been taking like four, five, six Percodans a day. I can't tell the difference between fact and fiction. I just don't think it's a good idea to write this story now, okay? I'm begging you just not to write the story.

JOHN Look, I gotta go to the . . . I gotta go back to the office. *(the elevator doors open, and John steps inside)*

GEORGE Shit. *(he sticks his hands between the closing doors)*

GEORGE — John, John, write your column. Because you're a critic, and critics kill everything. But not like animals who eat what they kill. You just let it lie there and rot and move on to your next self-serving column. Because you can't do it. But destroy everything around you that has any life, okay? Write it. You're a hack, John! Write your column. It's water off my back! Water off my back. I don't give a shit. *(the doors close)*

It is night, and George, Mark, and Karen leave the building and walk towards the Globe and Mail *box at the curb.*

MARK — I don't know why you attacked him so viciously. What was there to be gained?

GEORGE — It was a mistake. I was out of control, okay?

KAREN — Well, at least you didn't leave it on his voice mail.

GEORGE — Yeah. Anyway, are you sure the drop has been at this box?

MARK — Yep, yep. That's tomorrow's, that's tomorrow's *Globe.*

GEORGE — Good, good, good. Okay, okay, okay. *(he goes to the box, puts money in the slot, and takes out a paper)*

KAREN — I can't believe you actually called him a self-loathing hack.

GEORGE — Look, I'd taken some painkillers. I was in a very strange hallucinogenic state.

MARK — I thought the doctors cut you off when they found out you were doubling up on prescriptions.

GEORGE — Listen, that was taken care of, all right?

Okay, Haslett Cuff column inside. *(he nervously rips through the paper)* Here he is, here it is. Haslett Cuff, John Haslett Cuff. Here we go, okay. What's he saying here. American prime-time garbage . . . da-da-da. British brilliance . . . da-da-da. His old drinking problem, the sixties . . . Didn't mention me, didn't mention me!

KAREN You're kidding.

GEORGE Done, done.

MARK That's great.

George, Mark, and Karen are in George's office, still with their coats on.

KAREN I don't think you should phone a critic.

MARK Even, even if you're going to thank him. It's not a good idea.

KAREN Yeah.

GEORGE *(dialling)* Just trust me on this. John Haslett Cuff doesn't like a compliment, there's something wrong with the world, okay?

KAREN Yeah, but, you maybe shouldn't *phone* him with a compliment.

MARK Don't. I don't think it's a good idea.

KAREN Just wait until you see him again.

GEORGE Voice mail.

MARK *(together with Karen)* Hang up, hang up.

GEORGE John, uh, this is George Findlay, and I wanted to say, *(he consults a notepad)* you know, my explosion today was really, uh, was really uncalled for. I, I, as I said, uh, I'd taken some Percodans for a root canal *(Mark and Karen look at each other)* and I've really been one of your biggest fans for years. You are really quite brilliant and, uh, courageous, uh, you know, with a style that's a lot like Gore Vidal and, um, and Truman Capote. You know, all of you put your personal life into your observations, and I think that, um, I think that takes courage and, um, that's it. Give my best to your family and, um, we'll meet again. Bye-bye. *(he hangs up)*

I think that was good. I think that was fine.

KAREN Well, the Truman Capote thing might have been a bit over the top.

MARK It sounded like maybe you were sucking up to him.

KAREN Yeah.

GEORGE It's true.

KAREN Yeah, but you left it on his voice mail. See, he can play it over and over again, and when he does, it's gonna sound like you're kissing ass.

MARK Plus, you said, uh, "courage" twice.

KAREN Yeah.

MARK That's redundant.

GEORGE *(flipping through his notes)* Wrong, wrong, wrong. I did not say "courage" twice.

MARK I'm pretty sure you did.

GEORGE I said "courageous" and "courage."

KAREN Well, same thing.

MARK He will hear that.

KAREN He's a writer.

MARK You should have found another word.

KAREN It's the same thing.

GEORGE What, are we splitting hairs here? I mean, this is ridiculous. I gave the guy a compliment. The guy's gonna love a compliment.

MARK You read the guy a compliment.

KAREN It sounded like you were . . . like you were reading it. And then you said, you said, um, *(she grabs the notepad and reads from it)* I have taken some Percodans for a root canal and I've been one of your biggest fans for years. You ran those two together. They're two separate thoughts.

MARK Well, how 'bout this. *(he looks at George's notes)* You gave your best to his family. We don't know if he's got a wife or kids, I mean . . .

KAREN He might have no family.

GEORGE He's got parents, he's got cousins, everyone has a family, okay?

MARK So you just gave your best to his cousins and you don't think you were kissing his ass.

KAREN You should have hung up.

MARK You should have hung up.

THE END

EPISODE 10

"Meltdown," Part 1

First Aired: March 10, 1997

Karen comes out of the elevator with David Cronenberg and they walk down the atrium corridor.

KAREN Mr. Cronenberg, usually a spot like this would be covered by our entertainment editor, but when Jim Walcott heard that you were gonna be on the show to talk about *Crash*, he insisted on doing the interview.

DAVID Well, that's great. Terrific.

KAREN He's a big special-effects freak.

DAVID Oh, special effects?

KAREN Yeah, yeah. He, uh . . .

DAVID Listen, I hope he's not going to talk about effects and stuff and my film *Scanners*, you know, all that stuff.

KAREN Right, right. No, you're here to talk about *Crash*.

DAVID *Crash* is on this whole other plateau. You know, it's a different thing.

KAREN Right. Well, *Crash* won the Special Jury prize at Cannes, right? For, um, audacity and daring and, uh, originality.

DAVID Yeah. Very good.

KAREN I got that off the billboard.

DAVID I sensed that, yeah.

KAREN My ex-boyfriend is a huge fan of yours.

DAVID Ex-boyfriend?

KAREN Yeah, well, not that that had anything to do with us splitting up. Anyway, he basically force-fed me your films during –

DAVID Force-fed? *(they stop walking)*

KAREN Well, I mean, initially I was force-fed, but eventually, I mean, well, your artistry is just . . . and we had other problems.

I have to go to the bathroom, so, um, the studio is just, uh, down there to your right. And, um . . .

DAVID Listen, have you seen *Crash*?

KAREN *Crash*?

DAVID Yeah, you know, the movie that I'm here . . .

KAREN Well, not the whole thing.

DAVID No.

KAREN I saw the clip that was –

DAVID The clip, so that's like about twenty seconds.

KAREN Oh, it was good, yeah, yeah.

DAVID And the guy who's interviewing me? What's his name?

KAREN Jim Walcott.

DAVID Jim. Has he seen *Crash*?

KAREN *Crash*?

DAVID Uh-huh.

KAREN Um, well, he, I know he saw the clip.

DAVID So, he's rock solid on that twenty seconds.

KAREN Absolutely, absolutely. And, uh, he's a huge fan. I mean, I know he's seen your *Videodrome* and *Scanners* and *Rude*, and it's just endless, you know. He's a huge, huge fan. He'll be fine. Yeah, I really do have go to the bathroom now.

DAVID Okay.

She turns away and shakes her head. They part.

Mark, Karen, George, Audrey, and Graham are in the boardroom.

MARK — Okay, four Pickering "A" reactors were built with only one fast shutdown system. Now, the Atomic Energy Commission has since required all reactors like Pickering to have at least two fast shutdown systems. At Chernobyl there was a dual-mode failure. Now, in a dual-mode failure, containment pressure can be expected to get higher than, uh, containment chambers were designed to manage. Now, our source on site says that if pressure keeps building up at this rate, we could have a second Chernobyl on our hands in a matter of hours.

Everyone remains silent. Karen puts her hands to her mouth. George looks at Mark. Audrey looks at Mark and George.

GEORGE — *(waits a beat, then . . .)* Are we gonna pre-package the Cronenberg item?

MARK — *(shocked)* What?

GEORGE — Cronenberg.

KAREN — God, George.

MARK — What are you talking about?

GEORGE — Well, I've seen the clips from *Crash*, and I would say that they're just a bit too raw for the six o'clock news. Can we get a clip from, like, *Scanners* or something like that?

KAREN — You mean, like, exploding heads?

GEORGE — Yes, the exploding heads. Can we get that?

MARK — Wait a second. We're talking about heads exploding. Southern Ontario could explode.

KAREN — Cronenberg doesn't want to talk about exploding heads any more. He's gone beyond that, he feels.

MARK Can we not talk about Cronenberg? Can we talk about, oh, I don't know, nuclear meltdown, maybe?

GEORGE Fine, fine. Okay.

MARK We have a potential failure of a shutdown system at Pickering.

GEORGE Right. Yes.

MARK We could have a Chernobyl.

GEORGE Yes. What we don't have . . . there's no hook to this story.

MARK A hook?

GEORGE Something people can relate to. There's not a single dead body.

MARK Are you telling me people can't relate to a China Syndrome in their backyard?

GEORGE I didn't say that. China Syndrome they can relate to. I like that. That's a hook. Because there was a movie there. People saw the movie, they understand what you're talking about when you say China Syndrome. That's how you build a news story.

You know what we should do? *(Audrey frowns)* Rent five copies of *The China Syndrome*. We should watch the movie.

MARK We're gonna rent movies?

GEORGE I want to see how they cover the story in the movie. The problem with stories like this is there's way too much science and not enough production value. The audience can't relate to that.

Karen looks at Mark, not quite able to figure out George's angle.

MARK Shouldn't we do a double-ender with the guy at the plant? Maybe, uh, pre-record it with Jim in the studio?

GEORGE	"The Hot Zone." Let's call this thing "The Hot Zone." I love that.
AUDREY	"The Hot Zone" was the Ebola virus.
GEORGE	Very good. "The Hot Zone" was the Ebola virus. I need a title. Titles, titles, titles. Thank you very much.

Jim is with David Cronenberg in the make-up room. Jim sits in a make-up chair while David is attended to by a make-up artist.

JIM	So you probably heard, I do this great impression of when that guy's head explodes in *Scanners*. I've been doing it since I was a kid. *(he vibrates in an impression of the guy who's head is about to explode in* Scanners*)* I loved it when that head exploded. I loved it.
DAVID	You know, it's been so long since I did that stuff. I literally cannot remember how we did most of it, you know.
JIM	Really?
DAVID	Yeah. So I just want to make sure that we talk about *Crash* a lot, because that is really what I'm here for. *Crash*.
JIM	*Crash*.
DAVID	Did you ever see this movie before?
JIM	Yeah, yeah, that was, uh, audacious. An audacious, daring, and, uh, original film. But, you know, I'm a special-effects nut, so I'd love to know how you got that head to explode.
DAVID	I'm gonna have to insist, really, that we don't talk about *Scanners* or special effects or exploding heads, okay?
JIM	Yeah, absolutely. I'll see you out there, Dave.

David stands in the office corridor with an attractive female worker. She is mesmerized by his conversation.

DAVID Now, we're down to our last two heads. What are we gonna do? How are we gonna explode their heads in a, in a realistic way? And, uh, I could tell ya, you know, what we came up with, but you wouldn't believe it.

George and a Graphics guy are in the graphics room.

GRAPHICS Okay, that's the CNN graphic opening from the O.J. trial. *(a graphic of the famous scales-of-justice opening from the O.J. Simpson trial is on the screen)*

GEORGE Good. Now, what I want to do is copy this for the nuclear story, but I want to make some changes. See where the scales of justice come up there? I want Chernobyl in there. The destruction of the plant, but also the victims. I want it to be gruesome, okay? It's about death. I want to see horrors, I want to see death. See where Marcia Clark is there? Okay, I want the burn victims from Nagasaki where Marcia Clark is. And there, where Johnny Cochran is, put a nuclear explosion in. Nicole Simpson, another nuclear explosion. Ron Goldman, another nuclear explosion. Boom, boom, boom.

GRAPHICS I was thinking, replace O.J. with Albert Einstein. You know, the atom, nuclear –

GEORGE No, forget Einstein, Einstein won't work. Einstein's too friendly. I want something more gruesome here. Something related to death. Nuclear and death. Something about mutation. People are afraid of that.

GRAPHICS Mutated . . . babies?

GEORGE I love that! Yes! Can we get a shot of a mutated baby?

GRAPHICS Um, it'd be tight.

GEORGE Okay, forget the mutation. I've got a better idea. You know what we do? We hold O.J.'s face here.

GRAPHICS O.J.

GEORGE Just leave O.J.'s face.

GRAPHICS On a nuclear story?

GEORGE Yes, yes! You see, people watched the O.J. trial for a year. All the O.J. circuits are there. We show O.J.'s face, people say, Hey, we have to watch that, okay? And by the time this thing blows – if the plant does – and blows this city off the face of this earth, they'll forget that, uh, O.J. was on the screen. But O.J. got us to the dance, O.J. will get us there.

Jim sits beside Mark while Mark works at his workstation. Jim is anxious.

JIM This could contaminate all of Southern Ontario.

MARK Well, it's not as bad as the network's fall comedy line-up, but it's bad.

JIM Come on, don't mess with me. Is this a potential nuclear meltdown or not?

MARK Yeah.

JIM Think I should wear my tie loose or tight on air?

MARK Your tie?

JIM Yeah . . . on air. I've been thinking about this moment for a long time, you know. A story big enough to transcend the formal anchor image, and, and, you know, justify a loose tie. Something that conveys the gravity . . . and the immediacy of the situation, that says, Hey, folks, you know, this is the big one. And we're all in it together. Maybe even a coffee mug. Am I nuts? Is that over the top?

MARK Uh, I don't think a coffee mug with a nuclear holocaust would be over the top. Listen, just the staff knows about this, and, uh, we don't want to create a panic, but, uh, people are calling up close friends and loved ones. Give them a chance to, uh, drive west. So if there's someone you know, maybe now would be a good time to, uh, call them. *(he leaves Jim sitting at this workstation)*

JIM Yeah.

(mutters to himself) Friends or close loved ones. That's a good point. *(pauses and thinks)* Oh, shit. Aw, aw shit!

Audrey walks by. Jim gets up and turns to Audrey, who goes to her workstation beside Mark's.

JIM Shit. He's an asshole. He knows I have no one to call. This, this whole nuclear thing is all bullshit, isn't it? It's a joke, it's a joke to set me up! Just testing me to see who I could come up with.

AUDREY It's not a joke.

JIM What? What'd you say?

AUDREY It is not a joke.

JIM Um, I have to get my cat out of the city.

George is with Sid at an audio board in the music room. Sid plays the O.J. theme.

GEORGE That's good, that's good. All right. Kill it, kill it. That's the O.J. theme. That's the theme I want. I want O.J. and I want a nuclear holocaust twist to it.

SID	Nuclear holocaust twist.
GEORGE	Yes, yes.
SID	Don't you think O.J.'s a bit dated?
GEORGE	No, no, you don't understand. Do you know the circuitry of the brain? Circuits build up, okay? All these circuits are built up from people watching the O.J. trial, all right? That's an addiction. That's a habit. I want something to crank up that old addiction. Fire that old habit. Just send something new through the veins, right?
SID	*(smiles nervously)* Is this nuclear accident a real threat to Toronto? Could people die? My mother's visiting, and I could arrange to move her.
GEORGE	Death, death, death, death, death. This is it. I get it now. Death. I want to hear death through this whole thing, okay? O.J.'s the alarm bell. Gets people to listen, and then lay in the death. The holocaust.
SID	Are you talking about nuclear, a nuclear holocaust? Holocaust, Second World War . . .
GEORGE	I like that. Better, better, better. The other holocaust. Good, okay? Work on it. O.J., Holocaust, run to two. Death, O.J., death, O.J. I'll be right back. Just work on it.

Jim is sitting on a couch in the corridor. Karen stands nearby.

JIM	So you . . . *(clears his throat)* come to this big realization in your life. Who do you call? Who are your friends, who are your loved ones?
KAREN	You know, I should probably, um . . .
JIM	Just sit down for a second.
KAREN	Uh, no, I'm fine.
JIM	You know . . . maybe it's just the pressure that you can't think of anyone.

KAREN Yeah.

JIM But is that what it all comes down to? Huh? You know . . . being an anchor, you give your life up to this public persona, to that big nameless, faceless blob out there, the audience . . . They're your loved ones, they're your friends. But who are they? Who are they?! They're my friends, but I can't call them. Do they give a shit about me? The dirty goddamn secret about this face that everybody loves is nobody really loves it. It's a two-dimensional image.

KAREN Right. And, uh, George wanted to know it you're gonna wear your tie up or down.

JIM I was thinking down, shirtsleeves rolled up.

KAREN Great. *(she turns and walks away)*

JIM And a coffee mug.

KAREN *(she stops and turns back to Jim)* A mug?

JIM Yeah.

KAREN Great.

JIM Yeah. *(thinking about it)* Yeah.

George is hurrying along the office corridor followed by a visibly upset Bruce.

BRUCE Mark hands me this shit about nuclear clouds and the prevailing atmospheric wind patterns after Chernobyl, and he tells me I should get ready to read it on air tonight. I mean, what the hell's going on? *(George doesn't respond)*

George, is this real? Is this the real one?

George is trying to remember something and stops.

BRUCE Look, I have a cottage about fifty miles from that plant. I've got two brand-new hundred-horse-power

Merc engines I just put on my boat. I won't be able to go near those things for five thousand years! Do you know what that does to my goddamn resale? I can't handle this. I just can't handle this! *(he is in a panic spin)*

GEORGE *(looks at Bruce a beat, then . . .)* Can you do that on TV? On air?

BRUCE Do what?

GEORGE Lose it like this. Look, the anchor has to maintain self-control, but the weather guy, the weather guy can lose it. See, I like that. Knee-jerk self-pity in a crisis. That's a weakness, you know? That kind of spinelessness thing you're doing here, you know? That works for us dramatically. If you can show them the spinelessness, that takes real courage.

BRUCE You are such an asshole.

GEORGE I'm just, uh . . .

BRUCE I'll tell you something, though. I started out in Collingwood selling Evinrudes, all right? And I busted my balls to get the weather spot on some shit-ass local Barrie station. Eight years I spent in that piss-hole. Eight years, until I worked my way up into the biggest market in this country. You know what? I played golf with Mike Harris two weeks ago. *(George looks at him)* Yeah, we were suckin' back beers in the golf cart. The guy threw up on my golf shoes. That's how far I've come. And you want me to throw that away?

GEORGE "There's a man with a gun over there." I was just thinking while you were talking, sorry. That's the song. It's a Neil Young song.

George is with Sid in the music room.

GEORGE Something, "Hey, there, what's that sound, everybody look what's going down." You know that song?

SID I don't like it. That song was with the Vietnam War. You're mixing issues here.

GEORGE It's Canadian.

SID I'm a little nervous about this. No one's told me what's really going on. Are we in danger?

GEORGE Leonard Cohen. I'm hearing Leonard Cohen now, okay? Um, um, um, "Suzanne takes you down . . ."

SID What does that have to do with this?

GEORGE I love that. That's perfect. It's intuitive. You have to trust your intuition with this stuff.

SID That's the theory . . .

GEORGE I intuit Leonard Cohen, I intuit Leonard Cohen. He's great. It'll be perfect.

SID Good.

GEORGE He's wrong. Leonard Cohen's wrong. He's wrong.
The Doors. "Light My Fire." That's brilliant. *Apocalypse Now*. But keep it original, okay? Something from The Doors, maybe something from *Jaws*. Little bit of O.J. and the Holocaust, all right? Work on it. I'll be right back.

George, Mark, and Karen are at Mark's workstation. Mark and Karen run titles by George.

GEORGE Titles. Okay, hit me.

MARK "Metro Meltdown."

GEORGE Pass. Horrible.

KAREN "Candu, Can't Do." It's a Candu reactor, and I thought that . . .

GEORGE I get it. I get it. And I hate it.

MARK "A Risk Too High."

GEORGE What is that?

MARK	It's from *A Bridge Too Far*.
GEORGE	Oh, great. A really well-known movie. Twenty-five years old, and nobody saw that. Pass.
KAREN	"Pickering Mon Amour." It's off of *Hiroshima Mon Amour*.
GEORGE	Hir*osh*ima. I say Hiro*shi*ma.
MARK	I say Hiro*shi*ma.
KAREN	I think it's Hir*osh*ima.
MARK	Hir*osh*ima?
GEORGE	First, Hir*osh*ima's pretentious. Second, it's an art-movie title. I'm not putting that in a television show.
KAREN	Uh, "Chernobyl North." It's a play on Toronto's "Hollywood North." "Chernobyl North." I know it doesn't work, because Chernobyl is probably north of Toronto, but, I just . . . we'll keep working on it.

George and the Graphics guy are in the graphics room.

GRAPHICS	I brought the burn-victim footage from Hiro*shi*ma up over Mark Furhman. Held O.J., and right here, nuked out Marcia Clark. Nuked out Judge Ito. And right here where the scales of justice were *(explosions are seen on the computer screen)* . . . the ground-zero destruction of Nagasaki.
GEORGE	It's great, it's great. The titles?
GRAPHICS	*(shows graphic)* First is "One Million Dead?"
GEORGE	"One Million Dead" has a question mark after it. I thought we were going to put an exclamation mark.
GRAPHICS	I think an exclamation mark after "One Million Dead" is kind of redundant. And if it's speculation that a million might die, then a question mark makes sense.

GEORGE Look, if we're speculating, okay, fine, we'll put in three million. Let's do it, okay? It's brilliant. I love this. Let's see it from the top.

A Mail guy opens the door and comes in.

MAIL GUY Excuse me. I've got a video here for a George Findlay?

GEORGE Yeah, that's me.

MAIL GUY *(hands George a package) The China Syndrome.*

GEORGE Oh, great, great. That's great. Great, thank you, thank you. *(he stops the Mail guy from leaving)* Wait, wait. Come here, come here, come here. I want you to see something. Watch this. Run it. Okay, we have the O.J. opening. Okay, that's the regular O.J. opening. But what we've done is, we've nuked out Marcia Clark, boom. Nuked out Judge Ito, boom. Nuked out the scales of justice with an A-bomb, boom. And out. What do you think?

MAIL GUY What is it?

GEORGE It's an opening for a TV spot. I mean, you're a viewer, right? I mean, I'm doing a random sample here. Do you love this or do you hate it? Just tell me. Do you love it or hate it? Love it or hate it?

MAIL GUY I hate it.

GEORGE You hate it? *(the Mail guy nods)*

The Mail guy leaves. George switches to a seat on the other side of the Graphics guy.

GEORGE I hate this. I hate it.

GRAPHICS A Mail guy hated it.

GEORGE Yeah, well, the Mail guy was eighteen years old, okay? That's a very important demographic for us.

Without that demographic, we're dead. This is too much about death, this nuclear story, okay? This has to be more life-affirming. This is 1997. I'm guessing the audience is going to want upbeat, okay? The numbers for that Zaire thing – the whole exodus of refugees in Zaire – was just shit. Nobody watched that stuff, okay? I want to be upbeat. I want to be life-affirming. I want Marcia Clark replaced with, with, with . . . God. God.

GRAPHICS God.

GEORGE From the Sistine Chapel. The ceiling of the Sistine Chapel. Reaching his hand out. *(he holds out his arm and points)* I love that.

GRAPHICS You want the whole ceiling?

GEORGE No, no, no. Just the part where he's reaching out and touching, touching . . . Who's he touching? Who was God touching there?

GRAPHICS Adam.

GEORGE Adam, Adam, I love that. But Adam's not . . . local. Adam's not Toronto.

GRAPHICS He's Garden of Eden.

GEORGE I know he's Garden of Eden. He's touching, he's touching who? Who's he touching?

GRAPHICS Einstein?

GEORGE No, forget Einstein.

GRAPHICS O.J.?

GEORGE No, not O.J. He's not touching O.J. God is touching something in Toronto. He's touching . . . the tip of the CN Tower. This is about life now. This is not about death, okay? *(the Graphics guy slowly closes his eyes)* Take out burn victims in Hiroshima. I want a dog leaping for a Frisbee in a field, all right? Replace the nuclear explosions with . . . Cosby. Cosby.

GRAPHICS Bill Cosby?

GEORGE	Yes, Cosby, the image of Cosby. The image of Terry Fox. Terry Fox overcomes adversity. Terry Fox is Canadian. This is a Canadian thing. We can beat this as Canadians.
GRAPHICS	Cosby's a Canadian?
GEORGE	Well, Cosby's in syndication, and when you're in syndication you're virtually universal. I love this. Love, love this. Let's do it.

George and Sid are in the music room. Sid plays music for George on his keyboard.

SID	Death.
GEORGE	That's it?
SID	Yeah. You like it?
GEORGE	I hate that. It's all wrong. It's all wrong. No, no more death. Forget death. Life, that's what this is all about. Okay? Life. *(Sid picks up pencil and writes)* Um, Petula Clark. Um, you know, um, what is that? Uh, "Downtown." Uh, Billy Joel's "Uptown Girl." Um, uh, those are horrible. Uh, "Chariots of Fire." That's what I love. I love that Vangelis "Chariots of Fire." "Chariots of Fire," Vangelis. Okay, forget O.J. Forget the Holocaust. "Chariots of Fire." You know what? We could win a Gemini Award for this.

Audrey is on the phone at her workstation. She is upset and mad.

AUDREY	You are the fifth person I've been passed to with this question. Obviously there is no evacuation plan in case of a nuclear accident . . . Don't give, no, don't give me that shit. Excuse me. I can't say the word shit, but you can kill five million

people . . . Uh-huh . . . No, the fact is that we're airing in forty-two minutes, and I think it would be nice if we could give the people a number that they could call . . . An Internet number and no phone number? That is the stupidest thing I've ever heard! Oh, my skin is burning off, but no problem, because I can have a forum about it with other burning bodies on the Net!

She slams the phone down. Mark walks up to his workstation. Audrey lights a cigarette.

MARK Hey, you can't smoke here.

AUDREY Fuck off!

David Cronenberg and Jim are finishing up on air at the anchor desk.

DAVID . . . So what we actually ended up doing was using a real shotgun.

JIM Really?

DAVID Blew the head from behind low down so that the gelatin skin slid off the skull and hung down, inside out, swinging, you know, like a napkin. It was –

JIM Wonderful, wonderful. Gruesome.

DAVID It was fantastic.

JIM Great story.

DAVID Thank you.

JIM Thank you for being with us.

DAVID Okay.

JIM Our guest, of course, Mr. David Cronenberg. The director of the audacious, daring, and original *Crash*.

Cut. Good. *(gets something through his earplug)* Uh, we're getting another feed in right now.

Another pre-packaged item. They want to know if you'll stay right there. Do you mind?

DAVID — No. What's the story?

JIM — We could have a nuclear-plant meltdown within thirty-five minutes, twenty miles from here. Another Chernobyl, actually.

David stands and quickly walks off as Jim gets his cue.

JIM — *(to camera)* With us on site right now at Reactor Six, live, Mr. Paul Tinsley.

David leaves the studio, starts to walk down the corridor, then breaks into a run.

The on-site expert, Paul Tinsley, looks and talks like Jack Lemmon from The China Syndrome. *He's jumpy, distressed, expressing unfinished thoughts. He's inside a room at the plant with lockers. George and Karen are watching. Paul on the monitor in the control room.*

JIM — So what's happening in Pickering right now?

PAUL — Well, well, I felt this, uh, uh, vibration, and, uh, right then, well it wasn't so much a vibration as it was a shudder, a shudder.

GEORGE — Is this our guy?

KAREN — Yeah.

GEORGE — Oh, this guy's good. This guy's ridiculous.

KAREN — This is the key guy, George.

GEORGE — He's acting. This guy's acting. Look at this.

PAUL — . . . Two intersecting geological, uh, what would you call them, they're more like, uh, uh, faults.

GEORGE — You know what he's doing? He's doing Jack Lemmon. He's doing Jack Lemmon from *The China Syndrome*.

KAREN This guy's a nuclear engineer. I don't think he does impressions.

GEORGE Look at, just, look at him.

PAUL . . . the Niagara Magnet just comes up . . .

GEORGE He's doing Jack Lemmon. Look, it's totally obvious. And, you know, Jack Lemmon took me right out of that movie. This guy's taking me right out of the story the same way. In *The China Syndrome*, do you know what it was? I kept seeing *The Apartment*. I kept seeing *Irma La Douce*. This guy's doing *Grumpy Old Men*.

KAREN Did you see *Glengarry Glen Ross*?

The vibration starts again. An alarm sounds. Tinsley stops and looks around. George and Karen are not paying attention to the monitor.

GEORGE I hated that one. I mean, I didn't see it.

KAREN The movie was terrible, but it was more recent than *Grumpy Old Men*.

GEORGE The director is a horrible director. He made, um, that director made, um, what was that terrible Madonna picture, um, *Who's That Girl*. The director was the same guy who did that movie.

KAREN Did you see *Short Cuts*?

GEORGE Jack Lemmon was not in *Short Cuts*.

KAREN Yes, he was in *Short Cuts*.

GEORGE Jack Lemmon was not in *Short Cuts*.

KAREN He was in *Short Cuts*.

GEORGE No, no, he wasn't in *Short Cuts*. *Short Cuts* was, um . . .

KAREN The director?

GEORGE Yeah, yeah, yeah. He did, uh, no, no, no. What do you call it? He did *The Player*. Altman!

PAUL	. . . that would be the, um . . . *(he looks around nervously)*
KAREN	Altman!
PAUL	. . . that was the shudder I was referring to earlier, actually . . .
KAREN	Altman did *Short Cuts*, and Jack Lemmon was in *Short Cuts*.
GEORGE	He was not.
PAUL	. . . technically was designed to withstand . . .
KAREN	Yes he was.
GEORGE	He wasn't in, oh . . .
PAUL	. . . I can tell you that this is fairly severe.
GEORGE	Maybe you were right.
KAREN	He was somebody's father in *Short Cuts*.
PAUL	. . . remain calm of course . . .
GEORGE	He was the father of the kid that was hit . . .
KAREN	Yes!
GEORGE	. . . in the car . . .
KAREN	Yes!
GEORGE	. . . by . . .
KAREN	By . . .
GEORGE	Lily Tomlin.
PAUL	Oh, Jesus.
GEORGE	And you're absolutely right. It was Jack Lemmon.
PAUL	Oh, Jesus.

George and Sid are in the music room. They sit in silence. Sid is stumped.

GEORGE	Are you thinking?

TO BE CONTINUED . . .

EPISODE 11

“Meltdown,” Part 2

First Aired: March 17, 1997

George, Mark, Karen, and Audrey are in the boardroom.

GEORGE "China Syndrome" is perfect.

MARK "China Syndrome."

GEORGE "China Syndrome's" perfect. People can relate to that. They saw the movie. If we get a character out there who looks like Jane Fonda, the audience . . . we draw them in.

Audrey, get Casting on this. Find the woman who we could send out as the Jane Fonda type.

KAREN A Jane Fonda type?

GEORGE I'm going for a little production value, okay? I'm trying to build a story here. A little production value.

MARK We can't use an actor on a story this big.

GEORGE Why not? I mean, what does a reporter do? A reporter reads copy. Write the copy, get an actress, send her out there.

KAREN Why don't we, uh, get some experts?

GEORGE Yes, analysts.

MARK Yeah, okay. That makes sense.

GEORGE Okay? A man and a woman. Okay, I want some underlying sexual tension here.

MARK Well, we don't need, I mean, sex, we don't need sex. We've got a nuclear disaster.

GEORGE No, no, no, no. Sexual tension. You know what I want? The Greta Van Susteren character.

	Remember, from the O.J. trial? The two of them, the guy with the curly hair. The two lawyers . . .
MARK	You want, you want those two from the Simpson trial.
GEORGE	Of course not. I want the same relationship, okay? Those two, the two lawyers, okay? He's pro-nuke, wears a suit. She's anti-nuke, she's attractive, but she's ironic. He's on the right, she's on the left, but she still wants to sleep with him.
KAREN	She does?
GEORGE	The audience has to imagine she wants to sleep with him.
KAREN	Better.
GEORGE	Dress her in Donna Karan stuff. Heels, okay, I don't want the Birkenstocks. I want her legs shaved, and I don't want some woman in here who's forty-five years old and has decided to go prematurely grey to make a point.

George, Mark, and Karen are walking down the office corridor and along the atrium walkway.

GEORGE	I just want to make this work as a news story, okay? I want the Fonda character at the site. I want the Greta Van Susteren and the other guy in the studio. I want the casting director to have a copy of *China Syndrome*. And that Greta character, I want her to be Greenpeace, but I don't want her to be shrill. Roger Cossack.
MARK	What?
GEORGE	Roger Cossack, he's the guy, the other guy that was with Greta Van Susteren.
MARK	Oh, right, right.
GEORGE	Do I get a point for that?

KAREN You get a point.

GEORGE Thank you. I'll be in Casting.

In the boardroom, Mark reads off a list of previous Pickering accidents while George reviews casting photos with Audrey.

GEORGE This will not . . . Oh, this is total "Baywatch" time.

AUDREY What about this one?

MARK Okay, I got one here. August 1st, 1983. A pressure tube in Pickering Reactor Two ruptured with little warning. The metre-long break dumped seventeen kilograms of heavy water per second onto the floor of the reactor vault.

GEORGE Oh, she's got the right look. Can we get her?

AUDREY She's on her way in.

GEORGE Good.

MARK In November 1990, all moderator-room pumps were found seized at Pickering Unit Four.

GEORGE This does not resemble Jane Fonda.

Mark looks shocked that George is not listening to what he is saying.

GEORGE I like her, I like her hair.

AUDREY She's too pouty.

GEORGE I like those kind of lips.

AUDREY She's doing a Jean-Claude Van Damme picture.

GEORGE He's in town?

AUDREY Uh-huh.

GEORGE You see, why don't we have Jean-Claude Van Damme on the show? He's a big star, he's doing a picture in Toronto . . .

AUDREY We tried and he passed.

GEORGE He passed.

AUDREY He passed.

GEORGE Asshole.

MARK You know, instead of trying to get Jean-Claude Van Damme, why don't we get a nuclear physicist who could give this stuff some perspective.

GEORGE She does a paper-towel commercial, doesn't she?

AUDREY Tampons.

GEORGE Let's get her in, let's get her in.

George sits with Karen in a small studio with bleachers. They rehearse the first Van Susteren/Cossack team.

KAREN So just relax, this is just a rehearsal.
(whispers to George) This is the first Greta Van Susteren/Roger Cossack team.

GEORGE *(whispering back)* Do they know they're auditioning?

KAREN No, they think they're the only ones.

GEORGE Good, good.

KAREN *(to the team)* Okay. Go ahead.

SUSTEREN #1 Let's face some facts, Jim. The four reactors at Pickering "A," which have been operating since 1971 and 1973 –

GEORGE Uh, excuse me, sorry. Can you be a little less earnest? I, I, I know you're connected to Greenpeace, but you don't have to be that earnest, you know?

KAREN *(whispers to George)* George, she's not an actor.

GEORGE I'm looking for something here. Uh, just a little more energy. That's what I want. More energy.

SUSTEREN #1 Let's face some facts, Jim. The four reactors at Pickering "A" –

GEORGE Sorry, that's wrong, that's wrong, that's wrong. You gotta, you gotta project more.

SUSTEREN #1 Let's face some facts, Jim. The four reactors –

GEORGE But you're still doing the same thing.

SUSTEREN #1 Well . . .

GEORGE This is TV, okay? I think it'll just work a lot better if you're just a little bigger.

SUSTEREN #1 Okay?

GEORGE From the top, from the top.

SUSTEREN #1 Uh, let's face some facts, Jim. The four –

GEORGE Okay, um, did you watch the O.J. Simpson thing, the trial? Did you ever see the Greta Van Susteren character?

SUSTEREN #1 No, I didn't.

George looks at Karen. She puts her head in her hand.

GEORGE *(waits a beat, then . . .)* Okay, um. Louder.

SUSTEREN #1 . . . And it is not surprising that a dual-mode accident, such as this one, should eventually occur. The fact is, Candu can't do.

KAREN *(whispers to George)* Did you hear that? Candu can't do? You dumped on me when I said that.

GEORGE Okay, the lawyer? Just be yourself, be natural, be real. This is a news show.

COSSACK #1 All right, I'm not saying that, uh, we don't have a serious situation out there, Jim. But Adrian's right when she says that, uh, the plant's –

GEORGE Excuse me, sorry. You're agreeing with her. You can't agree with her. There has to be some kind of conflict here. We want to get a kind of crossfire here.

KAREN George?

GEORGE I know you're not actors, but just give me a little bit of conflict, okay? Okay. Here we go, here we go, here we go.

COSSACK #1 I know we've got a serious situation down there. And Adrian's right that, uh, the plant is old, but you are wrong about this . . .

GEORGE Thank you very much. Great, great. You'll be great.

Susteren #1 and Cossack #1 stand to leave.

GEORGE Okay? You can go.

George sees Susteren #1 and Cossack #1 out of the studio.

SUSTEREN #1 The make-up woman wants me to shave under my arms. What the hell is that?

GEORGE Well, you could wear a blouse with a longer sleeve.

SUSTEREN #1 That's not the point! The comment was totally unacceptable. Especially in a crisis of this magnitude.

COSSACK #1 Look, am I going on air or not? I mean, I didn't think I was auditioning.

GEORGE You're not.

COSSACK #1 *(stops walking and looks at his watch)* Well, look, I've got a busy law practice downtown, all right? So, like, am I on air or not?

GEORGE You're on air. You're both on air. Unless something unforeseeable happens.

Back in the small studio, George and Karen look at the second Susteren/Cossack team.

KAREN *(whispers to George)* This is the second team.

GEORGE Do they also think they're the only ones?

KAREN That's right.

GEORGE Good.

KAREN	*(to Susteren/Cossack)* Oh, you can go ahead any time. It's just a rehearsal.
SUSTEREN #2	All emergency planning scenarios, uh, assume that radioactivity can be held in containment chambers for several days –
GEORGE	Uh, one point. Excuse me. Um, this skirt. Can you just, just an inch, just an inch more leg?
SUSTEREN #2	What?!
GEORGE	It's just television. Did you see the O.J. Simpson trial? The Greta Van Susteren character?
SUSTEREN #2	Uh, well, yes, I did.
GEORGE	Well, she just had this . . . it's just there is this, sexual relationship between the, uh . . .
KAREN	*(to Susteren #2)* Don't do anything you don't feel comfortable doing.
SUSTEREN #2	Okay, great. Thank you.
GEORGE	No, don't. I just want it to be believable, all right? Um, okay, can we start from the top?
SUSTEREN #2	If this accident is as big as I think it is, that's not necessarily the case. And the fact is that the Candu can't do.
KAREN	*(to George)* Again?
COSSACK #2	Okay, there are gonna be risks if you want to have affordable and plentiful energy. Now, you people want it, but you don't want the acceptable risk. So then the nuclear industry's damned if they do and damned if they don't.
GEORGE	Um, on the word "energy," did I detect an accent of some kind?
COSSACK #2	Well, I spend some time in South Africa. It might've just sort of –
GEORGE	It just sounded a little, um, a little pretentious to me.
COSSACK #2	I can do a sort of Bronx thing if you want.

GEORGE You can do a Bronx accent?

KAREN George, don't make him do an accent.

GEORGE Okay, fine. Let's take a shot.

COSSACK #2 Okay, from, from, from the top, sort of a New York . . .

KAREN *(whispers to George)* If anybody knows this guy, if anybody knows this guy in the city . . .

GEORGE *(to Cossack)* That'd be great.

COSSACK #2 It's just a little more aggressive.

GEORGE *(to Karen)* I'm just trying to make the piece work.

KAREN He's humiliating himself. This is a prominent guy . . . George . . .

GEORGE Try the Bronx thing and dump the British South African thing. And the energy. And we'll go, and you guys are great.

Karen puts her head in her hands.

COSSACK #2 *(in an exaggerated New York accent)* Okay, we have a problem. No one's trying to cover that up.

Graham sits with George on a couch in the corridor.

GRAHAM We've got a possible Chernobyl twenty-five miles from the city. And I have got a budget request from a casting director for female reporters. George, what the heck are you doing? Where's the story?

GEORGE Did you get a copy of *The China Syndrome* that I sent your office?

GRAHAM I've seen it. Why did your intern drop a copy off on my desk? Why are we watching movies?

GEORGE Well, I wanted to send a reporter to the site who was like Jane Fonda on that movie.

GRAHAM That was a movie; this is the real thing. George! You're working on graphics openings, you've got music, casting. Where's the story?

GEORGE I'm getting it, I'm getting it.

GRAHAM You're in denial, George.

GEORGE Oh, I'm in denial?

GRAHAM Yes, you can't deal with your own mortality. You can't deal with the horror of this, so you're burying your head in the sands of over-production.

GEORGE The sands of . . . I absolutely can deal with my own mortality, okay?

GRAHAM Then get the story, and stop jerking off.

Fonda #1, her agent, and George are standing in the office corridor outside the studio.

FONDA #1 What's the story? If I don't know the story, I can't understand the motivation of my character, and I have to know my motivation.

GEORGE Uh, it's Jane Fonda in *The China Syndrome.*

FONDA #1 Oh, I love her.

AGENT Oh, Fonda was great in that. Um, the thing is, though, Carol's in the middle of shooting a Van Damme picture right now, and, uh, what you're asking her to do is go from one character to another. That's very difficult for an actor, so she really wants to see a script.

GEORGE A script?

AGENT Yeah.

GEORGE Um, you play a reporter. You'll be fine.

AGENT What does she do?

GEORGE Um, well, she reports. Okay?

George starts backing away, but the agent and Fonda #1 follow.

AGENT What does she report, though? We can't work like this. We need, you know, we need a script.

GEORGE I know, I have something to do right now, but she plays herself.

AGENT Oh, well, she played herself in a Cronenberg film, actually. She was killed in a car crash as herself. She was wonderful.

GEORGE That's exactly it. That's all you have to do, okay?

FONDA #1 Well, when do I get the script?

GEORGE Uh, very soon. Very soon.

Mark walks with George along the atrium walkway. George is dressed in a white shirt and black tie. He is putting on a black jacket. Rossini's "The Barber of Seville" plays underneath the dialogue.

MARK I've got two experts on their way in for live studio spots. One's a transit specialist who says Toronto has no adequate evacuation plan in place for a Chernobyl-like disaster.

A man appears, about fifty, hair slicked back, Italian, dark suit, silk tie, silk hanky in breast pocket. He's with two attractive, sexually playful younger women, also dressed for a party, giggling. They pass Mark and George.

MAN *(Italian accent, exuberant)* George, I have a fantastic new design idea for your anchor desk. I saw it in Milan. I want to talk to you about it. I'll see you downstairs at the reception.

GEORGE Good.

MAN *(to the women as they continue down the walkway)* How about a little drink, my . . .

MARK The seal rings that lead into the vacuum chambers of every nuclear plant in the province have deteriorated.

GEORGE Uh-huh.

MARK Now, what this means is that . . .

They pass Fonda #1 waiting on a couch. She rises quickly.

FONDA #1 Is there a script yet?

The music stops.

GEORGE Uh, not yet.

FONDA #1 Well, if I don't know the story, I can't understand the motivation of my character.

GEORGE Well, just play Jane Fonda from *The China Syndrome.*

FONDA #1 I'm doing a Van Damme picture right now.

GEORGE You'll be great in this. Don't worry about a thing.

FONDA #1 Thank you.

Mark and George keep going.

MARK Listen, George, uh, we could have a serious nuclear accident on our hands.

GEORGE I have a reception downstairs in fifteen minutes. I have to run. I'll be right back.

George turns and walks away from Mark. Mark leaves in the opposite direction. The music starts again, George is humming. A Jane Fonda candidate, Jessica Noble, stops him in this tracks.

JESSICA Are you George Findlay?

GEORGE Yes, I am.

JESSICA Jessica Noble. God, they gave me such a hard time down in Security. I mean, they're such jerks. Christ, it's not like they don't know who I am. I mean, I've only done about two hundred roles here. You know, this is the fifth anchor I've played.

GEORGE Oh, you're here for the Fonda character?

JESSICA Yeah.

GEORGE Oh, the anchor. You'll be perfect.

JESSICA Well, I mean, I'd be perfect if I could find a script and find a little about what the story is.

GEORGE Oh, it's a nuclear accident. Could you wear your hair up?

JESSICA Yeah, but this is for the news. What is it, like a dramatization or –

The music stops.

GEORGE Yes, it's a dramatization. Exactly. That's exactly it. You'll be perfect. Is that what you're wearing?

JESSICA No, but Wardrobe hasn't contacted me.

GEORGE I'll take care of that. I'll take care of it.

JESSICA We shooting on location or in the building?

GEORGE Uh, location, I think.

JESSICA Location you think? We're shooting today.

GEORGE You'll be perfect for this.

The music starts.

JESSICA Yeah, but, this, this reporter. Is she tough, is she sweet, is she a bitch, uh, Barbara Walters, Diane Sawyer, Pam Wallin? *(she stops walking)*

GEORGE — *(starting to back away)* She's you. Just play yourself. You'll be fabulous. I want reality. Just be real. Be yourself.

Audrey walks quickly with her ex-boyfriend, Sean, down the office corridor.

AUDREY — This is just a really bad time for you to be here.

SEAN — Audrey, look, man. I was just downtown. I thought I'd drop in, you know.

AUDREY — This is a job, Sean!

SEAN — We got to talk about this. *(they stop walking)*

AUDREY — I have to work.

The music stops.

SEAN — Okay, look. Just give me five minutes, okay? Five minutes.

AUDREY — Why, why? It's over. It's over. There's nothing to say. You weren't honest with me, it's over.

SEAN — Audrey, okay? It was an old charge, okay? I was a passenger in the car! I didn't even know the car was stolen!

AUDREY — There were other cars.

Audrey and Sean are smoking a joint in the washroom.

AUDREY — You know, it's not that you steal cars. It's that you care enough about them to steal one, you know?

SEAN — *(he drags on the joint)* Yeah.

AUDREY — Does that make sense?

SEAN — Yep.

AUDREY Okay, I shouldn't be doing this. I'm at work. I shouldn't be doing this.

SEAN Well, I'll tell you, this is very mellow and kind of relaxing.

AUDREY No. No, there is a nuclear meltdown twenty miles from here. *(starts laughing)* Everything could go off like a bomb, you know, which is not funny, but . . .

SEAN I know, I know, I know. You know, I saw this documentary on, uh, Hiroshima, and I remember that when the Japanese took all this footage after the bomb, they filmed all this stuff. People walkin' around half-burnt. And, like, wow, you know, it was incredible footage, but, you know. And I'm thinkin', you know, who's got the stomach to, to, to . . . Who shot it, you know?

AUDREY You see footage of burning people and, and you think about who shot it? That's it? The world has come down to footage. Do you get that?

SEAN Well, it's not a big thing. I think you think about it too much. It's probably the pot.

Audrey and George are in the newsroom, standing at workstations. Audrey looks stoned.

AUDREY I get what you're doing.

GEORGE I smell pot. Have you been smoking a joint?

AUDREY No, no. This is, uh *(smells her shirt)*, yep, it's the shirt. Probably from, you know *(sways on the spot)*, a club. I was out last night, um, anyways. This whole thing with the wardrobe and the actresses and the . . . I know what you're doing.

GEORGE You do?

AUDREY Uh-huh. Life is theatre. And theatre of the absurd is a meltdown, twenty miles from the biggest population in the country. And what do you do? You turn it into real theatre. Yes?

GEORGE No.

Music starts. George walks away and goes into his office. Karen is sitting on the coach with a woman from Hair, who is holding a wig. They stand when George enters. George goes through his desk, looking for cigarettes.

KAREN The analysts are driving me insane. No one knows whether they're in or not, and apparently they're all pretty pissed off, because people keep referring to them as Greta Van Susteren and Roger Cossack.

George leaves his office. Karen and the Hair woman follow.

GEORGE Oh, well, they should be that good.

KAREN They're all threatening to walk unless we commit to someone.

GEORGE Who do you like?

KAREN I like the woman from the first pair, the guy from the second.

GEORGE Fine.

KAREN I thought you'd agree. She has grey hair. You didn't want that, so I brought Hair along for some help. It's the only wig they could find to cover the grey.

GEORGE *(turning to look at the wig)* Perfect.

They come around a corner and meet Susteren #1. She is holding a blouse. They walk together towards the atrium.

SUSTEREN #1 I have to say that I'm opposed to a wardrobe change just because you're afraid the audience may see that I don't shave under my arms and that may provoke some anti-feminist bias. The whole notion is totally absurd. I'm not even going to discuss it. But we're moments away from a major nuclear disaster, which could contaminate half of Southern Ontario, and I'm not going to fight it. Well, I'm not gonna wear the wig just because you've got some idiotic and regressive notion about women who are prematurely grey.

The music stops.

GEORGE Okay, fine. Pass on the wig. You'll be perfect without the wig. *(he starts to back away)*

You have to understand that in these horrific disasters, no matter how much mass death there is, no matter how many bodies, there's still a very strong sexual relationship between the TV personality and the audience. Just stay focused.

Jim walks around the corner and into George. They walk. The music starts.

JIM Hi, okay. So, I decided to go with my tie down loose and a Styrofoam cup instead of a mug. I've been thinking that a mug would end up looking too stagey or something. What do you think?

GEORGE I don't know.

JIM You know, I mean, I did the Cronenberg piece without it, but, uh, so there's, you know, there's no match problem. But who's to say that somebody didn't hand me a cup during the break?

GEORGE Right, right.

Jim stops and George heads off around the corner and into Jessica Noble. Her hair is up and she's in a suit, holding a newspaper.

JESSICA There you are! I've been looking all over for you. Nobody will tell me what's going on. Do I have the *China Syndrome* part? I haven't even seen a script.

GEORGE Let me see your paper. Let me see it. Can you read that?

The music stops.

JESSICA Read?

GEORGE Gimme that.

JESSICA As a reporter or as an anchor? Is she a bitch, is she simpatico?

GEORGE Just be real. Be yourself.

JESSICA *(reading in a very theatrical, overly dramatic way)* Virtually every brain function can be enhanced by simply taking a pill. Welcome to the brave new world of anti-depressants and a whole lot more. *(she looks at George)* Is that what you want?

GEORGE I can't decide, sorry. *(he walks to the elevators, and Jessica follows)*

JESSICA You're a pig. I won't be humiliated like this.

GEORGE I'm just having a cigarette outside. *(he pushes the "down" button)*

JESSICA I'm a professional actress. This is nothing to do with dramatizing the news. This is all about you!

George slips into the elevator and Jessica follows.

JESSICA You don't understand what I've done. I've done feature films, I've done TV series, I've done voice-overs, I've done children's programming, I've done telethons . . .

The music starts. George puts on his sunglasses and Jessica's voice begins to fade out.

JESSICA . . . I've done hand modelling, I've done talk shows . . .

George walks along the atrium walkway and into Mark and Dr. Burgess. Dr. Burgess is forty-five, with greying shoulder-length hair.

MARK Oh, George, George. This is Dr. Burgess. He just studied the recent safety assessment at Pickering. *(they stop walking, and Mark leans in close to whisper)* George, are we going to get this on for six o'clock?

GEORGE Yes.

MARK Are you all right?

GEORGE Yes.

MARK Listen, we want to pre-tape this guy, so you should talk to him first.

GEORGE *(looking at Dr. Burgess)* Fine. *(he sits down on a couch)*

MARK *(to Dr. Burgess)* Tell him.

DR. BURGESS All emergency planning scenarios assume that radioactivity can be held inside the containment structure for a period of several hours to several days following a serious accident, giving residents time to evacuate before venting. But only at Pickering do eight reactors all connect to the same vacuum building. During a 1990 test, two seals ruptured at about half the pressure they were designed to withstand. It was estimated that –

GEORGE This is great, this will be perfect television. You're fantastic. I only have one problem. Hair.

The music stops.

DR. BURGESS What about it?

GEORGE It's Michael Bolton is what it is. Your hair is Michael Bolton. The audience is not going to believe Michael Bolton, okay? I can't have hair like this on television.

DR. BURGESS *(to Mark)* This is ridiculous.

GEORGE Of course it's ridiculous. Television is ridiculous. Television is a fraud. It's all garbage, it's all crap. The audience are morons. They gotta believe *scientist.* If they think you're Michael Bolton, they're not gonna believe you.

Know what I need? Los Alamos, Silicon Valley. I need a ponytail. Give him a ponytail. *(the music starts)* Can you do a ponytail? Do the ponytail, we'll do the item. It's brilliant.

Mark and Dr. Burgess watch George leave. Fonda #1 is sitting in a chair. She rises when she sees George.

FONDA #1 Is there a script yet?

GEORGE *(passing by her)* Very soon, soon.

A maintenance worker approaches carrying a piece of electrical equipment from inside a complex computerized machine. He accosts George, speaking excitedly in Italian about the part. George turns to looks at him and shrugs. The maintenance worker continues to talk at George as he walks away. George turns the corner and comes upon Karen and Dr. Morris, a man wearing small round sunglasses, black shirt, jacket, scarf tied loosely around his neck, and a ponytail. They walk with George.

KAREN George, this is Dr. Morris. He's a nuclear physicist. He was just out at the plant. He says it looks even worse than he expected.

DR. MORRIS The loss of coolant was serious enough, but the fact that they can't locate the source of the leak at this stage already –

GEORGE Excuse me. Do me a favour with the ponytail. Can you lose that?

DR. MORRIS I don't understand. *Lose* the . . .

GEORGE Well, we're just a little heavy on ponytails on the show. It's just about audience perception, that's all. *(they all stop walking)* I mean, the audience are morons, and television is ridiculous, I must admit. But if they see two ponytails on the same show, they're gonna think we have some kind of bias.

KAREN The guy just said the plant could blow. People could die.

The music stops. There is no sound. George looks up and sees an attractive young woman in a summery floral shirtwaist dress walk by. She is barefoot, carrying school books and her sandals, and looks directly at George as she passes in slow motion.

Graham walks with George down the corridor towards the elevators. Graham is holding a cigarette.

GRAHAM I'm up to my tits in actresses who think they're playing Jane Fonda in *The China Syndrome*. You've got two different graphic openings, and you don't know which to use. And I've got a bunch of post-production union people freaked out because they're about to die and you're treating them like shit. And all this when we've got a fall launch reception downstairs. *(they stop at the elevators)*

I want this story on the air at six o'clock, and I don't want any more of your bullshit.

The elevator doors open and George goes in, leaving Graham standing there. In the elevator, George puts his sunglasses on. It's very dark. In the shadows there is a Catholic archbishop, his sallow, dark-suited aide, and a CBC executive.

AIDE *(to the CBC executive)* The archbishop appreciates your allowing him to screen the sequel to "The Boys of St. Vincent" and admired the balanced approach your network took this time to a very sensitive and complex Church issue.

CBC EXEC Well, every little boy isn't a saint.

George is now in a limo, sitting next to the archbishop. George is contrite. The archbishop sips tea from fine china.

GEORGE There's a real chance of a huge nuclear accident that could take place within the next hour. It could virtually contaminate the entire city. The death toll would be immeasurable. Only a handful of people in our news department know about this. I'm the news director. I can't seem to make any decisions. People have said I'm in denial. I feel paralysed.

ARCHBISHOP It's death. You're finally facing it without preparation. Without faith, one can't face death on this scale. You have a grave responsibility. You must first have faith; only then can you take this monstrous event, and your role in it, seriously. Would you like some tea?

George looks to the seat across from them. A beautiful model in a French maid's outfit holds a silver teapot and smiles.

TO BE CONTINUED . . .

EPISODE 12

"Meltdown," Part 3

First Aired: March 24, 1997

George is trapped in a car that is filling with smoke. Wagner's "The Ride of the Valkyries" begins to play. He is banging on the window. A man in another car is watching. Gillian, also in a car, is with a man who is stroking her arm. An old man in a car beside them watches.

A wide shot shows people at the fall launch event in the atrium. The camera trucks by a number of people: a woman smoking; a woman holding a glass of wine, who nods; a black man in sunglasses looking around and taking a drink from his wineglass; two women chatting together and holding brochures that read "TV That's Proud To Be Canadian," who nod to the camera; the conductor, waving his baton to the orchestra; a woman putting a cigarette to her mouth while passing a blonde woman, who takes a sip of wine.

A line, two people wide, moves slowly and methodically towards the wine bar. Waiters, in unison, hand glasses of white wine to each wave of people as they approach the bar.

George, waiting in line, moves into frame, smoking. The music changes to Rossini's "The Barber of Seville." He's looking around, and pulls down his sunglasses to see the attractive young woman from the previous episode. The music stops, no sound. She is in the same summery floral shirtwaist dress, barefoot, carrying school books and her sandals. She walks in slow motion and looks directly at George as she passes. He smiles. The music resumes.

George is with a woman producer. He's slightly distracted as he listens.

PRODUCER #1 The Saskatchewan farmer, the mercy killing, it's a wonderful made-for-TV movie. I mean, it's that wonderful paradox of tragedy and humanity, giving your life to take another. I love the concept.

GEORGE The guy that kills his disabled daughter.

George's eye is caught by a tall, attractive woman in the crowd, who is looking at him.

PRODUCER #1 Yeah, yeah. It's a terrific story. We love the script. Uh, I mean, the guy got ten years for his first trial, but we're waiting for the appeal before we do the rewrite. It's a perfect concept.

GEORGE Oh, it's fantastic.

PRODUCER #1 Great.

George walks away.

The music changes to "Cha Cha Charlie," by Young. George is now with another woman producer in a different area of the party. He is sitting at a table, making a pyramid with the fall launch brochures. She is standing in front of him.

PRODUCER #2 How many black men have been shot by Toronto cops? This is a fantastic story. We were going to develop the script with Dany Laferrière, the black writer from Montreal, the guy who wrote *How To Make Love To A Negro*, but we couldn't get him. *(she sits at the table)* So we're looking at the writer who did "The Million Dollar Babies," about the Dionne quintuplets, or a Regina kid living in L.A. who's writing on "Home Improvement" but might want to do something important.

GEORGE I think the Regina kid's a terrific idea, because the farmer's from Saskatchewan, right?

PRODUCER #2 What farmer?

GEORGE The mercy killing. The one that kills his daughter.

PRODUCER #2 This is cops killing blacks.

GEORGE Oh, I'm sorry. You're right. That's a great idea, really. And I think it's long overdue.

His pyramid falls.

The music changes to "Lucky Mambo," by Delaney. Graham walks up to George and crouches down beside him.

GRAHAM What the hell are you doing down here with that nuclear plant about to blow?

GEORGE Don't worry. The story's under control.

GRAHAM There are some newspaper people behind us who want to talk to you. They're Europeans on a tour of North American news agencies. I don't want the nuclear incident mentioned until we know exactly what we have going on out there. I just hope you're getting the story.

Graham leaves.

The music changes to "Surprise Cha Cha Cha," by Gould. A French journalist is now seated with George.

JOURNALIST *(with an accent)* Do you think the monstrous horrors we see on TV news serve a basic need of the audience to experience human suffering from a safe distance?

GEORGE Perhaps.

JOURNALIST And, and do you think that the producers are as, um, the link in the chain between horror and viewer, also responsible for the crimes? That on one

	level the crime is committed for the audience, and as a guilty party the producers will some day be punished?
GEORGE	Punished by whom?
JOURNALIST	By God.
GEORGE	Oh, I don't believe in the existence of God.
JOURNALIST	What you believe has nothing to do with his existence. Only self-centred fools answer philosophical questions in terms of themselves.

A German journalist now sits with George.

GERMAN	*(with a heavy accent)* Can you image a story so horrible that you could not have the stomach to broadcast it?
GEORGE	Goldie Hawn expanding her Muskoka cottage.

German journalist looks at George, not understanding.

French journalist again.

JOURNALIST	*(speaks French, subtitles are shown)* Does the awareness of your own mortality influence how you cover your stories?
GEORGE	I'm sorry, I don't speak French.

The music changes to "The Blue Danube," by Johann Strauss. George is now seated at a table beside the tall woman he saw pass by earlier. She is seated with her mother, Suzanne, who is looking off.

TALL WOMAN	I work in film archives.
GEORGE	Oh, yes?

TALL WOMAN — But I think you know my mother. You had an affair with her when you were younger? Suzanne Davis.

GEORGE — The Suzanne Davis who claimed to be the Suzanne from the Leonard Cohen song? "Suzanne takes you down to a place by the river . . ." *(she turns to George)*

Oh, my God.

SUZANNE — Hi, George.

GEORGE — Oh, my God. It's you. *(turns to the tall woman)* You're her daughter.

SUZANNE — This is my perfect daughter.

GEORGE — Do you remember that apartment on The Esplanade, that big place?

SUZANNE — Yes, I do, that's right.

GEORGE — We stayed in the bedroom for three straight days, ordered in pizza, smoked dope, and had sex.

SUZANNE — No, we did not. *(she points at her daughter)*

GEORGE — The police raided the place because they thought that we were harbouring FLQ terrorists.

SUZANNE — That's right.

GEORGE — What are you doing now?

SUZANNE — I work for *TV Guide.*

GEORGE — Really?

SUZANNE — Yeah, yeah. I just went to L.A. for them. Uh, the four major networks have about thirty-nine new half-hour comedies for the next season. And they're really, really smart, and they're really funny, and . . .

GEORGE — I have to run.

SUZANNE — Okay.

His eyes shift from Suzanne to her daughter. He leaves.

The music changes to the minuet from Luigi Boccherini's String Quintet in E Major. George spots an old friend, Shaffik Harishi, at the wine bar. He walks towards him.

GEORGE Shaffik, Shaffik! *(they shake hands)*

SHAFFIK George, hey, you're still in the news game I see.

GEORGE Ah, it's a living. What are you doing here? I thought you quit.

SHAFFIK I did, I did. I'm only here because my second wife's family is connected to this huge telephone company. They might be carrying all public broadcasting when fibre-optic cable comes in. There she is. *(he points to a beautiful blonde of twenty-nine who is chatting with two men)*

Isn't she gorgeous? She was my assistant on that Mount Everest documentary two years ago. We had an affair in Nepal. I know, I know, she's twenty-five years younger than me, but something clicked. She is heir to about fifty million dollars and has multiple orgasms.

When we first met, I said, You could be a film star. And she said she can't act, and I said, Well, you don't have to act. All you have to do is play your natural supercilious self, and she said, That doesn't sound too hard, whatever supercilious means. "Whatever supercilious means!" You know what went through my head, She's gorgeous, she's rich, *and* she's not too bright. I hit gold. Is that a terrible impulse? I was being honest with myself. I find sex with stupid woman fantastic. I'm a pig, but I'm a happy pig. *(George smiles)* I'm bragging, but I haven't felt this good in years.

You know, her family owns this massive farm north of the city with horses and a private lake where we go and spend every weekend. She's also inherited this Paris apartment from an ancient aunt.

Ah, I left my wife and kids for her. Do you think I was wrong? I mean, I'm not getting any younger. Should I feel guilty? You only live once. I mean, this is the age of the massive heart attack.

I know, I know, it's all too scary to think about. I mean, not only is health a minefield, *(George puts a hand to his heart)* but the whole layer of civility seems to be getting as thin as the ozone. The other day, we were driving back from the farm and this guy cuts us off on Highway 403. So I leaned on the horn and he gives me the finger and screams, "Die, fucker!" You know what I did? I had the licence plates on my car changed immediately, and I had all records of the old plate wiped off the computer. Am I crazy? I don't know. I think there's something going wrong with this world. That's why I love the security of her family horse farm and Paris . . . Oh, it's so fucking civilized. I mean, the whole idea behind Paris is civility. In '68, when the workers and students rioted, it was for an idea that was basically humanizing.

George's Paris dream sequence: The music changes to original "French Café Music," by Sid Robinovitch. George is seated at a Paris outdoor café. He is smoking and reading the Herald Tribune. *A waiter places a small tumbler of Pernod and water on his table. George notices a gorgeous blonde woman at a table nearby having an animated conversation with a man whose back is to George. George folds his paper, takes off his sunglasses, and watches them. The man has scraggly salt-and-pepper grey hair, wears a tweed coat, scarf, and horn-rimmed glasses. He is about sixty-four. The woman looks at George, then rises and crosses to him. The music stops.*

WOMAN *(speaks in French, English subtitles)* You were looking at me?

GEORGE *(getting up)* I'm sorry, I thought I recognized the man you were with.

WOMAN That's Jean-Luc Godard.

GEORGE Oh, Paris is perfect.

The woman moves close to George and kisses him hard on the mouth. She then whispers in his ear.

WOMAN Human history is the struggle between culture and fascism, between humanity and bestiality.

She leaves. "French Café Music" begins. George notices Godard being punched to the ground and kicked by three skinheads.

Back to Shaffik and the fall launch party in the atrium.

SHAFFIK Now all we have are thugs. Thugs in government, thugs on the street. Without thugs, there can be no fascism. I remember reading that somewhere when I used to give a fuck about this world.

She has these orgasms, they don't stop. I can't walk around feeling guilty when the whole world's about to blow up. *(pats George on back)* Good seeing you again, George. Hey, I didn't let you get a word in . . .

GEORGE	Don't worry about it. *(they shake hands)* You're looking very good, Shaffik, very good.
SHAFFIK	Who knows what can happen to us?

Shaffik leaves, and George puts his hand to his chest. The music stops.

George, Karen, and Dr. Naylor meet in the hallway.

KAREN	This is Dr. Naylor. This is George, our news director.

They walk. "The Barber of Seville" starts. The lights flicker off and on.

DR. NAYLOR	Ah, when I worked for Nuclear Energy in November of 1990 . . .
GEORGE	*(pointing up at the ceiling)* Uh, okay.
DR. NAYLOR	. . . all moderator-room pumps were found seized at Pickering Unit Four. This situation effectively disabled the emergency core cooling system for that reactor. For the previous eleven months . . .

They are interrupted by Fonda #1 and her agent, who rise quickly from a couch.

AGENT	George, we've been waiting for you. Carol has to be back on set on the Van Damme film. She has no idea what you want her to do.
GEORGE	Uh, the Fonda character. The anchorwoman.
FONDA #1	You keep saying that, but there's no script.
AGENT	When does she get a script?
GEORGE	Very soon.

George hurries off with Dr. Naylor and Karen. Naylor continues, but George is preoccupied.

DR. NAYLOR Had an accident occurred in that time, the pumps would not have performed their function of recycling water to the ECCS to prevent the fuel from melting.

KAREN The China Syndrome.

GEORGE The China Syndrome?

DR. NAYLOR Uh, potentially.

GEORGE *(stops walking)* Do me a favour. Just make sure to use the expression "The China Syndrome" on the air.

DR. NAYLOR Oh, we're not there yet. And I don't think in all fairness we should use it now.

GEORGE *(to Karen)* Get him a copy of the picture, would you?

The music stops. George spots a tall, middle-aged woman, Heather Campbell, passing. He goes after her.

GEORGE Excuse me, Heather Campbell?

She turns and smiles at him, but continues walking.

HEATHER Hello, George.

GEORGE You still recognize me after, what, fifteen years?

The lights go out.

GEORGE Oh, that's a power failure.

HEATHER Yes, it's been going on for an hour.

GEORGE You know, I meant to call.

HEATHER Um, George. You see me here all the time. *(She stops walking)* You just turn away and deny I exist. Is it because I remind you of how old you are?

GEORGE No, no. Not at all. I, I . . .

HEATHER You know, it was only for the sex.

"The Barber of Seville" starts again.

HEATHER But mostly to satisfy you. But that's okay.

GEORGE *(pauses)* I just meant . . . to say hello.

HEATHER Oh, I'm sure you feel some guilt about never calling me again. *(George takes a seat on a box in the hallway)* Personal relations are like house plants to men like you. First you enjoy them, and then very quickly watering becomes a chore. And every time you pass one, there's a slight twinge of guilt at how much the plant has wilted, but the denial gets you past the guilt. But now what is it? You look tired. Defeated.

GEORGE I've been working hard.

HEATHER Is it the fear of your own mortality? Weakness and self-obsessiveness are a walk in the park compared to mortality. They're the easy little demons. Cute little cocktail-party demons. But mortality: mortality is like a psycho-nazi skinhead gang at your heels, isn't it? You have the mortality panic in your eyes.

George smiles. She leaves. The music stops, and the lights come back on.

George and the tall woman are in the newsroom boardroom. The lights are out. The only illumination is the glow from the TV monitor, where the VCR plays one nuclear explosion after the other. They are leaning on the table in front of the monitor, smoking cigarettes. Quiet, soft music plays.

GEORGE See, this footage is all wrong. It's wrong.

TALL WOMAN This is what you asked for.

GEORGE No, I know, I know. But do you know what, uh, would work better than this? Footage of the burn victims from Hiroshima. Have you ever seen it?

TALL WOMAN Uh-huh.

GEORGE You see, this story isn't about the marvels of science. This story's about death. This story's about hell, about the inferno. This story's about burning human flesh. Can I ask you a question?

TALL WOMAN Uh-huh.

GEORGE Is there some kind of a sexual attraction . . . here?

TALL WOMAN *(smiles)* Yes.

GEORGE No, I know there's an age difference, but the fact that I had an affair with your mother a number of years ago, and this attraction, uh, I find that kind of interesting. Do you think that's crazy and horrible?

TALL WOMAN Slightly perverse, but not crazy and horrible.

GEORGE Really?

The music stops and the phone rings.

GEORGE Oh, God.
(picks up the phone) Yeah?

AUDREY Your ex-wife is downstairs.

GEORGE *(groans)* Oh, no.

Outside the building, George's ex-wife – tall, elegant, wearing dark angular horn-rimmed sunglasses, a big white soft sweater under a leather coat – puffs on a cigarette. George smokes too as they pace. The wind is strong.

EX-WIFE	I was shopping nearby, and thought I'd say hello. You look tired.
GEORGE	Well, I'm working on a big story.
EX-WIFE	Is it interesting?
GEORGE	Well, after a while they're all about the same thing.
EX-WIFE	Death?
GEORGE	You're still happy.
EX-WIFE	Of course.
GEORGE	You know, this place where you and your new husband go, up North Carolina? I read the other day that microbes wash up on the beach and you can breath them in and they'll kill you faster than botulism. But you're still happy.
EX-WIFE	Are you still so obsessed with your own unhappiness? That's why our marriage broke up. You had to find some terror lurking in every corner of your existence. It was just a matter of time before you found it in me. Why did you marry me in the first place?
GEORGE	You tanned beautifully.
EX-WIFE	And now tanning kills us, right?
GEORGE	That's it. That's the change. Tanning kills us now.
EX-WIFE	I watch your news show, and I'm always amazed at how much you lie.
GEORGE	Well, you have to have access. You have to play the game or they'll cut you off.
EX-WIFE	When we were young, you felt the truth would set people free and to tell it would make you happy. You always used to quote some line from an art

movie: "The truth will bury everything that is death within us."

The wind picks up, forcing her to speak up to be heard.

GEORGE I'm sorry, I can't hear you. The wind.

EX-WIFE "The truth will bury everything that is dead within us."

GEORGE I'm sorry. *(he starts to back away and points behind her)*

EX-WIFE "The truth will bury everything that is dead within us." What movie is that from?

The camera pans, following the ex-wife's gaze to the huge fan and the film crew behind her. Daniel Murphy, the first assistant director, moves up and yells over the wind.

DAN Listen, he hasn't got time for this now. He's got a big story to get out about a nuclear meltdown in Pickering. We're less than ten minutes to air, and he hasn't even dealt with his mother yet.

Dream sequence in a white hospital room: George sits at his mother's bedside. Sheer curtains surround the bed, and on the other side is a bright light. In the background, an organ plays "Kiss Me Again," by Herbert.

GEORGE You're looking good today.

MOTHER I hate it here. Why am I here?

GEORGE We thought it was best for you. Everyone agreed.

She is elegant, old, beautiful. She lies in white and is

connected to a life-support system. The camera moves in and out, as in Fellini's 8 1/2.

MOTHER The food here is horrible. You used to help me cook. I always said you had the most fantastic palate. You could detect the subtlest taste in anything that I made. But now I'm hooked up to this intravenous, and all the food they bring me is cold and mashed.

GEORGE It's what's best for you.

MOTHER You come here in your car, thinking, "Maybe she's already dead. Maybe it's all over."

GEORGE Oh, I don't want to have this conversation every time I come here, okay? I don't want to hear this any more.

MOTHER Who makes the decision?

GEORGE What decision? What are you talking about?

MOTHER To pull the plug? It must be you. I hate it that you should have that hanging over you.

"Kiss Me Again" fades into "The Barber of Seville."

GEORGE That's not even on my mind.

George's eyes shift down and sees his leg entangled in the cord for the life-support system. He tugs it to extricate himself. The plug wiggles in the wall socket.

MOTHER I always wanted you to be happy. It's all I lived for. Now this death of mine that won't happen. *(George struggles with the cord)* I torment you by staying alive, when all I lived for was to make you happy.

A nurse enters and places a tray of cold, mashed, colourless stuff next to the bed. A doctor enters.

DOCTOR Time for your mother's meal.

(whispering to George) She's actually doing remarkably well, considering her condition. She knows you want her to die. She's very sharp. She's just bothered by one thing, your incessant unhappiness. So maybe the next time you come by, you could be a little more *(puts his hand on George's shoulder)* upbeat.

The doctor leaves. George looks at his mother. The music stops.

"Carlotta's Gallop," by Nino Rota, starts to play. Dr. Naylor, wind blowing in his face, is being interviewed outside the building. There are long cream-coloured sheers on scaffolding behind Dr. Naylor, blowing in the wind.

DR. NAYLOR *(talking to a camera)* In November 1990, all moderator-room pumps were found seized in Pickering Unit Four. *(George comes out of the building, trying to light a cigarette in the wind)* The pumps were unable to perform their function of recirculating the water to prevent the fuel from melting.

FONDA #1 There he is!

A mob of reporters surges towards George. They are all the women in George's life.

DR. NAYLOR . . . potentially a China Syndrome.

The women walk fast behind Dr. Naylor. Mark and Graham run up to George, taking one arm each. George balks, he doesn't want to go. Mark and Graham drag him to the women.

GRAHAM We're 8 1/2 minutes from air time.

MARK We want to do the interviews with the experts now.

GRAHAM You've got to do this now.

The women run up to George, stick microphones in his face, and fire questions. The women are all really, really angry at him.

JOURNALIST We've put up with your indecision for long enough. We want some answers!

GRAHAM Answer them, say something.

GEORGE We're going to air with the nuclear story in a matter of minutes.

JESSICA Not that story. That's not the real story. The real story is how you treat women.

EX-WIFE Your relationships with woman have only been about you, right?

George, with Mark and Graham, split through the crowd. They trail after them.

MARK I'll tell you how to get out of this. Kill yourself now.

Graham jumps up on an abutment. George sits down on it and lights a cigarette.

GRAHAM He's willing to answer all your questions now.

PRODUCER #2 How about you stop treating women like objects?

GEORGE — No comment.

SUZANNE — Did you ever once tell me that you loved me in the nine months we were together?

GEORGE — No comment.

HEATHER — You couldn't love us because none of us were perfect, am I right?

GEORGE — No.

GRAHAM — Your questions are hostile. They have nothing to do with the story.

EX-WIFE — You could never love a woman who was her own person. A fully defined human being. Yes or no?

GEORGE — Is there something wrong with that?

FONDA #1 — You haven't a clue what you want in a woman, and we're supposed to wait around at your beck and call till you figure it out?

PRODUCER #1 — He's afraid to admit that he can't love anything because he's dead inside, am I correct?

GEORGE — No.

MOTHER — He's not dead. Someone who agonizes the way he agonizes over me is not dead inside.

SUZANNE — He agonizes because you remind him of his mortality.

GEORGE — I want her to be young again. Is that so terrible?

EX-WIFE — *You* want to be young again. That's what you really mean.

GEORGE — I have a show to do.

George stands up and leaves. The music stops.

The huge door of Studio 40 opens, throwing a shaft of blazing light across the floor. The group from the last scene and two network executives enter with Graham. Some smoke cigarettes and are talking. George leads the pack as each person walks in and takes a seat in the bleachers.

Graham walks in with two executives.

GRAHAM It's a big story. George is an old pro. He knows what he's doing. I trust his instincts. He, he's never failed us when it's come to the numbers.

Heather and George's ex-wife walk in.

HEATHER But he's always self-obsessed. You know, I think this . . . all of us here together, he's out of control.

EX-WIFE He's lost his romantic vision and is left only with the truth. He can't deal with that, so he pulls us up out of his imagination, looking for answers.

Jessica, Fonda #1, and the agent walk in.

JESSICA He said all I had to do was play myself, I'd be perfect.

FONDA #1 He said the same thing to me.

AGENT He hasn't got a clue what he's doing. I can't believe I got you into this.

Mark, Audrey, and Karen walk in.

AUDREY Does he really have the story?

MARK I have no idea.

KAREN What are we doing here? I just talked to the guy at the plant, who said the pressure in the containment is alarmingly higher than what the chamber was designed to hold.

Susteren #1 and Susteren #2 walk in.

SUSTEREN #1 I feel ridiculous and manipulated.

SUSTEREN #2 Uh, look. I have done a number of TV shows on the environment, and I have never been treated like such a piece of meat.

Cossack #1 and Cossack #2 walk in.

COSSACK #1 I've got clients waiting for me in my office right now. I've killed the whole goddamn day here, for what?

COSSACK #2 I think they pay about a hundred and twenty-five dollars if you're on air. It's a goddamn joke.

The studio door closes.

GRAHAM *(whispering to George, who's seated in front of her, the two executives behind her)* This is the biggest story of your life. We're two minutes away from air time. I had the brass on my ass and they want to see something.

GEORGE I said don't worry.

GRAHAM *(sits back and talks back to executives)* He's got it all under control. I told you he'd come through for us. He's a genius.

(leaning forward to George and whispering again) This'd better be good or I'll have you killed.

George waves a finger in the air for the show to begin. A spotlight crashes on, exposing only the extreme close-up of a gaunt, smiling man in white make-up, a top hat, and a wing-collar tuxedo. It's Jim.

SMILING MAN (JIM) Welcome! We're here on this big stage because this is a big story. But why do they call news "stories"?

After man takes care of his basic animal needs, he indulges in a behaviour not imposed by nature but invented by him. Emerging as it does from his imagination, can we not then call all invented human life – this building, literature, freeway, wars – a fiction? If so, then television news must be theatre, and this nuclear accident just one more scene in the human drama.

That said, let the show begin!

Jim extends his arm. A glaring spotlight crashes on, revealing three singers in skintight, floor-length, sequinned gowns. They start to sing "Soldier Boy," by The Shirelles, to the stunned faces of the watching crowd.

George is smiling. Images of nuclear explosion and other footage are seen. George turns in his seat to Graham, smiling and hoping for a positive reaction. Nothing. He turns back. We see the image of the mysterious girl in the floral sundress, then the screen goes to black.

THE END

EPISODE 13

"Campaign"

First Aired: March 31, 1997

The following documentary was shot shortly after the collapse of public broadcasting.

George, Mark, and Jeremy are seated at a table in "Campaign Headquarters." George is on the speakerphone, while Mark and Jeremy listen.

VOICE	So, why did you leave news for politics?
GEORGE	You know, there's this thing that happens. When you work in the news and you get a story of three hundred and fifty people killed in a train crash in India, you know, it's just another story, right?
MARK/JEREMY	Right. Yeah.
GEORGE	Because that's the big lead. You get the film, you get the bodies. You know, you get excited by that.
JEREMY	Right.
GEORGE	And after a while, you just become so, you know, completely cynical and hardened, you know? But I think in politics, uh, the angle you take on a story like that would be, Hey, we, can do something about that. Um, and we build a better train.
MARK	Build a better train.
GEORGE	And we, and we, uh, sell, sell India a better train. And, uh, you're not gonna have three hundred and fifty people killed, maybe. You know, and that's what we can do in politics.

Audrey is on the phone at a desk in the campaign office.

AUDREY Okay, so you would like to know if Jim Walcott is in favour of eliminating child poverty in Canada. I'll ask him for you. *(puts the caller on hold)*

(Jim approaches her table) Jim, it's the guy from the *Star*. Are you in favour of eliminating child poverty in Canada?

JIM Child poverty in Canada? This is a provincial election.

AUDREY Is that a yes or a no?

JIM Jeremy, Jeremy.

Jeremy is at a desk on the phone. He looks up at Jim.

JIM Just a sec. Guy from the *Toronto Star* wants to know if I'm in favour of eliminating child poverty in Canada.

JEREMY It's a provincial election.

JIM Yeah, that's what I said.

Jim gets out of a campaign van on a street and spots only a white-haired couple on the sidewalk. He walks directly to them and hands them a pamphlet.

JIM Hi, how are you? I'm Jim Walcott. I'm running for the Liberal party in this district, and I hope I can count on your support.

MAN We're from Detroit, up for a week of gambling in Orillia.

JIM Oh, you're Americans. I'm sorry. Well, I hope if you ever decide to take up residence here, I'll have your support.

WOMAN We love Canada.

JIM We love having you.

MAN We don't have the coloured problem here.

JIM — No, but you don't get our horrible winters, huh?

MAN — That's true.

JIM — Have a good one.

MAN — Thank you. *(they leave)*

JIM — Uh, the pamphlet?

Aw, keep 'em. They're yours. Souvenirs.

George, Jim, Mark, and Jeremy sit in the back of the campaign van and are being driven somewhere.

DRIVER — Ah, politicians today. You know the best politician this country ever saw? Pierre Trudeau, man. Even if you didn't agree with him, at least he did something. He had the balls to do something. Conviction. They don't, uh, they don't do that any more. Maggie Trudeau screwed him up, huh? She was a fruitloop. Hippy-dippy. You know, that ruined everything.

Mark, George, Jim, and Jeremy exchange looks.

DRIVER — Man, politicians nowadays, eh? Every single one of them, just an idiot. Morons.

Jim and George are standing outside the campaign van.

JIM — Can we get another driver?

GEORGE — It's his van. He's cheap, okay?

JIM — The guy thinks I'm an idiot, come on.

GEORGE — He's one guy who thinks you're an idiot. When the majority of the voting public starts thinking you're an idiot, then we'll worry. Trust me on this.

Driver walks up and hands them coffee.

GEORGE Coffee is here. Coffee, coffee, coffee.

They are all back in the campaign van. The driver keeps talking. Jim tries to ignore him as he, George, Jeremy, and Mark eat take-out from McDonalds.

DRIVER You just look at 'em now, eh? Politicians now. Just garbage. Douche-bags.

JEREMY Oh, he's not talking about you when he says "douche-bags." Don't worry, you're gonna be the next premier of the province.

JIM Oh, shit. Look at this. I get the Hamburgler again. Can you believe they do that? I've got, like, four of these. What'd you guys get?

GEORGE I didn't get the Happy Meal.

MARK Yeah, I didn't get the Happy Meal.

JEREMY Oh, I got the Roger Rabbit roadster. This is a great toy.

JIM Let me see that. Oh, I don't see anything.

JEREMY You've gotta hold it up to a light source. You've got to point it towards the window.

JIM Oh, yeah. That's great.

George, Jim, Mark, and Jeremy have arrived at a Liberal fund-raising party at a home in Forest Hill, Toronto. They talk at the front door before entering.

GEORGE There's a lot of money here today. Don't discuss any complicated issues. Just say cut the deficit, create jobs.

JIM Cut the deficit, create jobs.

GEORGE Cut the deficit, create jobs.

JIM Cut the deficit, create jobs.

GEORGE Okay, good, good.

MARK Be yourself.

JEREMY Don't say a lot. Let your image talk for you.

George knocks on the door.

JIM How's the hair?

GEORGE *(together with Mark and Jeremy)* Good, good, good.

The hostess, Adelle Grossman, CEO *of Can-Wiz Educational Software, answers the door. She's in her forties, rich, energetic, urbane, and kisses Jim as he enters.*

HOSTESS Hello, hello, hello! Jim Walcott! Well, this is really such an honour for Jerry and I. Jerry, as you know, has done a tremendous amount of fund-raising for the federal Liberals.

JIM Oh, terrific.

HOSTESS Yes. Can I have your coat?

JIM Yeah. *(he hands her his coat)*

HOSTESS Oh, no, no, no. Roselda!

A photographer takes their picture. They all walk about and mingle.

MARK Are you hungry?

JEREMY Oh, yeah. Let's get something to eat.

JIM Well, I really appreciate you contributing your house like this.

HOSTESS Oh, don't be silly. At Christmas we had a thing for the mother of Shidane Arone, you know the Somali boy who was killed by the Canadian Armed Forces in Somalia. *(she smiles and waves at someone)*

JIM	Oh, the, the, um, Somali Commission. I remember doing that story.
HOSTESS	Yeah, yeah. Well, we flew her over here, and it, uh, was the dead of winter. She didn't have a warm coat. So I gave her an old mink. Now, I won't wear fur any more. But I'm sure you can wear fur in Somalia. I mean, they don't have that Disney relationship to animals in Africa that we do over here.
JIM	Oh, no. I'm sure they use every part of the animal over there.
HOSTESS	Yeah.

Elsewhere the crowd, Mark talks with a man.

MAN	I was in New Delhi for this conference on child poverty. The statistics were horrible. Anyway, the guy in the room next to me is from Mozambique, an incredibly poor place, and I see on his sink Gillette clear gel antiperspirant.
MARK	That's the kind where you turn it and it comes up through the holes.
MAN	Right. Now, he's from Mozambique, so I phone up my broker and buy a thousand shares of Gillette at sixty-two and it closed today at seventy.
MARK	Don't you find a build-up with the clear gel?

Back to Jim and the hostess. They walk through the house and eat.

HOSTESS	Well, we built the sauna so that you can go directly to the pool without, uh, walking through the house.
JIM	Oh, that's great.

HOSTESS — But, more importantly, we have to win this election. There are too many people without jobs, and too many families living in shelters.

JIM — My gosh, this house is beautiful.

HOSTESS — Six thousand two hundred square feet, not including the, uh, the pool house. Jerry and I just love the concept of a news anchor running . . . *(noticing a waiter's empty tray as he passes between them)* slow down on the salmon!

I want you to meet someone with a lot of money, who's heart's in the right place. There he is!

Jim is drinking wine with a rich woman.

WOMAN #1 — Hutus killing Tutsis; Tutsis killing Hutus; and Serbs and Croats killing each other. Arnold and I used to travel everywhere. Think you can travel anywhere any more? Paris, maybe.

JIM — Um, apparently there's a travel advisory out there right now for Canadians in Mexico.

WOMAN #1 — Probably the Zapatistas.

JIM — Oh, right. That's the little, um, in the water, right? The organism?

WOMAN #1 — The revolutionary movement. *(she laughs)*

JIM — Right, right, right.

Mark and Jeremy are talking to the hostess.

MARK — Jim's a real thinking candidate. I've worked with him for the last four years, and I've gotten to know the real guy.

JEREMY — He's compassionate, he's highly intelligent, and he's focused on the really big issues that matter in this campaign.

Jim sits in a small lounge area and talks to four people sitting with him.

JIM — Well, you take a campaign sign and pound it into a lot and then take it out a couple of weeks later. It only takes, you know, a day or two for the grass roots, for the grass to grow back over the little hole. But, I mean, it's really no different than a divot on a golf course. But so often you'll see, uh, you'll play a golf course and you'll see all these divots hanging around. I mean, a guy will take a divot and put it back without pressing it down, you know?

Jim is now talking with a woman.

JIM — Yeah, I've always been pro-choice, but I've got to think about this one for a second. You're saying that the decision should always be between the woman, her doctor, and her dog?

WOMAN — Her God, not her dog.

JIM — Oh, oh, oh! Okay, I thought you said "dog."

WOMAN — We believe the decision should be left between the, uh, woman, her doctor, and her God. *(she leaves)*

JIM — Right. I thought "dog" was a little bit weird.

Jeremy, Mark, and George are talking with the rich woman.

MARK — The thing about politics in Canada right now is that they're so right-wing, you know? It's like the United States.

JEREMY — All the politicians screaming for capital punishment is pathetic.

GEORGE You're right, you know. We, uh, we believe that Jim is gonna bring politics here back to the moderate liberal centre.

WOMAN Well, personally, I think all sex offenders should be hung.

Mark, Jeremy, and George pause and exchange looks.

JEREMY *(together with Mark and George)* Yeah, yeah.

JEREMY That's what we were saying.

MARK Absolutely. Hang 'em.

George and Jim are now talking quietly on their own.

GEORGE Okay, she told me that you thought that she said when she was talking about abortion that the choice was between a woman, her doctor, and her dog. And that you were willing to think about this, to consider this?

JIM No, I thought she said "dog," not "God."

GEORGE I know you thought that. That's my point, okay? You're discussing abortion. And not quite sure what a person says –

WOMAN *(walking in between them)* Excuse me.

GEORGE Then you said "dog," when she said "God." It doesn't take a genius to figure out they said "God."

JIM No, she could have said "dog," she could have said "God." I don't know. I didn't hear her.

GEORGE Let me put it this way. Someone says to you that they believe in an all-knowing God. But you don't quite hear that. Are you gonna think, Oh, maybe they said, I believe in an all-knowing dog?!

JIM No, I thought she said "dog," that's all.

GEORGE I know, I know you thought that, okay? Someone's gonna have an abortion. What are they gonna do? Consult a dog?

JIM No.

GEORGE Stay away from those issues, all right? Just cut the deficit, create jobs. That's all you gotta say. Cut the deficit, create jobs.

JIM I know.

GEORGE Okay? That's it.

George is talking with the hostess in the kitchen while she arranges food on a tray.

GEORGE In news, um, every human tragedy is a story. And every idea is a commodity. And after a while you become incredibly cynical. You stop believing in everything. And, um, I guess I wanted to believe in something again. I hope that doesn't sound trashy.

HOSTESS No, no! I know exactly what you mean.

GEORGE And I hope this doesn't sound even more trite, but I think I believe in Jim Walcott.

HOSTESS Yeah, that cynicism, that everything's a commodity . . . You know, I had exactly the same feeling after our software company went public. There was just so much money that I personally made off the public offering on a children's educational undertaking. See, it started out as an act of love for children's books and ended up so hugely successful with offices here and in New York and in Vancouver. Uh, I came home from that first meeting, from the brokerage firm that underwrote us, five million dollars richer. But, something was missing, you know? I felt empty. So you know what I did? I went up to my daughter's room and took out an old copy of *Charlotte's Web*, and I curled up and I read it. Just for me. Know what I mean?

GEORGE — Five million?

HOSTESS — Yes. Stock has doubled since then.

The hostess is now walking towards the front door as the doorbell rings. She talks to people on the way there.

HOSTESS — There's still more salmon . . . Good, good . . . Hey, you! Where have you been? I miss you. Need to talk to you. *(she opens the door and doesn't know the woman standing there)*

HOSTESS — Oh, I'm sorry, this is a private party.

SQUEAKY — But I'm a supporter of Jim's campaign, and I'm pregnant with his baby.

HOSTESS — Thanks for your support. *(she closes the door on her)*

The hostess gives a toast to Jim.

HOSTESS — To Jim Walcott! And a Liberal victory!

JIM — Here, here.

ALL — *(raising their glasses)* Cheers!

JIM — Thank you.

HOSTESS — Cheers. *(she gives Jim a kiss on the cheek)*

George, Jim, Mark, and Jeremy are sitting around the campaign office.

JIM — Yesterday we were pro-choice, today we're pro-life, I mean . . .

MARK — We're just listening to our polls.

JIM — Well, yeah. But doesn't that change now damage our credibility?

JEREMY — Inflexibility damages our credibility.

MARK Look, our polls show that a slim majority of people are pro-choice, but only half of them actually vote. On the other hand, 95 per cent of the pro-lifers actually take the time to fill out a ballot.

JEREMY I don't remember talking about listening to people who care enough to vote. Hell, if that's a crime, lock me up.

JIM Yesterday you were all saying that pro-choice is a morally superior position.

GEORGE We've got the morally superior candidate.

MARK Exactly.

JEREMY Yeah, okay?

GEORGE Now, you can take all the moral issues in the world. You can take the Ten Commandments to the polls. But if you can't sell them Moses, "Thou shalt not kill" is no better than tits on a bull. Look, let's win this thing first, then we'll part the Red Sea.

JIM So, so when does life begin for us on this campaign?

MARK Um . . .

GEORGE Well, when does life begin? Well, you know, it begins at, uh, life at, uh . . .

JEREMY It depends on how badly you want to win.

GEORGE Exactly. It depends on how badly you want to win.

The point is, you've got to keep it simple. You start talking about first trimester, third trimester, rape, incest, you know what happens? The voters start to think. So, you keep it simple. If you can't define life in one word, you don't belong in a political campaign, okay? You've just gotta figure out what the word is.

They all look around and pause, then . . .

MARK I think we have to go back as far as insemination.

JEREMY Insemination.

GEORGE Insemination.

JIM When the sperm hits the egg.

GEORGE Absolutely.

MARK Shit, shit. The literature. The first mailing, Jim's pro-choice in it.

GEORGE Well, just cancel it.

MARK It's already gone out.

GEORGE *(walking up to Audrey, who's sitting at a desk)* Audrey, the truck with the literature. Where is it? Is it gone, is it here, where is it?

AUDREY They just picked it up. What's the problem?

GEORGE Come with me, come with me. *(she stands and follows George)*

The problem is, it has the literature with Jim as pro-choice, okay?

AUDREY I thought that he *was* pro-choice?

GEORGE He's gonna change, okay? From now on, if anyone asks, life begins at insemination.

They walk through the hallway to the back of the building, where Hugh McCaully, a campaign worker, is loading a van with boxes of pamphlets.

AUDREY Silly me. I thought life began with the viability of the foetus.

GEORGE Not if we want to win this election, it doesn't.

(to Hugh) Hey, hold on a sec. Whoa, whoa. Uh, this stuff can't go out. This stuff is all wrong.

HUGH What?

GEORGE Well, this is Jim pro-choice, right?

HUGH He *is* pro-choice.

GEORGE	No, there's been a change, okay? From now on, life begins at insemination, okay? I don't want a single truck that goes out of here pro-choice. Every truck from now on, life begins at insemination.
HUGH	Okay, this is the second truck. The first truck is already gone. It's pro-choice.
GEORGE	Oh, God. This is ridiculous, okay? Okay, from now on, life begins at insemination, all right? Tell the drivers.
HUGH	Yeah.

Jim is outside on various streets, handing out pamphlets to various people walking by.

JIM	Hi, Jim Walcott. Cutting the deficit, creating jobs. Hope we can count on your support in the upcoming election . . .
JIM	Hi, I'm Jim Walcott. I'm running in the upcoming election. I hope I can count on your support . . .
JIM	When you vote, when you go to vote, when you see this name, J-I-M W-A-L-C-O-T-T, that's me, yeah? So you go and you say, Jim Walcott, yes. Check. Maybe you remember me from the news. I did the six o'clock news? "Good evening, I'm Jim Walcott." You don't remember that? . . .

Jim and Jeremy are in the campaign office. Jeremy is seated behind a desk. Jim stands in front of him, holding a Jim Walcott lawn sign with his face on it. Jim has also placed on Jeremy's desk one of those plastic Jesus statues whose eyes follow you as you pass.

JIM	Yeah, you pass by the poster and I'm looking off in that direction, right? There. I'm only making eye contact if you're standing right in front of the poster.

JEREMY Right.

JIM But here, with Jesus . . . I got this in Little Italy when I was campaigning. A guy just gave it to me. His eyes seem to follow you as you pass by. See that? He keeps looking at you. Right?

JEREMY Right.

JIM So, I'm just wondering if we could get this on my poster so if you're standing over there, Jim Walcott is smiling at you. And if you're standing over *there*, Jim Walcott is still smiling at you. I'm making eye contact for that much longer. Right? I don't know what the process is that gets Christ's eyes to do that, but it can't be that hard to get on a poster. Jesus: eye contact. Jim Walcott: no eye contact. *(he demonstrates by passing the poster and Jesus statue in front of Jeremy)*

See the difference?

George, Mark, Jeremy, Jim, and Audrey are seated around a table. Audrey reads from news-wire copy.

AUDREY The Conservatives are calling Jim Walcott's flip-flop on abortion the most cynical, opportunistic manoeuvre they've ever seen in Ontario politics.

GEORGE *(grabs copy from Audrey)* Cynical opportunism, that's bullshit. Opportunistic? If that driver hadn't taken two more minutes and had a leak, okay, "where life begins" wouldn't have been an issue in this campaign. Really.

JIM Look, I've been thinking about this. I think that maybe what I should say is what I feel in my heart about abortion, period.

ALL No.

JEREMY That's a bad idea, Jim.

GEORGE	Remember in *Jesus Christ Superstar*? Remember that show? Remember that? Uh, there's a character in there . . . the woman . . . Mary, uh, and she was a hooker, and . . .
MARK	Mary Magdalene.
GEORGE	Mary Magdalene. She started as a hooker and then something happened. She saw Christ or the Resurrection or something like this.
MARK	Well, she became holy, right? She became holy.
GEORGE	Okay, Mary Magdalene can flip-flop; Jim Walcott can flip-flop.
JEREMY	Right.
GEORGE	Let's forget about the whole flip-flop thing.
JEREMY	Okay.
GEORGE	All right? So be it. That's it.
JEREMY	So it is written, so it shall be done.
GEORGE	I like that. Who said that? St. Paul?
JEREMY	No, that was Yul Brynner. *Ten Commandments.*
JIM	You know, Yul Brynner was brilliant in *The Magnificent Seven.*
JEREMY	Yeah, he was good in that.
GEORGE	Great movie. This is what's good about Jim. Say *The Ten Commandments*, you know, forget it, right? But, you know, bang, I love *The Magnificent Seven.* Yul Brynner, *The Magnificent Seven*, that's the kind of stuff he comes up with, right? So he says, I love the movie, I love the candidate. It's that kind of mainstream, middle-brow sort of association that you make. I think that's great.
JEREMY	Appeals to the common man.
GEORGE	Appeals to the common man. Got to tap into that. Tap into that.

Outside the campaign office, Jim is cornered by reporters as he makes his way to the campaign van.

JIM	*(to the reporters)* If Mary Magdalene flip-flopped when she saw the light, then fine. Jim Walcott flip-flopped on the issue of abortion. I also want to say that I loved Yul Brynner in *The Magnificent Seven.* Okay? Thanks. *(he gets into the van as the reporters fire questions)*

George and Jim are in the campaign office. Jim is eating soup with noodles at the "war room" table. George is standing.

GEORGE	Look, you just can't blurt out that you love Yul Brynner in *The Magnificent Seven*. It means nothing to anyone, okay? *(he takes a seat at the table)*
JIM	Wait a minute, wait a minute. You said that the Yul Brynner thing worked.
GEORGE	I did Yul Brynner as an example. I mean, it was about an idea. It was about populist thinking, that's all. Yul Brynner in *Magnificent Seven*, it doesn't mean anything to anyone, okay? You can't just stand up there and start talking about Yul Brynner in a campaign in 1997!
JIM	So, so what if I tied the Yul Brynner thing into the campaign somehow. Like, Yul Brynner's courageous fight against cancer inspired me in this election fight.
GEORGE	What do you mean, tie it in? I want you to think clearly about this, okay? We're out there talking to people about jobs, we're talking to people about welfare, and you're talking to them about Yul Brynner. He's not even a Canadian.

JIM	So, Raymond Burr, Ironside, and his struggle. People associate him with a wheelchair the whole time, so that's a struggle.
GEORGE	Nobody knows Raymond Burr in a wheelchair. I mean, nobody even remembers that show. I don't even . . . Perry Mason, he wasn't in a wheelchair.
JIM	Everybody remembers "Ironside."
GEORGE	You're gonna tie "Ironside" into this campaign?
JIM	Lorne Greene, I don't care, whoever.
GEORGE	Lorne Greene? You don't even know how he died. He could have fallen off a horse. He could have died instantly, all right? There may have been no struggle at all.
JIM	Christopher Reeve fell off a horse. Yes, still in a struggle.
GEORGE	He's not a Canadian.
JIM	Oh, what? He played Superman. So, um, who is the woman? Margot Kidder, Lois Lane.
GEORGE	You're gonna tie Margot Kidder into this?
JIM	Well, yeah. That's what you want, isn't it?
GEORGE	Forget about Margot Kidder and Christopher Reeve, forget about Raymond Burr. We're running Jim Walcott, okay? We're not running Yul Brynner, all right? *(he stands.)* Okay?
JIM	All right.
GEORGE	Okay, then we're going back out, right?
JIM	Yep.
GEORGE	Are you gonna wear that tie?
JIM	Yeah.
GEORGE	Don't eat soup with a tie then, okay? You get soup on the tie, we don't have a tie for today.
JIM	Well, here. I'll . . . *(tucks a napkin in his shirt collar like a bib)* All right?

GEORGE All right.

George, Mark, Jeremy, Jim, and the driver in the campaign van.

MARK And the pro-lifers are real important to us. We want them to know you're a serious pro-life candidate. Not knee-jerk. No bullshit. You're a guy who's thought about – long and hard – about the abortion issue and has come to a very strong religious and philosophical pro-life conclusion.

JIM Right, right.

MARK So life begins at insemination, okay?

JIM Yeah. I find it hard to say insemination in front of a crowd.

MARK Why?

JIM It's a weird word thing. Whenever I say insemination, I think masturbation. It's weird, it's weird, I don't know. It's the same number of syllables or something.

MARK Well, they're totally different things.

JIM I know, I know.

MARK So forget masturbation.

JIM Yeah.

MARK Life begins at insemination.

JIM Yeah, I just, I just think masturbation.

MARK Insemination, not masturbation.

JIM Insemination.

They make a stop at a pro-life protest at an abortion clinic. Jim hops out of the van and talks to picketers. One woman holds a sign that reads "Satan is pro-choice."

JIM Hi, how's it goin'? Little chilly out here, isn't it? I'm Jim Walcott. I'm a pro-life sympathizer, and I'm with you in your struggle. And I hope you support me in my campaign. I also want to say that I believe life begins at masturbation. Oh, shit, shit! *(he bangs his forehead with his fist.)*

Back in the campaign van.

GEORGE *(to Mark)* I blame you for this. You kept saying "masturbation" over and over and over again.

MARK All I said was that he's gotta get it out of his head.

JIM Look, why can't we make this simple. Why can't we just be pro-choice?

GEORGE Because you believe in the sanctity of human life, okay!? I thought we were straight on that.
(to Mark) I blame you for this.

MARK All I said was that he had to get masturbation out of his head.

JEREMY Well, there! You just said it again. You keep saying it, he's gonna keep thinkin' it.

MARK All right, insemination then.

JIM You know, you know what it is? It's the root word "semen" in insemination that's giving me all the trouble. That's all it is.

GEORGE Okay, then don't say insemination. Just say you're pro-life. You're pro-life, all right?

JIM Yeah, fine.

GEORGE Forget insemination. Forget semen. Forget masturbation. You're pro-life, okay?

JIM Yeah.

GEORGE Are we getting those donuts, there? Mike?

DRIVER Yeah.

GEORGE Okay, who wants what?

JEREMY Gimme, uh, gimme the ones, uh, two of the ones with the, uh, the yellow filling on the inside.

DRIVER Lemon donut.

JEREMY The lemon donut. The lemon-filled donut.

DRIVER Lemon-filled donut.

JEREMY That's the one.

GEORGE Yeah, I'll have the Hawaii, okay? Give me two of them. It's the one with the, um, with the sprinkles on top.

What are you having?

MARK Uh, I'll have a Boston semen, uh, cream.

JIM Well, you know, if, you know, if you're gonna make fun of this whole thing, I mean . . .

MARK No.

JIM All right, I'm not gonna say it again. It's just that root word. And it's out of my head, it's gone.

GEORGE All right.

They make a stop at another Toronto abortion clinic. There are a few people outside the clinic. A man sits in a chair with a cooler, coffee urn, and shoebox beside him. Several women stand around.

JIM Hi. How are you all? Little chilly out tonight, isn't it? Um, I'm Jim Walcott. I'm a pro-life sympathizer. I want to say that I'm with you in your struggle. And I hope you support me in my campaign.

(to the man in the chair) Hi. Is that, uh, is that a dead human foetus in that shoebox?

PROTESTOR No. Those are my other shoes.

JIM Well, if it was a dead foetus, I'd support you a hundred per cent, all right?

Keep warm guys. Bye-bye.

Jim does a phone-in spot at a radio talk show.

HOST — We're here with Liberal candidate Jim Walcott. The lines are open, go ahead.

The phone doesn't light up.

HOST — If you'd like to hear Jim Walcott's views, uh, give us a call. The lines are open, go ahead.

Again, the phone doesn't light up.

HOST — Um, find out what's on Jim Walcott's mind. This is the show to do it. Jim, um, is sitting here waiting to, to discuss, uh, what his views on, uh, on the political situation are today. Give us a call, go ahead caller.

Again, the phone doesn't light up. The man in the control booth shrugs.

George, Mark, Jeremy, Jim, and Audrey are in the campaign "war room."

GEORGE — You guys, you guys, we've got a problem on this campaign, okay?

JEREMY — Right.

GEORGE — You know what our problem is?

JEREMY — What?

GEORGE — We're losing. We're dead here, okay?

JEREMY — Okay.

GEORGE — If we don't come up with something, if we don't, you know . . . I think we got to find out what it is that we just . . . what, as a human being, what we love in this guy. Aside from his image, aside from the hair, and aside from, you know, the broadcast image, what we really love about this guy, the person, and we capitalize on that.

They all look around at each other. Audrey cracks her knuckles.

GEORGE *(to Audrey)* What?

AUDREY Sorry.

GEORGE What are you doing?

AUDREY I was cracking my knuckles.

GEORGE *(to Jim)* Can you think of anything that you've done in your life that has been of value.

JIM Yeah.

GEORGE Okay . . .

JIM You want it, you want it right now? I mean, can I, I'll get back to you on it.

GEORGE Yeah, okay. Good, good, think about that.

JIM I'm going away this weekend, but . . .

GEORGE Okay, I know, I know.

JIM So, not Monday, but Tuesday.

GEORGE Fine, okay.

Jim, Mark, Jeremy, and George are sitting in a booth at a coffee shop. Jeremy eats chicken wings.

JIM Look, maybe this whole campaign was a mistake.

MARK *(reading from a newspaper)* I'll tell you what. The Conservatives are killing us. They're eighteen points up.

GEORGE They've won it. The Conservative ideology, they've won everything, right? So we just end run 'em here. Okay, we win this thing, we go way beyond that. Like, we're crossing the finish line and they're still

	standing on the track, going, Hey, what happened to us, you know? We steal their platform.
MARK	Okay, how 'bout we, uh, we try to get government out of the health-care business.
GEORGE	Kill medicare, one hundred per cent. Okay, they'll be standing there, scratching their heads. Work fair, not welfare. I like that. Work fair, not welfare. Let's play that card. And stop pussyfooting around. Kill their kids. Kill their kids and adult jails, all right? And if they kill again, we kill them. Hang 'em. I think you can do that.
JIM	Kids kill; kill them.
GEORGE	Okay, what else?
MARK	We should just keep hitting "market economy." That's a big market.
GEORGE	Hit market economy. Hit 'em, hit 'em, hit 'em.
JEREMY	Create some jobs.
GEORGE	You're right, but not civil-service jobs. Not touchy-feely shit.
MARK	No, no, no.
GEORGE	Not counsellors counselling unwed mothers, you know. What we do is we create jobs so that unwed mothers will be out there producing goods and services, not babies.
MARK	I love that. *(Mark jots some notes)*
GEORGE	Produce goods and services, not babies, all right? We've got to carry a big stick or we're dead in this province, all right?
JEREMY	Big stick like Joe Don Baker in *Walking Tall.*
JIM	I could tie in Joe Don Baker instead of Yul Brynner.
GEORGE	*(together with Jeremy and Mark)* No, no, no. Don't do that. Don't do that.
GEORGE	Don't do that, please. Thank you.

Mark, Jeremy, George, Jim, and the driver are in the campaign van.

MARK *(looking at another party's pamphlet)* They've got Jim's marks here. His high-school marks, his junior-high marks. Fs and incompletes. They're using them in their campaign literature.

GEORGE Yeah, okay, listen. We'll stick to the real issues in this campaign, let them stoop to that kind of crap.

Their guy had an AIDS test, didn't he?

JEREMY Well, he was speaking to a high-school class and the issue of safe sex came up. And he said once he'd been tested for an insurance policy.

MARK I don't think that's an issue, though.

GEORGE Look, that's about lifestyle, right? And lifestyle goes to character, and character's going to be an issue in this campaign. Now, what lifestyle was this guy leading when he felt he had to be tested for AIDS?

MARK Jesus, Jim got an F in spelling.

GEORGE Uh, Jim Walcott might not know how to spell AIDS, but Jim Walcott, you know, doesn't have to spell AIDS. I like that. Jim Walcott doesn't have to spell AIDS. I like that. Use that.

JIM *(dozing off, gets woken by a passing car sounding its horn)* Are we there yet?

GEORGE What else?

JEREMY Religion, church?

MARK Well, he doesn't go to church.

GEORGE Well, we'll get him a church, all right?

JIM *(getting in on conversation)* Wait a minute, what kind of church?

GEORGE Well, I don't know. You know, nothing too churchy, nothing too religious.

MARK Well, we're pretty weak on family. Jim, Jim's been separated for six years.

GEORGE	Look, two adults made a choice and handled it with sensitivity for each other's feelings and needs. We can make that work for us. You respect each other, we can sell that, right Jim?
JIM	That bitch still costs me ten grand a year.
JEREMY	What if we give her fifteen, will she get back together with you?
JIM	Uh, she might.
GEORGE	Done. Okay, get him an AIDS test. Make sure it's negative. Get him a church. You know, no wailing, no guilt, no suffering, none of that, all right?
MARK	Should there be a God?
GEORGE	Yes, there should be a God, and I want you to pay off the wife, all right? Pay off the wife, call it support. Make sure we get our money's worth. I want her to smile a lot.

In a press room, Marlene Radner (a Gennifer Flowers type) and her lawyer field questions at a podium as flashbulbs flash.

LAWYER	Miss Radner has a statement, and then she'll take your questions.
RADNER	Thank you. I was Jim Walcott's mistress for a period of ten years. That was the same time that Jim was married. His sexual preferences included bondage, whipping, slave/mistress submission, and a lot of sex-role reversal. That's all. Thank you.
REPORTER	Is it true you were paid twenty thousand dollars by a local paper for an exclusive on this story?
RADNER	I have no comment.

George, Jeremy, and Mark are in the campaign "war room."

GEORGE	Okay, we have a problem with this woman, you guys. She's a nutcase, she's a publicity freak, and I have no idea how low she'll stoop to kill us on this. I mean, do we have anything on her?
JEREMY	No.
MARK	No, she's pretty clean.
GEORGE	I mean, can we lay anything on her? What can we come up with?
MARK	How about a mental-health problem? That shouldn't be too hard.
GEORGE	I like that, mental health.
JEREMY	Toss in a drug addiction.
GEORGE	Okay, that's good. Drug addiction, mental health problem, but we've got to be sensitive about these things, okay? So we'll have Jim pray to God for her speedy recovery.
MARK	Sounds good.

Jim is with his wife outside the building, speaking to the press.

JIM	You know, I feel very sorry for this woman . . . No, I never met her before in my life. She's, she's obviously mentally disturbed, perhaps due to drug use, I don't know. My wife and I can only pray to God for her speedy recovery. Thank you, that's all. Thank you.
	Jim and his wife get into a cab as reporters fire questions.

George, Jim, Mark, Jeremy, and Audrey are in the campaign "war room."

GEORGE — Anything from your youth that we can capitalize on, something courageous that you did? Something extraordinary?

JIM — You know, um, eighteen, nineteen, twenty, something like that, I met this girl. She was maybe a little younger, I don't remember. Seventeen, sixteen. She got pregnant and, um, and I just assumed that she was using something. Birth control or something. I didn't even think about it. *(Jeremy looks at Jim, then at George)* And then she's harping on me to do something about it. So I went to my mother, who had been gathering money up for a charity food-drive thing, and I somehow talked my mother into giving me the money and I sent it off. I gave it to this girl.

GEORGE — For what?

JIM — Take care of, uh, for an abortion, I assume.

GEORGE — What? You mean you never . . .

JIM — God, no! I never saw her again.

GEORGE — Um, I don't know if we can use that.

JEREMY — No. We need something a little more heroic.

MARK — There's parts of it we can use.

JIM — Maybe she wasn't really pregnant, uh, at all.

GEORGE — What, you mean it was, like, a false pregnancy? Maybe she was, like, crazy.

MARK — And then not seeing her, if we could, if we could massage that so that you've maintained steady contact.

GEORGE — I love the food-drive part of it, all right? So I think that, um, maybe we can work the hooker, Mary Magdalene thing in there. You had an older brother, you know, he had a couple hundred bucks 'cause he wanted to spend it on two-hundred-dollar hookers or something, right?

JIM Right.

GEORGE And some night, or a buddy, that wants to do this and get some drugs together, get some alcohol for hookers. And you said, and you took the money . . .

JIM And put it to better use.

GEORGE . . . and you gave it, you gave it for the food drive, for the food drive.

JEREMY That's great.

GEORGE Okay? I mean, that's the whole story.

JIM So forget the whole bit about the pregnancy . . . ?

GEORGE Yeah, yeah, but basically it's a true story.

MARK Yeah.

GEORGE Very good. Okay.

Jeremy and Mark jot notes.

Mark and Jeremy sit in a booth at a coffee shop with Jim's wife and her agent.

MARK You agreed to get back together with Jim for fifteen thousand dollars. Now, it's twenty-five, and you have an agent.

JIM'S WIFE That other woman's getting twenty thousand for her story.

JEREMY That's not confirmed, and we had a deal.

MARK You're his wife.

AGENT Uh, I've spoken to the other woman's people and confirmed the twenty thousand.

JEREMY Oh, great. She's got people too.

AGENT Look, Saundra is willing to be a terrific, loving wife to Jim through election night. But sex wasn't part of the original deal.

JEREMY How did sex get into this? This is new to me.

AGENT Jim wants it three times a week.

MARK	So you're representing her sex life.
AGENT	I'm giving her full-service representation. Sex is part of it. Sex once a week, and twenty-five thousand.

Mark and Jeremy exchange looks.

JEREMY	We should have hired a hooker for five hundred bucks a night. It would have been cheaper. *(to Jim's wife)* No offence.
MARK	I mean, what kind of sex are we talking about?
JEREMY	Exactly.
JIM'S WIFE	Straight sex.
JEREMY	You mean, like missionary, that's it?
MARK	Come on! It's Jim Walcott.
AGENT	You tell us what you want.
JEREMY	Okay, well oral should . . . that, that to me is part of regular . . .
AGENT	Are you sure you're okay with that?
JEREMY	Oral is fine?
MARK	Oral's all right?
JIM'S WIFE	Uh-huh, oral's good.
MARK	Twenty-three thousand, twice a week.
JIM'S WIFE	Twice a week.
AGENT	We have a deal, we have a deal.

Marlene Radner is in the press room again, talking to the press.

RADNER	Look, if I never met Jim Walcott, then how do I have this picture of us together in Hawaii with our arms around each other? *(she shows an 8 x 10 photo)* I have nothing to gain here. I have no axe to grind. All I want is to tell the truth, that's all.

Flashbulbs go off.

George, Mark, and Jeremy are in the campaign office. George is pacing as Mark and Jeremy sit in chairs.

GEORGE Okay, so they got a picture of this woman with Jim, what, sitting on Jim's lap or something? I sat on Santa Claus's lap, I have a picture of that. Was I sleeping with Santa Claus? You know what I mean?

MARK I don't know, were you?

GEORGE No, I wasn't. Now we've got a sympathy problem here, okay? We're losing the sympathy for Jim Walcott, all right? So we have to build that up, okay? You know what I need here? I need, um, I need a wheelchair. We need a wheelchair in this campaign. That's how we do it.

Jeremy looks at Mark, who frowns back.

GEORGE I want Jim's wife in a wheelchair.

MARK Uh, hold on. I just saw Jim's wife on TV this morning. She was walking.

GEORGE Shit. Okay, get anyone in the wheelchair. Give me anyone in a wheelchair, all right? That can't be too hard.

JEREMY Okay.

GEORGE Get a person in a wheelchair, put them on the campaign.

JEREMY Okay.

GEORGE I don't want anyone who's off-putting.

JEREMY Off-putting?

GEORGE I don't want an off-putting disability.

MARK What do you mean, "off-putting disability"?

GEORGE — Image is important here, okay? I don't want to sound too harsh. But I don't want, you know, a Stephen Hawking type, okay? I want an injury that people can feel good about.

JEREMY — You mean, like a spinal sports injury?

GEORGE — Yes, exactly. I want a disability that people don't feel threatened by. A disability people can feel good about, okay? Good, good. That's it.

Jim, his wife, and a man in a wheelchair are getting out of the campaign van outside the office.

JIM — *(to the assembled reporters)* Look, when I said I never met Miss Radner, I was mistaken. I was mistaken. I did meet her, once. Ten years ago at a party. So if Miss Radner thinks that constitutes a relationship, she is in need of some serious psychological help. My wife and I are praying for her recovery every day. As is one of the newest members of my campaign team, one of my best old school-friends, who recently had a tragic skiing accident and who's strength and courage are a daily source of inspiration to me. That's all. Thanks.

Jim and his wife step inside the building, leaving the man in the wheelchair outside.

Marlene Radner steps out of an elevator holding a baby. The press are waiting.

RADNER — Jim Walcott is the father of my baby. I have nothing else to say.

At campaign headquarters, Jim, his wife, the man in the wheelchair, and a person to sign for the deaf are at a podium before the press.

JIM All right, um, I just want to say that I do in fact recall now that Miss Radner and I were lovers on, um, a couple of occasions, but I am confident that blood tests will prove beyond a shadow of a doubt that I am not the father of this woman's child. This is a seriously disturbed woman in need of help. And my wife and I are praying for her recovery twice daily, as is one of my best school-friends, who recently had a tragic skiing accident and who's strength and courage are a daily source of inspiration for me. That's all. Thank you for coming out.

Jim, his wife, and the sign person leave the podium as reporters fire questions, leaving the man in the wheelchair behind.

George, Jeremy, the man in the wheelchair, and his agent are in the campaign "war room."

GEORGE What's he getting now?

JEREMY Two hundred an appearance.

GEORGE Okay, and you want?

AGENT #2 Six hundred with a guarantee of six appearances.

GEORGE Six thousand dollars?

AGENT #2 That's right.

GEORGE Oh, please. Come on. This is a political campaign. We can't afford that. That's a joke. Are you an agent or a lawyer?

AGENT #2 I'm an agent.

GEORGE *(to the man in the wheelchair)* You came here with an agent? You're Jim's friend. You come in here with an agent?

MAN She's protecting my interests.

AGENT #2 That's right. I'm here to represent my client.

GEORGE No, forget it. It's too much.

AGENT #2 You want to exploit him?

GEORGE I'm not exploiting anybody, okay? And you know something, I don't need him, I don't need him. Forget it then.

JEREMY No, no. Hang on, hang on, hang on.

(leans in to George) Relax, my God, we need the guy. Sympathy, look at him.

GEORGE Okay, okay, okay.

Let me ask you a question. Can you absolutely, for sure, not walk?

MAN Absolutely, can't walk a step.

AGENT #2 That's right.

GEORGE And this was a skiing accident?

MAN Yes, I was skiing. Uh, we were drinking on the drive home and, uh, we got into a car accident.

GEORGE Oh, well, this . . .

MAN I was, I was skiing first.

GEORGE Oh, forget this! This is a drinking-and-driving accident. This wasn't a skiing accident. We wanted an athlete here.

AGENT #2 You wanted a guy in a wheelchair.

GEORGE The guy was drinking and driving. He had an accident. I'll give him three hundred and a guarantee of five appearances, tops!

AGENT #2 Five hundred with a guarantee of ten.

JEREMY Four and seven.

AGENT #2 Four and a half with a guarantee of eight.

GEORGE Four and a quarter, guarantee of seven.

AGENT #2 We'll, take it.

JEREMY All right.

GEORGE Done. I just want to make sure that when this campaign is over and I'm walking down the street, this guy doesn't come walking towards me.

MAN You won't. I promise I'll never walk again.

AGENT #2 Okay, thank you.

At a government office, a Crown prosecutor is addressing the press.

PROSECTOR Jim Walcott is under investigation for misuse of public broadcasting funds between the years 1991 and 1996.

PRESS What was the money spent on?

PROSECUTOR Personal air fares, ski trips, alcohol, personal car repairs. Excuse me.

PRESS Where are any charges?

The prosecutor leaves.

Jim, his wife, the sign person, and the man in the wheelchair are at a podium in the campaign headquarters.

JIM *(clears his throat)* Pardon me. This criminal investigation against me is a ludicrous fraud. The police and prosecutor are so far off base here. I'll tell ya, I'll tell ya, if I had done something wrong, let them arrest me here and now.

My wife and I can only pray for these people, as will my best school-friend, Dave, who recently had a tragic skiing accident and who's courage and strength are a daily source of inspiration for me.

MAN Jim Walcott has been there for me all through this traumatic experience after my skiing accident. And my struggle has been as difficult as Yul Brynner's when he was dying.

George, Mark, Jim, the man in the wheelchair, and Jeremy are in the campaign "war room." George is angry.

GEORGE "... and my struggle has been as difficult as Yul Brynner's when he was dying."

MAN Look, he told me to say that.

JIM Yeah, yeah, I thought we could finally tie in the whole Yul Brynner thing.

GEORGE What do you mean, tie in? I said just drop the Yul Brynner thing, okay? Drop the Yul Brynner thing.

MAN I said, you know, I need more of a segue between my struggle and the Yul Brynner part.

JEREMY Segue? Now you're talking about segues?

MARK Look, just do the wheelchair.

MAN You know what, screw it, okay? I don't need this. I've got a regular job.

GEORGE Okay, just settle down, okay? From now on, every speech goes by me first, all right?

JIM All right, no problem.

GEORGE Thank you very much. Very good.

JIM Look, it's been a very long day, and I feel, like, a certain responsibility for this, and, uh, I saw a documentary once on group dynamics so I suggest that we all hug.

Jeremy moans.

JIM All right? We'll all have a hug. Just, you know, bring the team back together as a kind of ...

Jim walks over to Mark to give him a hug. Mark keeps his arms folded.

JIM — We're a team, right?

Jim walks over to George, arms extended. George backs away.

GEORGE — No, no, okay, fine. Okay, it'll work. Everything will work.

JIM — Okay, yeah, no problem.
(he gives a seated Jeremy a handshake) Great, thanks for all your help.

JEREMY — Okay.

JIM — We're back together. Jim Walcott team, yeah?

A doctor giving a press conference stands at a bank of microphones.

DOCTOR — We ran a blood test on both Jim Walcott and the child, and Mr. Walcott is beyond a shadow of a doubt the father of Miss Radner's baby.

In the campaign office, Mark and Jeremy sit with Jim's mother. She's sixty-two, and tough.

MARK — So you're Jim's mother, right?

MOTHER — That's right.

JEREMY — And you haven't seen your son in twenty-two years.

MOTHER — Well, you know how it is. People get busy, especially in families. But I've been watching his problems on TV, and I thought it was time to come and help, if I could.

MARK — We pay a hundred dollars per appearance.

MOTHER Five.

Jim, his wife, the sign person, the man in the wheelchair, and Jim's mother are at the podium at campaign headquarters.

JIM I have no idea where they got my blood. This doctor clearly has either a vested interest in my downfall or has some serious mental problems. I want to say "physician heal thyself," but instead my wife and I are gonna pray for him as we are praying for Miss Radner and the prosecutor in the misuse-of-funds charge. Most of all, our deepest prayers are going out to the child who is being manipulated in this whole mess. Joining us in our prayers is, of course, my old friend and school chum, Dave. And as well, now, my mom. My mom single-handedly raised four young boys as a single mother after the tragic death of my father. And we will make it through this. Thank you.

Jim's mother is being interviewed by Pamela Wallin on her show.

MOTHER Jim's father was having an affair with my second cousin. Her husband came home, caught them in bed. Jim Senior tried to jump out the window. The guy shot him in the leg. Jim's father fell on his head, he was brain dead for a few months, until they pulled the plug. Now, mind you, in those days, there wasn't much problem about pulling plugs.

In the newsroom building, a young woman speaks about Jim on camera.

WOMAN #1 — I've worked here in the news department for about two years. Um, Jim Walcott, without my consent, kissed me on the mouth and touched me several times while I worked as a researcher on his news show.

Another young woman being taped in her car.

WOMAN #2 — Um, I joined Mr. Walcott's campaign, and on the second day he propositioned me. When I refused, he had me kicked off the campaign team.

Another young woman is being taped in a coffee shop.

WOMAN #3 — I was on a school tour of the TV station where Jim Walcott was an anchor, and I asked him for an autograph. He said he'd give it to me in his dressing room. When I refused, he tried to kiss me. I ran away and told my teacher, and he propositioned her as well. That's it.

Jim and Mark are outside the broadcast centre in front of the press.

JIM — My wife and I are praying for everyone. You know, my wife has been a pillar of support for me throughout this whole thing. Without her love and amazing loyalty, I really couldn't have kept going. Thank you. *(he enters the building as reporters fire questions)*

Jim's wife is sitting in her car. Reporters stick microphones through the car window.

WIFE I'm leaving Jim. I have nothing more to say other than, uh, he has shown a very depraved and vile side to his nature, which I never knew existed. I can only pray for his soul.

Outside a shopping mall, Jim addresses uninterested shoppers with the sign person. George, Mark, and Jeremy stand by.

JIM My wife's mental stability has been stretched to the limit by the false and scandalous accusations that have been against me in this campaign. And I only hope that this terrible time hasn't driven her back to her alcohol and drug dependence. I'm praying to God for –

Suddenly there is a loud pop and the camera swishes in the direction of the sound. Someone who looks like Cindy "Squeaky" Fromme is scuffling with a man trying to wrestle a gun out of her hand.

JEREMY Oh, my God. Jim's been hit! They shot him, somebody shot him!

The camera swishes back to Jim, who is on the ground. George, Jeremy, and Mark are gathered around him.

MARK Get an ambulance, get an ambulance!

GEORGE You're gonna be okay, Jim.

This could work for us, am I right?

MARK You're right.

Squeaky Fromme, in handcuffs, is led by two police officers.

SQUEAKY (*to the press camera*) I loved Jim Walcott. He was the only candidate who was really willing to cut taxes and at the same time balance the budget.

Mark and George are in the campaign "war room."

MARK The doctor said the bullet is lodged in the centre of Jim's brain.

GEORGE Is this a big problem?

MARK Well, they can't get it out.

GEORGE No, but is this a problem for us?

MARK Well, I imagine so. It's in the middle of his brain.

GEORGE No, um, what I'm getting at here is, is there serious impairment?

MARK The doctor say he's brain dead.

GEORGE Oh, that's gonna hurt us. That's gonna hurt.

Mark, Jeremy, Audrey, and George are in the campaign office.

AUDREY (*on the phone*) Mr. Walcott is definitely alive. Can you hang on a sec?
(*covering the receiver with her hand*) Jeremy?

JEREMY Yeah?

AUDREY Guy from the *Globe* heard that Jim's brain dead. What are we saying?

JEREMY Hey, Mark?

MARK Yeah?

JEREMY Are we using brain dead?

MARK Uh, George?

GEORGE (*on a cellular phone*) I saw Jim about an hour ago. He looks fantastic. Hold on a second.
(*he covers the receiver*) Yeah?

MARK Are we using brain dead to the press?

GEORGE No, no, no. He's resting, he's resting. He's not brain dead.

(back on the phone) Yeah, I think what we've got here is what I would call a Canadian Christopher Reeve situation . . . Yeah, well, we have a, um, we have a celebrity with a certain amount of trauma. And this guy's still got a tremendous contribution to make to public life . . . That's right, well, we're having faith in Jim right now. That's what we're doing. Faith in Jim, faith in God, and faith in the democratic process . . . That's right. We're moving straight ahead. Which means, we think we can win this. And we know we can win this thing . . . That's right. Thank you very much.

George, Mark, and Jeremy are in the "war room."

MARK This is a poll they did after Jim's shooting. We're up sixteen points.

GEORGE Wow, great!

JEREMY Was I right booking him into that mall? Sixteen points in political terms, that's huge!

GEORGE That's huge.

MARK Yeah, just like the hole in his brain.

GEORGE I don't want to mention the term brain dead, okay? There's too much negative spin on that. Jim Walcott is still very much alive in this campaign.

JEREMY He's alive on paper.

GEORGE What do you mean, "on paper"? You make it sound like he's in some kind of birdcage or something. The man's body is in perfect shape. He's got one small hole in his head. No exit wound, okay?

JEREMY That's because his brain absorbed the impact.

GEORGE	His brain did absorb the impact, okay? But that shot got us something. You know what it did? *Bang* – sexual abuse charge, off the front page of the paper. *(Jeremy and Mark exchange looks)* *Bang* – the fraud thing, gone. *Bang* – the paternity suit, gone. So, without losing sight of the real tragedy of this thing, the shooting is about the best goddamn thing that could have happened to this campaign.
MARK	Are you saying that we're gonna run a brain-dead candidate?
GEORGE	Forget about brain dead. Forget about all that stuff, right? We've got to think of a positive spin we can give to this. Something we can sell.
JEREMY	How about: Jim Walcott, who is sleeping peacefully –
GEORGE	No, no, no. Not peacefully. Makes him sound like a pacifist. We're not running a pacifist. We're running a fighter. Jim's a fighter. Okay, I've got words like battle, courage, guts.
MARK	I've got one: Jim's silent war.
GEORGE	I like "war." I don't like "silent."
JEREMY	Quiet.
GEORGE	No, wrong.
MARK	Jim's private and courageous war.
GEORGE	Private and courageous struggle.
MARK	Jim's private and courageous struggle.
GEORGE	Struggle. Good, good.
JEREMY	Campaign.
GEORGE	Better, better. Okay, I like that. Jim's private and courageous campaign. I love that. The campaign, the courage, and it's private, right? He's got the whole brain thing going for him, but you know, we're keeping it down. He's not flaunting it.

MARK	Not like Karen Ann Quinlan did.
GEORGE	Let's get a poster. How long for posters?
JEREMY	Couple of days.
GEORGE	Couple of days? Okay, you know what I love? Those posters of Jean-Claude Van Damme. Those penetrating eyes. "Never Say Die." I love that. Jim's a fighter. "Never Say Die."
JEREMY	How about "Never Say Anything"?

Pamela Wallin interviews Hugh Segal and Jeffrey Simpson.

PAMELA	Hugh, politics can be a bizarre game, but have you ever seen anything like this campaign, with a brain-dead candidate?
HUGH	Pamela, I've seen some very strange things in politics in all the major parties. But the notion of running Jim Walcott in a brain-dead context, running him as a brain-dead candidate, is the most offensive thing I've ever seen. Even for the Liberals, it's offensive.
PAMELA	Jeffrey Simpson in Ottawa, your take on all of this?
JEFFREY	Pamela, I've been following politics and covering them for twenty years in Canada, and I've never seen anything more ridiculous than this. It's a complete hoax, perpetrated on the Canadian people.

Outside the campaign office, George and Mark walk towards the campaign van as reporters close in on them.

GEORGE	*(to the reporters)* We'd no sooner pull the plug on this campaign than we'd pull the plug on Jim's life support. We're fighting two campaigns right now, and we're gonna win both of them. We're gonna

win this election and Jim's gonna win his much more courageous and private campaign.

MARK Jim Walcott is a fighter, he's a symbol of sacrifice. He's not a quitter, he's the kind of symbol people want in government right now.

GEORGE That's right. We believe in the sanctity of all human life. We're pro-life, we're pro-Jim Walcott. Thank you.

They get into the van as the reporters fire questions.

Bob Rae is on the TV in Jim's hospital room.

BOB This Jim Walcott thing . . . this savage brutal exploitation of a brain-dead man . . . this political freak show makes me thankful that I left politics when I did.

Audrey, George, Jeremy, Mark, and Jim are in Jim's hospital room. Jim is on life-support. A recurring beep is heard. Audrey, Jeremy, and Mark are all on separate phones while George watches the TV. Stephen Lewis is commenting. It is election night.

AUDREY *(on a cellular phone)* Half the polls are counted and we're leading by 12 per cent.

STEPHEN *(on TV)* This whole thing is a complete travesty. You've got a bunch of manipulative donkeys who don't give a tinker's damn about Jim Walcott. They're just trying to squeeze as much sympathy out of the Ontario public as they can. If Jim Walcott is elected, you can write off democracy.

ANNOUNCER That was ex-Ontario leader Stephen Lewis, commentating from New York.

Now let's go back up to . . .

MARK (*on the hospital phone*) Yeah, Jim's encouraged by the early returns, but, typical Jim, he's not overreacting.

JEREMY (*on a cell phone*) I don't think there's a happier man in the province tonight than Jim Walcott. How can I tell? 'Cause he's got a twelve-point lead with over half the votes counted.

GEORGE Here it comes, you guys. Here it comes.

ANNOUNCER Here's Bob Davis with the returns from East York.

The beep on the life-support turns to a single tone. They all look at the flat line on the monitor.

BOB DAVIS It seems that we have another projected winner with 18 out of 20 polls counted. The Liberal candidate Jim Walcott has taken East York.

GEORGE We won! We did it you guys! We won!

JEREMY Yeah! Yeah! Yeah! (*he high-fives Mark*)

MARK We did it! That's great!

JEREMY Yeah, we won!

AUDREY Oh, my God.

JEREMY Yeah, Walcott's our man!

MARK Yes, Jimbo.

AUDREY Cool.

The camera freezes on Jim, lying lifeless in the bed.

THE END